AZTECS ON STAGE

AZTECS ON STAGE

Religious Theater in Colonial Mexico

Louise M. Burkhart

Translated from the Nahuatl by
Louise M. Burkhart, Barry D. Sell, and Stafford Poole

UNIVERSITY OF OKLAHOMA PRESS : NORMAN

Also by Louise M. Burkhart

The Slippery Earth: Nahua-Christian Moral Dialogue in Sixteenth-Century Mexico (Tucson, 1989)

Holy Wednesday: A Nahua Drama from Early Colonial Mexico (Philadelphia, 1996)

Before Guadalupe: The Virgin Mary in Early Colonial Nahuatl Literature (Albany, 2001)

(co-ed. and -trans. with Barry D. Sell) *Nahuatl Theater, Volume 1: Death and Life in Colonial Nahua Mexico* (Norman, Okla., 2004)

(co-ed. and -trans. with Barry D. Sell and Stafford Poole) *Nahuatl Theater, Volume 2: Our Lady of Guadalupe* (Norman, Okla., 2006)

(co-ed. and -trans. with Barry D. Sell and Elizabeth R. Wright) *Nahuatl Theater, Volume 3: Spanish Golden Age Drama in Mexican Translation* (Norman, Okla., 2008)

(co-ed. and -trans. with Barry D. Sell) *Nahuatl Theater, Volume 4: Nahua Christianity in Performance* (Norman, Okla., 2009)

Library of Congress Cataloging-in-Publication Data

Burkhart, Louise M., 1958–
    Aztecs on stage : religious theater in colonial Mexico / Louise M. Burkhart ; translated from the Nahuatl by Louise M. Burkhart, Barry D. Sell, and Stafford Poole.
        p. cm.
    Includes bibliographical references.
    ISBN 978-0-8061-4209-8 (pbk. : alk. paper) 1. Nahuatl drama—Translations into English. 2. Religious drama, Nahuatl. 3. Mary, Blessed Virgin, Saint—In literature. I. Sell, Barry D., 1949– II. Poole, Stafford. III. Title.
    PM4068.75.E5B87 2011
    897'.4522—dc22

                                                        2011005982

The paper in this book meets the guidelines for permanence and durability of the Committee on Production Guidelines for Book Longevity of the Council on Library Resources, Inc. ∞

CONTENTS

ILLUSTRATIONS

ACKNOWLEDGMENTS

Many thanks to Barry D. Sell, Stafford Poole, and Elizabeth R. Wright, collaborators on the Nahuatl Theater project, for their previous work on these plays and their comments on parts of this volume. I am grateful also to Camilla Townsend, Robert Haskett, and anonymous reviewers for the University of Oklahoma Press for their very helpful suggestions, and to Jonathan Truitt for his transcription of an archival document on theatrical suppression. I thank the various colleagues who expressed an interest in using this book in the classroom; I hope the result proves adequate.

For permission to publish these plays, I thank the Biblioteca Nacional de Antropología e Historia, Mexico; The Latin American Library, Tulane University; and the William L. Clements Library, University of Michigan. For photographs and publication permission, I am grateful to the John Carter Brown Library at Brown University, the Benson Latin American Collection at the University of Texas, and the Archivo General de la Nación. The Department of Anthropology, University at Albany, SUNY, helped to fund the publication of this book. The National Endowment for the Humanities (NEH), an independent federal agency, funded part of the earlier research on which this volume is based. At the University of Oklahoma Press, I thank Alessandra Jacobi Tamulevich, Emily Jerman, John Drayton, Jo Ann Reece, and copy editor Pippa Letsky for their support of the entire Nahuatl Theater project and this final volume.

AZTECS ON STAGE

INTRODUCTION

America's First Theater

The show would go down in history. The cast acted out the Final Judgment, or Judgment Day, when the world would come to an end and the souls of the dead would return to their bodies. The year was 1533. The place was Tlatelolco, just to the north of Tenochtitlan, the former capital of the Aztec Empire and now the capital of New Spain. These island cities were home to the Mexica, one of the many Nahuatl-speaking groups that dominated Central Mexico before the Spanish Conquest. Decades later, native historians recalled this Final Judgment performance as a "great marvel," at which "the Mexica were very amazed and astonished." This was apparently the first time Aztec actors put on a Christian-influenced play for other Aztecs; in any case, it is the earliest theatrical production in the Nahuatl language for which any record survives. And it made a big impression.[1]

Only a dozen years earlier, in 1521, Tenochtitlan and Tlatelolco lay in ruins, their streets and canals choked with corpses. Between 1519 and 1521 the Mexica-dominated Aztec Empire had disintegrated, as longtime enemies and then its own vassal states one after another threw their support behind Hernando Cortés. With Cortés's diplomatic and tactical successes backed up by reinforcements of men and weapons from Cuba and Spain, many native leaders were persuaded—or compelled—to join what looked like the winning side. The Mexica, led by their valiant young king, Cuauhtemoc, defended the twin cities as long as they could. Exhausted and starving after a brutal three-month siege that laid waste their beautiful island home, they surrendered to Cortés and his allies on August 13, 1521.[2]

But the end of the Aztec Empire was not the end of the world. A colonial era began, which would last for three centuries, until Mexico became an independent nation in 1821. Despite massive population loss and many other challenges, indigenous communities accommodated themselves to Spanish colonial rule and survived, retaining their languages and many other aspects of their culture. Spaniards who studied the Nahuatl language in depth admired its elegance and the richness of its metaphors. Today, speakers of contemporary Nahuatl number about a million and a half people, making Nahuatl the most widely spoken indigenous language of Mexico. While this group's preconquest civilization is commonly referred to as Aztec, anthropologists and historians use the term "Nahua" for people of the colonial and modern eras.

By 1533, friars of the Franciscan order, the first religious order charged with bringing the newly conquered peoples into Christianity, had been studying Nahuatl for ten years. Dominican friars came in 1526, Augustinians in 1533. These missionaries decided at the very start that they would preach to the peoples of Mexico in their own languages. They thought this would make it easier to persuade people to abandon their old gods and rites in favor of Christ, the Virgin Mary, and the ceremonies of the church. Jesuit priests, who first came to Mexico in 1572, would also be dedicated learners of Nahuatl. The diocesan church hierarchy—clergy who did not belong to religious orders—also supported preaching in native languages, but without the level of commitment demonstrated by the friars.

Franciscans enjoyed the most success with the Nahuas, as linguists and as evangelizers. Early on, their greatest success was with young boys, mainly sons of the elite, whom they brought into their residences to educate in reading, writing, and Christian doctrine. In 1536 they founded a college for indigenous boys in Tlatelolco, where they educated many teachers and leaders.

Most Nahuas, especially in the larger towns and cities and especially those of the nobility or upper class, realized that in order to get along as best they could under Spanish rule they would have to cooperate with the friars on at least a minimal level. This meant learning the basic teachings, becoming baptized, participating in some rituals and festivals, and building and maintaining churches. Some Nahuas became devout and well-indoctrinated Christians; others stuck to the old ways as much as they could. Most people found a middle path, participating in forms of Christianity adapted to their language and culture while maintaining many of the values, attitudes, and devotional practices of previous generations.[3]

Preconquest Nahua religion featured elaborate ceremonies that brought gods and sacred narratives to life. Priests dressed sacrificial victims in clothing, adornments, and face paint that did not simply resemble a given deity but actually *assembled* the god out of the constituent parts. These parts included the impersonator's body, thought to have been stripped of its personal identity. These preparations brought the deity into the temple precinct for the duration of the ritual. The ceremonies often in some way enacted or referred to events from the mythic past. The deity impersonators, once emptied of the divine presence, were then dispatched, usually through heart sacrifice, and dismembered.

Although professional priests were in charge of channeling sacred forces into the desired outlets, many people participated in the rites by preparing ornaments and food, taking part in songs and dances and processions, sweeping and adorning the ritual spaces, and observing the parts of the rituals that were performed in public. Less elaborate—and less bloody—rites were conducted in smaller settlements and in urban neighborhoods and homes.[4]

Catholic priests believed that the Nahuas' gods and goddesses were actual beings: devils who had tricked the people into serving them. Though repulsed by the bloodier aspects of native religion, they admired the devotion of these deeply religious people who, ignorant of Christianity, had been misled by opportunistic demons. But given how attached the Nahuas were to their old ceremonial life, how could they be persuaded to direct their devotional impulses to new stories, new festivals, and new personages?

The closest thing Europe had to the Aztec temple rituals was religious theater, a type of performance that developed during the Middle Ages and was very popular at the time Spain conquered Mexico. Costumed impersonators memorized a script and spoke their lines in front of an audience. Each drama told a story, with a beginning and an end, drawn from the Bible or saints' legends or illustrating a point of moral teaching.

Plays were performed on religious festivals such as Christmas, Easter, and especially the feast of Corpus Christi. This feast celebrates the Roman Catholic rite of transubstantiation: the conversion of bread into the body of Christ (*corpus Christi* in Latin) through the ritual of Mass. When Protestants rejected the belief that the bread really becomes Christ's body, Catholic areas like Spain defended it and made their Corpus Christi celebrations more and more elaborate. Actors performed plays as the consecrated bread, or host, was carried along a processional route.[5]

Franciscan friars were seeking effective tools of evangelization. Nahuas relished extravagant performance, impersonation, costume, and verbal art. Listening to friars preach sermons in clumsy Nahuatl could hardly compare to the excitement of the old ceremonies. The friars and Nahuas who put together that Final Judgment performance in Tlatelolco (as well as any unrecorded predecessors) had found a way to meet the needs of both groups: Christian teachings could be presented in dramatic form, by indigenous performers, in their own language. There could be costumes, props, elaborate stage sets, singing, dancing, and fireworks. The people "were very amazed and astonished."

So, Aztec and European traditions merged in the invention of Nahuatl theater, the first true American theater. It is American because the civilizations of Mexico were now part of a place called America, the New World "discovered" by Europe and propelled into the global exchange of ideas, organisms, and objects. It is American because it is not simply European theater transplanted to new soil. Despite its Roman Catholic models, Nahuatl theater belonged to the Native American people who responded with such wonder to that first performance, who learned to stage the plays as part of their communal religious life, and who passed the scripts from generation to generation. It is theater in the Western or European sense of the word, because like European drama—whether in ancient Greece or sixteenth-century Spain—it consists of the performance of plays, written scripts memorized by actors who temporarily assume the identity of characters and speak in front of an audience.[6]

This book presents six Nahuatl plays in English translation. They number among the twenty scripts published in a larger work, the four-volume *Nahuatl Theater* set. The translations have been edited to make them easier to read, and to read aloud. Additional plays, transcriptions of the Nahuatl, and more information and analysis can be found in the earlier volumes.[7]

Types of Plays

Nahuatl plays can be divided into two broad categories (see the appendix for a list of plays, their locations, and published editions). The first consists of morality plays. These star fictional human characters whose virtuous or sinful behavior leads to heavenly reward or damnation to hell. Angels, demons, and sometimes Jesus Christ and the Virgin Mary play parts, but the main characters are ordinary people. These dramas share a formulaic ending: a wicked person who has been condemned to hell laments his or her fate and implores the audience to avoid the behaviors that led to this end.

Morality plays typically stress the importance of confession. Colonial Nahuas were supposed to participate in the Catholic sacrament of penitence once a year, during Lent, the forty-day period leading up to Easter. This required that they confess all their sins to a priest, receive the priest's absolution, and carry out whatever penance or restitution the priest prescribed.[8] Morality plays were performed on Sundays during Lent, to encourage people to fulfill this obligation—or frighten them into it. Some plays also reinforce other death-related obligations: making a will, carrying out the terms of a deceased person's will, financing Masses for the souls of the dead, and praying for these souls in order to shorten the time they must spend in purgatory before going to heaven.[9]

The second, and larger, category consists of plays that tell stories drawn from the Bible, the apocryphal gospels (early Christian texts not included in the standard Bible), saints' legends, and other religious literature. In these plays, the main characters are historical or sacred figures rather than ordinary humans. Most numerous are Passion plays, which reenact the last days of Jesus Christ's earthly life, culminating in his crucifixion. Nahuas also liked the story of the Three Kings or Wise Men, pagan rulers who visit the infant Jesus in Bethlehem and accept him as their savior. This visit is celebrated on the Feast of Epiphany, January 6. Old Testament stories, other episodes from the lives of Jesus and the Virgin Mary, and medieval saints' legends also saw dramatic reenactments. Some of these are mentioned in historical sources but left no known scripts.

Battles were also enacted, some historical and some imaginary, in which pagan, Jewish, or Muslim enemies of Christianity were vanquished. Often these were more pantomimed, with stage combat, than scripted in lines.

A Nahua man, in the clutches of a devil, confesses to a Franciscan priest. Sixteenth-century woodcut in fray Alonso de Molina's *Confessionario mayor*, 1565 edition, f. 71r. (Courtesy of The John Carter Brown Library at Brown University.)

But two works that could be called "history plays" survive, one about the Roman destruction of Jerusalem in 70 A.D., and one about Constantine, who conquered Rome in 312 A.D. For Nahuas, both stories resonated with their own history of conquest.[10]

A beloved and appealing story homegrown in Mexico tells of the Virgin Mary appearing to a Nahua convert named Juan Diego, in 1531. She asks that a shrine be built to her, as Our Lady of Guadalupe, at a site on the lakeshore north of Mexico City. Although there is no reliable historical evidence that this story existed before the mid-seventeenth century, it later came to be seen as a true and sacred narrative. Many Mexicans, as well as Roman Catholics from other countries, find much solace in the story of a Nahuatl-speaking Virgin appearing to a humble indigenous man. Pope John Paul II canonized Juan Diego in 2002.[11] Two colonial dramatizations of the apparition story are known.

Most Nahuatl plays have a single act, without intermission, like sixteenth-century Spanish plays. However, later developments in Spanish theater influenced some writers of Nahuatl plays to make the productions longer, divide them into acts, and include foolish servants or other humorous characters. In this volume, the Guadalupe drama and *The Animal Prophet and the Fortunate Patricide* have three full acts and comic, low-class characters.

Literacy and Scripts

The native people of Mexico had books. They made paper, called *amatl* in Nahuatl, from the bark of fig trees. Nahuas used their picture-writing mainly to keep track of calendrical cycles, history, and ritual obligations, and to tell fortunes: to predict a person's fate based on his or her date of birth, to determine whether a young couple were suitable marriage partners, and the like.[12]

Nothing like a written script for a play existed in the New World until Catholic clergymen began writing down native languages using the roman alphabet and taught native students to do the same. To write out every word of a script for, say, an hour-long play would have been a cumbersome process even in the very sophisticated Mayan writing system, which had signs that could be read phonetically as syllables. In the much more limited Aztec picture-writing it would have been impossible. Therefore, as theatrical as the old rituals were, they were not scripted in this sense.

The Nahuas and other native people readily adopted alphabetic writing. Though not as beautiful as the old writing, it was much more efficient and precise. Nahuas applied their own words for paper, book, ink, reading, writing, and scribe to the new techniques and do not seem to have thought there was any meaningful discontinuity.[13]

The new literacy spread widely—though not deeply—through colonial Mexican society. In every community of any size there would be someone who could read and write. In part, this was a result of Spanish colonial government.

Nahua communities, called *altepetl*, were corporate, landholding bodies that could include several settlements of different sizes plus the lands around them. People identified closely with their altepetl; this affiliation was much more meaningful than an identity as "Nahua" or "Indian." The Spanish forced these communities to reorganize their government on the model of the Spanish *cabildo* or town council, a body of elected officials. Members of the local nobility tended to dominate these posts.

Each cabildo required a clerk or notary, who recorded the council's proceedings, and so every altepetl had to have at least one literate man. Church staff also included a notary; the same man sometimes filled both posts.[14] In addition to the professional notaries, many men of the nobility learned to read, in schools run by Catholic priests or from other literate Nahuas. Few non-noble men could read; literate women of any class were nearly unknown.

So, even though play scripts were written out, not everyone who performed in a play could necessarily read his or her lines. However, there would be some people available who could read the parts aloud. Non-literate actors would have to learn their parts by ear.

In addition to serving as a memory aid while people learned their lines, written scripts allowed a popular performance to be repeated year after year. Catholic priests had their own reasons to demand the use of written scripts: with these they could supervise and control the content of native performances. In this way, play scripts were tools of colonial domination.

Priests feared that, if left to compose their own oral literature, Nahuas would perform texts with idolatrous or diabolical content. Or they would use such complicated, metaphorical language that priests would not even be able to tell what the words really meant. In the case of music, friars wanted the native people to sing songs in their own language that the friars were sure had suitably Christian content. To fill this need, the Franciscan Bernardino de Sahagún worked with graduates of the Franciscan college to produce a book of Nahuatl songs for Christian festivals. This *Psalmodia christiana* was published in 1583.[15] Written play scripts functioned for drama as this book did for song: Nahuas could put on performances, and priests could assure themselves that they were singing or speaking approved lines.

Theater Talk

Just as Nahuas did not invent new vocabulary to describe alphabetic writing, for the most part they talked about theater with words they already had. This was a bit challenging, for Nahuatl had no specific words for theater, play, actor, act, perform, script, cast, audience, role, director, prompter, aside, or stage. A verb meaning "to play a part in a farce" (*ixehua*) appears in scripts only when an actor is playing a sort of

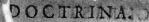

DOCTRINA.

TOtatzine huicac timoietztica, ma-
nouiã mach , cacēquizcaqualli imo,
tocatzin. Inī ini eühca momacuex, inic,
cētetl tlaçotl, ca teuiutica quetzalitztli.

Maoallauh in motlatocaiutzin , ma-
üeltchoatzin xitechmopachilhui, mano
yoan totech xiemopouili in motlatoca
iotzin. Ic vntetly, in momacuex tlaunca
iutia

A page from the *Psalmodia christiana* of 1583, f. 3v. The text is the Lord's Prayer in Nahuatl. The woodcut shows Christ praying in the Garden of Gethsemane; his disciples sleep in the foreground, Peter with his sword. (Courtesy of The John Carter Brown Library at Brown University.)

double role, for example in *The Nobleman and His Barren Wife* when an actor plays Jesus disguising himself as a priest.

When Nahuas needed a word for "play" they most often used *neix-cuitilli*, or "example": something from which one learns a lesson. To perform a play was "to make [*chihua*] an example." Sometimes Nahuas combined *neixcuitilli* with *machiyotl*, meaning sign, comparison, or model, making *neixcuitilmachiyotl*, "example-sign" or "exemplary model." They also used words meaning "marvel" or "wonder," like the chroniclers who described that early Final Judgment play in Tlatelolco.

The word *tlapechtli* (platform or bed) expanded to mean "stage." Various other verbal conventions took root, such as verbs for "coming out" on stage (*hualquiza*) and "going in" as one exited (*calaqui*). "Wind instruments will be played" (*tlapitzaloz*) or "drums will be beaten" (*tlatzo-tzonaloz*) frequently embellish the action. A verb meaning "to practice" or "to test oneself" (*mo-yeyecoa*) worked well for "rehearse."

Writers also simply borrowed Spanish nouns, referring to a drama as an *auto* (one-act religious play) or *coloquio* (dialogue) or *comedia* (three-act play). In plays with multiple acts, the sections bear the Spanish label *acto*. For asides, remarks addressed directly to the audience rather than to another character, the Spanish *aparte* (apart) was borrowed. Two eighteenth-century copyists refer to scripts using the Spanish word *original*. One of them also noted that a local nobleman's son served as the production's *apuntador*, or prompter—a job with extra importance when not all the actors can read.[16]

Nahuatl theater began in the 1530s; surviving scripts date from approximately 1590 through the mid-1700s. Over this period of time, Nahuatl changed under the influence of Spanish. Surviving play scripts speak in what Frances Karttunen and James Lockhart define as Stage Two Nahuatl, which characterized Nahuatl texts from about 1540 to about 1650. During this period, the only Spanish words that entered Nahuatl were nouns, borrowed to refer to ideas or objects that were new to the Nahuas. Occasionally, a Spanish idiom is translated directly into Nahuatl. For example, the Spanish phrase *quiere decir*, "it means" or, literally, "it wants to say," gave rise to Nahuatl *quitoznequi*, "it wants to say it," employed frequently to refer to translated words. After 1650 Spanish influence increased: Nahuas borrowed Spanish verbs and particles, syntax changed, and many more idioms were adopted.[17]

The later play scripts do not reflect these changes, with rare exceptions.[18] Nahuas apparently chose not to update the scripts but kept copying the same wording, or they wrote new plays in the same speech style. Sometimes Spanish words adopted in stage directions are kept out of the characters' dialogue. Plays must have started to sound old-fashioned to their audiences, the way a nineteenth-century novel does to readers today. This style may have seemed to be more authentic or authoritative than everyday language. Also, priests may have discouraged innovation, distrusting impromptu revisions to an accepted text.[19]

Playwrights, Translators, and Copyists

When Nahuatl plays are attributed to a specific author (as opposed to a copyist), this author is always a priest. However, this does not mean that priests wrote all the plays or wrote them by themselves. Priests relied on native speakers of Nahuatl to help them write texts in the language, to translate materials from Spanish, and to make copies. Priests often entrusted educated Nahuas with the actual writing, while putting their own name and authority to the final product. Few priests who did not grow up as bilingual speakers of Spanish and Nahuatl were fluent enough to write, on their own, the polished Nahuatl found throughout the dramas.

Two priest-playwrights did grow up speaking Nahuatl as a native language. Don Bartolomé de Alva adapted four early-seventeenth-century Spanish plays into Nahuatl, including this volume's *The Animal Prophet and the Fortunate Patricide*. Alva was of mixed Spanish and Nahua descent. The other was don Manuel de los Santos y Salazar, a Nahua nobleman, scholar, and parish priest from Tlaxcala. In 1714 Santos y Salazar "wrote down, putting it in order," the drama about the Roman emperor Constantine and his mother, Saint Helen. Few men of indigenous or mixed ancestry were ordained as Roman Catholic priests because of bias against their attaining this high-status position, so these men were exceptional.[20]

Spanish sources are known for a few Nahuatl plays. Comparing don Bartolomé de Alva's plays to the Spanish works that he adapted shows he carefully tailored his works to fit their new performance context. Another play, a dialogue between Jesus Christ and the Virgin Mary, was translated from a Spanish play but diverges from its source in ways that indicate native authorship.[21] Similarly, the Nahuatl play *The Destruction of Jerusalem* is far from a mirror image of the Spanish narrative on which it was based.[22] These examples show that native speakers of Nahuatl, even when they worked directly from Spanish, made innovative adaptations.

Of all the Nahuatl plays written and performed in New Spain, surely only a fraction survive in colonial era scripts with currently known whereabouts: twenty-two complete plays (twenty-three, if a second copy of one is counted) and four partial scripts (one of them a single leaf). Photocopies exist of another two, and later copies of two more (see the appendix for a list of the known scripts). More plays are sure to turn up in archives, or come out of private document collections, so these numbers are subject to change and may already be out of date. Colonial texts describe—often very briefly—over thirty other specific dramas.[23]

More than a hundred printed works in Nahuatl were published in Mexico during the colonial period, totaling about ten thousand printed pages. These were, overwhelmingly, religious texts, such as catechisms, sermons, and confession manuals.[24] But all known play scripts are handwritten manuscripts. No plays made it through the printing presses—unless some imprints have vanished without a trace. If plays had been published, more of this material might survive.

At least one Franciscan priest intended to publish plays. Fray Juan Bautista wrote in 1606 that he had three volumes of plays ready to go to press.[25] Collaborating on the project was Agustín de la Fuente, a Nahua scholar and teacher from Tlatelolco who probably prepared the actual Nahuatl texts. Some of the surviving plays might be versions of works that fray Juan Bautista and Agustín de la Fuente included in their compilation. But those volumes were never printed.

Colonial authorities disagreed about what sorts of materials could appropriately be translated into native languages, and how much of this material should be published in printed books. Especially problematic, in the wake of the Lutheran and other Protestant movements that translated the Bible out of Latin, were any translations of the holy scriptures into native languages. And some dramas, like the Epiphany and Passion plays in this volume, did tell Bible stories.

Among Spaniards, Franciscan friars held the most liberal opinions about native-language literature. But other priests—as well as the bishops, judges, and viceroys who had to issue approvals for published books— may have considered Nahuatl drama too controversial for the printed page, regardless of how useful it was at the local level. Although written scripts gave priests some control over native performances, making such texts too readily available could undermine that control. So access was limited, and people who wanted plays had to go to the extra effort of copying the scripts by hand.

To at least some extent, the texts did get away from priests and into the control of native communities, where scripts were kept by local leaders and recopied as needed by local scribes. Overt digressions from Christian models suggest local innovations not condoned by priests, as in the Passion play from Tepaltzingo (in this volume) where Jesus Christ rubs ointment on Mary Magdalene's head, instead of the other way around, as it is told in the Gospels. A man named Carlos de San Juan, who copied a play in 1717, noted that a former governor of his altepetl paid him to reproduce a script held by another local nobleman; no priest is mentioned. Officials from the Mexican Inquisition pulled various Passion plays out of Nahua hands during an eighteenth-century investigation.[26] The small number of surviving scripts does not mean that plays were rare or unusual. Plays circulated in a kind of literary underground, and over time many got lost or wore out, were confiscated, or were simply forgotten as performance practices changed.

Performing Christianity

All the dramas enact Christian stories. It may seem surprising, therefore, that colonial authorities would be at all suspicious of them. It is not as if the Nahua actors were openly performing their old myths.

Catholic priests never had much confidence in native Christianity. They had little tolerance for the ways that native people adapted Christianity to their own preferences and did not completely abandon their old customs. One of these preferences was their love for performance, pageantry, and paraphernalia—costumes, images, ornaments—over more spiritual or contemplative forms of devotion.[27] Hence theater, though useful as a way to make Christianity appealing, also pointed to the limitations of the evangelization program. People loved the show, but did they really get the messages priests wanted them to learn?

Spaniards' understandings of native Christianity were constrained by a worldview that imposed dual categories on reality, in particular the division between good and evil. If there was something different about native religion, this was not the normal result of cultural diversity, or slightly different understandings of the same basic ideas. The native forms were inferior, evil, the work of the devil. For the devil still held native people in thrall, poised to reclaim their souls if granted the slightest opportunity. If not from the devil, the differences stemmed from inherent weaknesses in the people's moral character. Spaniards, like all colonial powers, justified their rule based on their presumed superiority to the colonized people, and this disdain for native character was one way they expressed their supremacy. So if native people put tremendous effort into performing spectacular plays, this just showed that their faith was superficial, a matter of showmanship rather than deep devotion.

Christian stories did become different when they were told in Nahuatl. Priests, limited by their moral dualism and their persuasion that the Word of God was universal and unchangeable, could not really understand or accept these cultural differences. Nahuatl words meant slightly—sometimes very—different things from their closest Spanish or Latin equivalents. Nahuas lived in a different social universe, where relations between men and women, parents and children, rulers and subjects, and people and gods were not the same as in Spanish communities. As colonized people with limited political or economic power, they needed to construct and maintain these barriers of cultural difference in order to survive. Nahuas understood dramas and other Christian stories by inserting them into their own world as best they could, finding and favoring elements that resonated with their own experiences.

Here are just a few ways in which Nahuas integrated Christian ideas into their worldview, ways actually facilitated by some of the symbolism and metaphors presented to them in Nahuatl texts, and by use of the same words for god, temple, offering, festival, and so forth. Nahuas linked Jesus Christ with the sun, the world's animating force and source of all heat and light. His mother, the Virgin Mary, they associated with the dawn, with light, and with flowers, and eventually with the earth, fertility, and pulque, the native alcoholic beverage. Flowers refracted the sun's life-giving radiance into brilliant colors and intoxicating perfumes. Nahuas created sacred space by filling the sites of their rituals with flowers, a practice the friars could accept as "decoration." Brightly-colored tropical birds were another manifestation of solar energy and power; angels could be slotted into the same sky-dwelling niche.[28]

The yearly round of saints' festivals replaced the old festival calendar, with saints at least roughly filling some of the same roles as the old gods and becoming associated with local places such as sacred mountains. Thus Saint Anne, Mary's mother, provided a grandmother figure along the lines of the goddess Toci, "Our Grandmother." Saint John the Baptist had an obvious association with water, for he baptized Jesus in the River Jordan, and his June 24 feast day happened to fall at the beginning of the rainy season, so he could bear something of the nature of a rain god. Christ, Mary, and the saints did not demand blood offerings; they were content with flowers, food, candles, and incense. Indeed, Mary offered kindness and compassion unknown in preconquest religion and seemingly appreciated by her Nahua devotees. But the old contract between humans and the sacred forces—under which people celebrated the festivals, prayed, and made offerings in return for rain, crops, and other blessings—was not essentially changed.[29] Theater provided a new way not just to add pomp to the festivals but to bring sacred presences to life.

Good and evil for the Nahuas were not absolute forces. Nahuatl had no way of referring to evil except by saying something was "not good." The Christian notion of sin was assimilated to a broader concept of damage or disorder, individualized moral taint to broader concepts of cosmic decay and pollution. Nahuas had strict moral rules, but these were followed in order to ensure an orderly and wholesome life on earth, for one's loved ones as well as one's own self, not to please a god or to gain reward in the afterlife. A life force based in the heart was equated with the Christian idea of the soul. The underworld was turned into the place where bad people's souls went, while others went to heaven, or "in the sky." Devils, embodiments of evil, received the name *tlatlacatecolo*, or "human horned owls" (singular *tlacatecolotl*), in previous usage a type of malevolent, shape-changing sorcerer and now a category that included the disgraced old deities. Nasty creatures these are indeed, but not the very principle and embodiment of evil.[30]

Spaniards and Nahuas lived side by side for three hundred years in their different worlds. They did so by minimizing their differences and operating on the assumption that they actually knew what the other side was up to. This assumption encompassed the convenient fiction that *tlatlacolli* really meant "sin" (*pecado*), *mictlan* really meant "hell" (*infierno*), and so on. Historian James Lockhart calls this situation "Double Mistaken Identity" and describes it as "a partially unwitting truce . . . in which each side of the cultural exchange seemed satisfied that its own interpretation of a given cultural phenomenon was the prevailing, if not exclusive one."[31] It was only by misunderstanding one another that natives and non-natives could go through their lives acting as if they understood one another. Colonists could lord it over natives, thinking they were in charge, their superiority self-evident. Native people could appear to be in compliance while quietly continuing to do things in their own way.

Nahuas who put on a play presented themselves in public as Christians, as good and pious subjects of the colonial system. They also brought the community together for an enjoyable event that expressed its solidarity. An impressive play also glorified one's own altepetl, and thus one's own group identity, over others. It attracted visitors and drummed up business for local merchants. In this way theater played a role similar to the imposing churches that native Mexicans constructed for their communities. A play or a church was a public, visible assertion of political legitimacy, community pride, and devotion to the sacred powers—however people actually conceived of those. Within the community, nobles or relatively well-off individuals who sponsored a performance, paid for the sets and costumes, fed the actors, and so on would gain prestige, as would the actors themselves if they did a good job. All of these benefits existed on top of whatever spiritual or moral messages priests hoped the audience would absorb.

Another reason for colonial authorities to be suspicious of Nahuatl drama lay in the very nature of theater. Even if priests scrutinized the scripts and checked to see that people recited their lines correctly, they were ceding power to the performers. Actors are themselves and their characters at the same time. Plays tell stories yet at the same time comment on the local setting, the place and people around the performance.[32] Theater allowed Nahuas to become Jesus, Mary, saints, angels, devils, Jews, Romans, soldiers, priests, and every other sort of character, right in the centers of their own communities, while also remaining themselves—looking and talking like ordinary native people, one's friends and relations, not foreigners who spoke Nahuatl with Spanish accents, if they spoke it at all. Most statues and paintings in Nahua churches had European features, but the actors did not. The performance space—typically the churchyard, at the community's symbolic center—became Jerusalem, Bethlehem, Rome, heaven, hell. Cosmic events were made local; sacred powers, both helpful and harmful, were embodied in Nahua persons.

If playing the part of a sacred being retained some of the sense it had in the old ceremonies, the actors would have absorbed, temporarily at least, some actual essence of these sacred personages, rather than simply imitating them. One piece of evidence for such a belief is that people reportedly collected the fake blood "shed" by actors who played Jesus

Christ in Passion plays, because they thought it had healing powers. They also kissed and offered incense to these men in their guise as Jesus.[33] These actors must have, to at least some extent, really turned into Jesus—into a god—in the eyes of their neighbors. An indigenous Jesus, dying at the hands of colonial (Roman) authorities, makes a powerful nativist symbol.[34]

Theater worked against the priests' attempts to impose their own worldview in another way as well. Nahua philosophy was monist, not dualist. Not only was there no grand division between good and evil, there was only one world. Sacred forces inhabited it and flowed through it, manifesting themselves in concrete form, in natural phenomena like water and sunlight and mountains, in statues, in ritual impersonators. Gods (and then Christian saints) were not removed from the world to some ethereal, spiritual, invisible, and intangible plane of existence. Spirit was not opposed to matter. Theater, by presenting Jesus, devils, heaven, human souls, and everything else in such tangible form, reinforced this down-to-earth, this-worldly orientation.

Theater was a risky business in yet another way. Priests might control the script, but they could not control every gesture, every facial expression, or every intonation that actors used as they brought their parts to life, expressing their own attitudes toward the material in subtle ways that priests might not understand. Out of the hearing of any Nahuatl-speaking outsiders they could also improvise new lines, however they pleased. Unfortunately, written scripts provide no direct insight into these spontaneous actions.

In 1698, a friar stationed in Tlatelolco, explaining why he thought the local Nahuas should no longer be allowed to perform their Epiphany and Passion plays, complained about the public drunkenness that accompanied these events. It was not just a matter of the audience getting a bit rowdy. It was the actors, too. The previous year, for example, he had yanked most of the apostles out of the Passion play because they were drunk.[35] Colonial Nahuas did have serious problems with alcohol, as have many peoples living under colonialism or other forms of domination. But part of the problem was how they drank rather than how much they drank. They got thoroughly drunk to mark ritual occasions, sobering up when the festival was over.[36] Spaniards—who also drank but disapproved of any public loss of control—deplored this behavior. And any time anyone wanted to criticize native people about anything, they could simply dismiss them as a bunch of drunks.

Sympathetic observers could see Nahuatl theater as a sincere and pious tradition that taught people about the faith, instilled reverence for Christian teachings, and promoted good morals. Hostile observers could find indecencies, superstitions, and idolatries—as well as booze. And they were not necessarily watching different plays. It was a matter of how one viewed native Christianity—as basically good, or as basically bad. By extension, it was a matter of how one viewed native people themselves. Few outsiders considered them their equals.

So, even though all the scripts tell Christian stories, colonial authorities found plenty of reasons to be suspicious of Nahuatl theater. They responded by policing it in various ways. One way was to keep performances out of the church building itself. Another was by insisting that all play scripts be reviewed and approved in advance of the performance. Another was simply to ban certain types of performance outright. Repeated edicts making the same demands suggest that people might not have been paying much attention.[37]

However, the period from the 1750s to the 1770s saw a more concerted campaign against native theater, especially Passion plays. Influenced by the Enlightenment and its emphasis on reason and logic, churchmen rejected elaborate, emotional, extravagant spectacles. Such things may have been appropriate in the early days of evangelization, but native people should not need them anymore. They should simply listen to preaching. Some scripts were confiscated (and some of these therefore survive in archives). Some communities actually translated their plays into Spanish in the hope of skirting the restrictions on Nahuatl theater, but some of these Spanish plays were confiscated too.[38] All popular spectacles of this kind were now suspect. And some communities abandoned their annual productions or toned them down. They could, for example, substitute a procession with statues of Jesus Christ and the Virgin Mary for a drama in which people played these roles. This is what that friar in Tlatelolco recommended. But it was hardly the same thing as a play.

No known colonial scripts survive from after the middle of the eighteenth century. Nahuatl writings in general became rarer as most people educated enough to be literate could speak and write Spanish. Nahuatl literacy barely survived after Mexican Independence, although there are some later texts. The only play scripts made by Nahua hands in the nineteenth century are copies of colonial plays written out by Faustino Chimalpopoca Galicia, who taught Nahuatl at the University of Mexico and transcribed texts for the historian José Fernando Ramírez. He made these copies for scholarly, not performance, purposes. Native communities continued to perform elaborate ceremonies on Christian religious festivals, as they still do today. However, these lost their connection to the old scripts.

Stages and Sets

Nahuatl theater was not performed in enclosed buildings or actual theaters. Even in Spain, permanent performance spaces did not exist until the second half of the sixteenth century, and their name (*corrales*) accurately describes their outdoor, rudimentary nature. Nahuatl plays were performed outdoors, or in covered spaces open to the air, with the audience outdoors.

Nahuas built their churches with large open patios where they carried out many of their religious activities. These patio areas typically included an open-air chapel, smaller chapels in the corners, and a roofed porch at the entrance to the attached *convento* or friars' residence.[39] All of these spaces could be used as settings for dramatized action, with the audience spreading around the churchyard, as could other public plaza areas. The *Three Kings* play in this volume uses the inside of the church as well, but this use of sacred indoor space could meet with priestly disapproval. The cloisters inside the conventos provided another possible performance space, in which painted murals could serve as backdrops.[40]

At least in the eighteenth century, Passion plays were sometimes performed in the local cemetery. Priests disagreed about whether this was appropriate. Defending the practice, the Dominican fray Francisco Larrea opined that this was a good spot, more sacred than other spaces but not *too* sacred, as the church itself would be.[41] Nahuas may have believed this an appropriate staging ground for the death of Jesus.

Nahua stage crews erected temporary buildings, some quite elaborate, some perhaps just a wall with a door. Stage directions instruct actors to knock on, and go in and out of, the doors of these mock-up houses and palaces. The stage set for hell is sometimes called "the house of hell" (*mictlancalli*), suggesting an actual building, into which the demons could drag their victims. Temporary buildings could be as elaborate as the five-towered fortress Tlaxcalans built to represent Jerusalem for a 1539 performance. A Nahua historian in Mexico City was so impressed by a temporary building erected for a mock battle performance in 1572 that he painted a picture of it in his book.[42]

Stage sets could also include elaborate re-creations of natural settings. Tlaxcalans constructed a lavish Garden of Eden set for a 1539 play about Adam and Eve, complete with rivers, mountains, and live animals, including two jaguars restrained by ropes.[43] When plays had scenes in gardens, such as the Garden of Gethsemane in Passion plays or Malintzin's garden in *The Animal Prophet and the Fortunate Patricide* (in this volume), Nahuas probably took the opportunity to create flower-filled mock gardens. The hilltop of Tepeyacac in Guadalupe plays and Mount Calvary in Passion plays invite the construction of temporary "mountains."

When Nahuas began to set up actual stages—temporary wooden platforms—is not clear, but some scripts refer to the *tablado* (in Spanish) or tlapechtli (in Nahuatl). Hell could be represented by the space under the stage, while raised platforms above the stage represented heaven. The raised open chapels found at some churches could also make good heavens. From such spaces Jesus or Mary could speak to other characters, or characters could climb a ladder to enter heaven. Small platforms were even moved up and down with ropes, so that angels could come down from heaven, speak their lines, and go back up again, and so that Jesus or Mary could ascend to heaven.[44] Stage directions for the Guadalupe play in this volume call for the use of a curtain (with the Spanish word *cortina*). This is the only place a curtain is mentioned explicitly.

Permanent spaces dedicated to public performances may have existed in rare cases. A church in the altepetl of Zumpango, completed in 1728, had an attached platform, six meters long, with a vaulted roof, which may have been an open-air stage. A similar structure in the church patio in San Pedro Atocpan could have had the same function, although a colonial text referring to it mentions only the playing of music there.[45]

Actors and Action

Spain began to have professional acting companies in the 1540s,[46] but Nahua performers were not full-time professionals. Early on, with the Franciscan friars in charge, all roles were played by boys or men. Jesuits also supervised schoolboy productions at the schools they ran for native youths.[47]

As Nahua communities built and staffed their Christian churches, people took on professional or semi-professional roles as church personnel, called *teopantlaca*, or "church people." The highest-ranking church people were the *fiscales*, general assistants to the Catholic priests, who oversaw church affairs and finances. Among their many responsibilities, they made sure people came to church, got baptized, went to confession, and lived with partners they had married in church. Especially in communities with no resident priests, the fiscales would teach catechism classes, announce festivals, supervise burials, and even perform baptisms if necessary.[48]

Next in importance was the *maestro de capilla*, or "chapel master," who was in charge of a group of singers, or *cantores* (*cuicanime* in Nahuatl), which could include young choirboys. These men and boys often came from the local nobility. Spanish colonial law limited the number of cantores in any one town to just one or two, but Nahuas frequently defied this limit. Cantores gained prestige; they also had to pay only half as much tribute as other men.[49] Among other, loosely defined duties, the cantores provided choral and instrumental music for church services and festivals. They learned to sing the Latin chants from the Roman Catholic liturgy. They also learned to play European instruments such as wooden flutes, oboe-like *chirimías*, and different kinds of trumpets, adding new musical sounds to those of the native clay flutes, two-tone and standing drums, and rattles.

A few colonial sources refer to the cantores putting on plays.[50] Directing community shows would have been a logical extension of their other performance- and festival-related duties. Church notaries very likely copied scripts and helped people learn their lines, but there is no direct evidence for this. Nahuas who were leaders of religious confraternities were also likely to be involved in theater. Confraternities were voluntary, club-like groups devoted to some Christian personage or theme, such as the Holy Cross, the Virgin Mary, or the Souls in Purgatory. Nahua women and men participated enthusiastically in these organizations. A confraternity in Tlaxcala sponsored the Adam and Eve play mentioned above.

Plays with large casts would require volunteers from the community as well as religious leaders. Thus, cantores or confraternity leaders may have been in charge of productions, but other people—such as members of confraternities and their children—must have played parts, built sets, prepared props and costumes, and so forth. Some plays call for various "extras" with nonspeaking parts, such as soldiers, guards, attendants, servants, and silent angels—such that directors could include in the show as many people as they liked.

At some unknown point before 1698, women began to play female roles. In that year the same Tlatelolco friar who complained about drunken actors also wrote that, in his opinion, women should no longer be allowed to play the Virgin Mary and other female roles.[51] So, obviously, they had become accustomed to doing so. Offstage, women undoubtedly had always sewed costumes and prepared food and drink for the participants.

When Mexican Inquisition officials collected testimonies about Passion plays, they gathered some fascinating information about this controversial performance tradition. In the altepetl of Ozumba, rehearsals started halfway through Lent. Summoned by a drummer, participants gathered around nine o'clock in the evening and rehearsed until after midnight.[52] Women played the female roles. The same people, often members of the local nobility, would sometimes play the same parts year after year. People interviewed in the large altepetl of Huejotzingo in 1770 reported that they had stopped performing their Passion play some years earlier. They had used Nahuatl manuscripts for their play and performed it in the church patio. Two brothers and a sister from one noble family, the Guevaras, said they used to play Jesus, Peter, and the Virgin Mary. Another noblewoman, doña Lorenza Donado, reported that she had played Mary Magdalene.

One Huejotzingo nobleman claimed that the bishop had made them stop doing the play, but the Guevara brothers had a different explanation. They told the inquisitor that a man named Bernabé Bustamante, who had played the part of Judas for years, drank himself to death. Then no one else wanted to take over the role, because people thought that God may have punished this man.[53] Here is another piece of evidence that Nahuas thought actors took on something of the identity of their characters: playing a villain could bring on divine retribution. It is also interesting that the Guevaras did not give Bernabé Bustamante the noble title "don." Perhaps nobles claimed the "good" parts and stuck commoners with playing the villains.

European images—woodcuts, paintings, statues—and native artists' copies of them provided models for the costumes of characters from the Old World: Jesus, Mary, saints, Old Testament figures, Romans, angels, demons, and so on. Angel costumes would include wings; devil costumes would include horns, hooves, and a tail. People playing ordinary humans probably dressed in ordinary clothes matching the social position of the character, people playing priests in a friar's habit.

Sometimes people borrowed clothing from statues in the church when they were to represent these figures in a play. Some outsiders considered this sacrilegious, but fray Francisco Larrea defended the practice. In his view, native people had, if anything, too much reverence for their religious statues, identifying them too closely with the holy personages they depicted (an expression of native people's monist worldview, interpreted as spiritual weakness by priests). They would never treat the images disrespectfully. Actors wanted to have the right gear for their parts, Larrea wrote, and were too poor to make their own costumes.[54] Considering the special status of these garments, the actors wearing them might share in the holiness they and their fellow Nahuas ascribed to the images.

Music added excitement to the plays. In addition to the drums, flutes, and trumpets that provided musical flourishes as important personages entered or exited the scene, sometimes the action was accompanied by singing. Although a few plays have Nahuatl songs, most songs were Latin chants from the church liturgy, which the cantores and other educated boys or men knew how to sing. Characters chant Latin responsories for the dead in plays meant to model proper mourning rituals. Most spectators would not understand these Latin words. But the music would nevertheless add to the spectacle and enhance the aura of holiness around the production. Two plays call for the ringing of the church bell, an object treasured and sometimes even named by colonial Nahuas. Someone had to be stationed at the bell, ready to ring it on cue.[55]

Dance was also very popular before and after the Spanish conquest, but churchmen sometimes viewed it with suspicion. Morality plays, typically performed during Lent, would not have been suitable occasions for dancing. But an Epiphany play witnessed by a Franciscan in 1578 included a dance of angels and another of shepherds.[56] Dances may have been performed before or after other plays that were part of holiday celebrations. Mock battle performances could be considered a combination of dance and drama.[57] Two surviving scripts explicitly call for dancing. The Guadalupe drama in this volume does so twice, for the intermissions between acts. In the play about Emperor Constantine, the celebration of his victory includes a *tocotin* dance, a native dance so named for its characteristic drumbeat.[58]

Plays demand a wide variety of props, as the scripts in this volume demonstrate. These props could be household items such as tables, chairs, a broom, dishes, and food; paper, pens, and ink with which notaries take dictation or demons record a person's sins; weapons, such as swords, knives, bows and arrows, and the lance to pierce Christ's side; crowns,

scepters, banners, and staffs of office; books, letters, and written procla-
mations; torches, lanterns, and candles; horses, a donkey, a turkey; the
Star of Bethlehem on ropes or on a pole; gold, frankincense, and myrrh;
Jesus' manger and Mary's cradle; money and the purses or strongboxes
to keep it in; the flowers Juan Diego plucks on the stage set of Tepeyacac;
censers and aspergilla (for sprinkling holy water); whips and chains and
nasty objects with which demons torture sinners; fake flames of hell; fake
blood for Christ, or to drip from a murder weapon; and objects of partic-
ularly sacred quality such as Christ's cross and crown of thorns, and the
chalice, wine, and bread he would use for the Last Supper. All these
things had to be procured or manufactured, stored safely, and provided
to the actors at the right moment.

A favorite special effect was fireworks. Even today, Mexican villagers
enjoy using elaborate fireworks displays in their festivals. In colonial
morality plays, fireworks accompany scenes in which demons carry
sinners off to the underworld, or in which the Antichrist appears. There
would not only be frighteningly loud noises and flashes of light. The
gunpowder would leave a sulfurous odor suggesting the stench of hell.
In addition to setting off fireworks, playing musical instruments, or
ringing the church bell, sound effects helpers might need to imitate the
clamor of battle (by bashing things together and yelling), thunder, or
animal noises (mooing, bleating, crowing like a rooster).

Nahuatl plays yield rich information about how colonial Nahuas experienced Christian teachings, and how they spent their holidays. But
scripts project mere shadows of live performances, stripped of color
and sound, stripped of faces and gestures. Nor can they convey all the
behind-the-scenes bustle as people rehearsed, built sets, and prepared
props and costumes. Readers today can only guess at the prestige that
directors and actors might gain from their work, or conflicts they might
have with one another or with a supervising priest or community official.
People working together to put on a show surely experienced some
degree of cheerful camaraderie; they might also have gotten annoyed
at folks who forgot their lines, or who fell asleep at late rehearsals.
Spectators picked up some version of the Christian messages, and also
other messages about their community, their leaders, their neighbors,
and their place in the whole colonial social order. Whether they were
amazed, amused, frightened, or bored, they saw religious stories brought
vividly to life, in elegant Nahuatl, during the set-apart time of ritual, in

the sacred centers of their community. Readers of this book are encouraged to peer beyond the scripted lines and to ponder as well the non-scripted activities that went into the staging of a Nahuatl play.

Notes

1. Sahagún 1950–1982, 8:8; Horcasitas 1974, 562; the Nahua historian Chimalpahin (quoted in Horcasitas) gives the year as 1533.

2. On the conquest, see Clendinnen 1991b, Townsend 2003, Restall 2003, Hassig 2006.

3. On the evangelization program and Nahua responses, see Burkhart 1989, Klor de Alva 1982, Díaz Balsera 2005, Gruzinski 1993, Pardo 2004. What Ricard 1966 presented back in the 1930s as a "spiritual conquest" is now interpreted as a process of negotiation, accommodation, and contestation. On colonial Nahua religious practice, see Lockhart 1992, ch. 6.

4. Clendinnen (1991a) provides helpful insight into the sacrificial rituals. López Austin (1988) explains how Nahuas viewed human nature and the cosmos. For descriptions of the temple rituals, see Sahagún 1950–1982, 2, and Durán 1971.

5. Good sources on Spanish theater of this era are Greer 2004, Shergold 1967, McKendrick 1989. For scripts of sixteenth-century Spanish plays, see Rouanet 1979 and www.cervantesvirtual.com/servlet/SirveObras/89558283741231033 413846/index.htm.

6. Some European theater did not use memorized scripts: in Italian commedia dell'arte, actors played stock characters and followed standard plots, but they improvised their actual lines.

7. In addition to the *Nahuatl Theater* set (2004, 2006, 2008, 2009), see Burkhart 1996; Ravicz 1970; Horcasitas 1974, 2004; Arróniz 1979; Sten 1982; Sten et al. 2000; and Williams 1992. Partida (1992) reprints some of Horcasitas's Spanish translations. Guzmán Bravo (2007) reproduces Horcasitas's 1974 transcription and translation of the *Three Kings* play in this volume, with costume designs and suggested scores for choral accompaniments.

8. On Nahua confessions, see Burkhart 1989, Gruzinski 1989, Klor de Alva 1988.

9. On wills and other death-related customs see Burkhart essay in *Nahuatl Theater*, vol. 1; Cline 1986, chapter 3; Kellogg and Restall 1998.

10. See Burkhart essay in *Nahuatl Theater*, vol. 4, and Burkhart 2010.

11. On the history of the Guadalupe devotion, see Poole 1995, 2006; Burkhart 1993; Noguez 1993; and Taylor 1987, 2003. For the Guadalupe story in English, see Sousa et al. 1998; for a good Spanish translation see León-Portilla 2000.

12. On Aztec writing see Boone 2007, 2008.

13. See Karttunen 1982 on Nahuatl literacy. On the range of colonial Nahuatl documents, see Lockhart 1992, especially chapters 7–9.

14. On colonial altepetl organization and government offices, see Lockhart 1992, chapter 2; on notaries see especially pp. 40–41; on church notaries see pp. 217–18. See Haskett 1991 for an in-depth study of government in one altepetl.

15. This book has been translated into English (Sahagún 1993) and Spanish (Sahagún 1999).

16. *Nahuatl Theater*, 4:122–23, 384–85.

17. Karttunen and Lockhart 1976; Lockhart 1992, chapter 7.

18. For example, some informal Spanish phrases are used in the Guadalupe play in this volume.

19. On the Nahuatl used in the plays, see Sell essay in *Nahuatl Theater*, vol. 4.

20. *Nahuatl Theater*, vol. 3, is dedicated to Alva's work. On Santos y Salazar, see *Nahuatl Theater*, vol. 4; Lockhart 1992, 384, 592–93; Townsend 2009, 21–28; Zapata y Mendoza 1995. Poole (1981) discusses church policies on the ordination of native and mestizo men.

21. See Burkhart 1996.

22. See *Nahuatl Theater*, vol. 4; Burkhart 2010.

23. This estimate includes descriptions in Horcasitas 1974, plus scripts unknown to him. It is an approximation, because some brief descriptions may refer to dances or tableaux vivants rather than to scripted plays.

24. On colonial Nahuatl publishing see Sell 1993, and Sell's essay in *Nahuatl Theater*, vol. 1.

25. Bautista 1606, prologue.

26. Records are in Mexico's Archivo General de la Nación, Inquisición, vol. 1072, exp. 10. Some documents are published in Ramos Smith et al. 1998, 260–62, 299–319; see also Leyva 2001, Mosquera 2005.

27. On this performative focus of Nahua religion, see Clendinnen 1990, Burkhart 1998.

28. On solar associations see Burkhart 1988; on flower and bird symbolism associated with the Virgin Mary, see Burkhart 1992, 2001.

29. Wake (2009) explores continuities in these basic religious principles.

30. These Nahua-Christian adaptations are discussed more extensively in Burkhart 1989.

31. Lockhart 1991, 22. See also Lockhart 1985, 447, and 1992, 445.

32. Schechner (1985) discusses this "in-between" nature of theater.

33. From document in the Archivo General de la Nación, Mexico City, Bienes Nacionales, vol. 990, exp. 10, transcribed by Jonathan Truitt.

34. Bricker (1981) explores attempts by native people in Mexico and Guatemala to create an Indian Christ.

35. From document in the Archivo General de la Nación, Mexico City, Bienes Nacionales, vol. 990, exp. 10, transcribed by Jonathan Truitt.

36. Taylor (1979) discusses colonial drinking patterns.

37. For example, different archbishops of Mexico issued edicts suppressing theatrical performances in 1704, 1757, and 1769. See *Nahuatl Theater*, 4:9–12. For documents on the suppression of theater in colonial Mexico, see Ramos Smith et al. 1998.

38. One of these Spanish plays is published in Leyva 2001; see also Mosquera 2005.

39. On the various meanings that friars and Nahuas built into these church complexes, see Lara 2004 and Wake 2009.

40. Edgerton (2001) suggests this use for the cloisters.

41. Larrea's defense of Nahua Passion plays is part of the Inquisition documentation. See Ramos Smith et al. 1998, 307–17; cemetery use is mentioned on p. 311.

42. Motolinia describes Tlaxcala's "Conquest of Jerusalem" (1979, 67–72). The temporary building is depicted in the *Codex Aubin*, folio 58r (Lehmann et al. 1981, 37). See also Horcasitas 1974, 122, 124, 505.

43. Motolinia 1979, 65; Horcasitas 1974, 175–84.

44. For more on stage sets, see Horcasitas 1974, chapter 9.

45. Horcasitas 1974, 122–23.

46. McKendrick 1989, 43–46.

47. On the Jesuits, see Pérez de Ribas 1645, 639, 742. In Spain at the time (in contrast to Elizabethan England), women were permitted to act in plays—provided they were married and did not play male roles.

48. Lockhart 1992, 210–18; Ricard 1966, 97.

49. Haskett 1991, 118. Haskett notes that not all communities placed a maestro de capilla in charge of their cantores.

50. Horcasitas 1974, 154.

51. From document in the Archivo General de la Nación, Mexico City, Bienes Nacionales, vol. 990, exp. 10, transcribed by Jonathan Truitt.

52. Ramos Smith et al. 1998, 300.

53. Leyva (2001, 19–20) summarizes the Huejotzingo testimony.

54. Ramos Smith et al. 1998, 316–17.

55. Bells are rung in *Souls and Testamentary Executors* and *The Merchant*; responses for the dead are chanted in both those plays, *How to Live on Earth* (all three in *Nahuatl Theater*, vol. 1), and in *The Nobleman and His Barren Wife* (this volume). I thank Camilla Townsend (personal communication, April 27, 2010) for her comments on the significance of bells.

56. Ciudad Real 1976, 2:101; Horcasitas 1974, 141.

57. On mock battles, see Harris 2000.

58. *Nahuatl Theater*, 4:300–301.

READING GUIDE

Notes on Nahuatl in Translation

The following notes describe some characteristics of Nahuatl style and some issues relating to the translation of Nahuatl terms. Reading these notes will be helpful for understanding and interpreting the plays.

1. Parallelism. Speakers display verbal skill by stating the same idea two or more times in slightly different words, or by stringing together phrases with a similar grammatical structure. Repetition can create a pleasing rhythm, and the extra emphasis allows important ideas to sink in. This is a common feature of Native American oral performance.

2. Diphrases. Sometimes, a pair of words became an often-repeated verbal formula with a particular, figurative meaning. For example, "earth, mud" means the human body; "tail, wing" means people of the commoner class; "eagle, jaguar" means warrior; "sticks, stones" means punishment. Ángel María Garibay Kintana, a Mexican pioneer in the study of Nahuatl literature, invented the word *difrasismos* for these figures of speech.[1] Footnotes in the plays explain diphrases that do not have an obvious meaning.

3. Vocatives. When talking to someone politely, a male Nahuatl speaker adds a vocative suffix, *-e* (pronounced like Spanish *e*, or "ay" in English), to the person's title or name, accenting this syllable. So Pedro would become Pedroé (Pedro-AY). A female speaker accents the last syllable (Pe-DRO instead of PE-dro). In the translations, this feature is shown by putting the word "O" before the term of address: "O my beloved mother," "O teacher," and so on. This may seem stiff or formal, but it indicates that the characters are speaking to one another with respect and esteem. People can also be addressed politely as "you my mother," "you who are rulers," and the like. But to say simply "mother" is very rude. Where such direct forms of address occur in a play, the character is displaying a lack of respect. This form is not always used with personal names, however, so just saying "Pedro" is not necessarily rude.

4. **Fictional kinship.** Nahuas sometimes politely addressed one another using kinship terms that did not describe their actual relationship.[2] A relative might be addressed with the wrong kin term, or an unrelated person might be addressed as kin.

5. **The altepetl.** Where the word *altepetl* occurs in the plays, it is retained in the translations. The altepetl, or corporate community, was the primary source of group identity for colonial Nahuas. Some altepetl centered on a city or a large town, but some included multiple settlements of different sizes, including villages, hamlets, and the farmed or open lands around them. Thus "city" or "town" is not a very accurate parallel for this important concept.

6. **Four hundred**. The number "four hundred"—*centzontli*, a basic unit in the Nahuas' vigesimal counting system—had the sense of "a whole lot," or "innumerable," like English "gazillion."

7. **Gods and devils.** In Nahuatl texts the Christian God is called by the Spanish name *Dios*, but described as a *teotl*, the Nahuatl term for gods or for sacred and mysterious forces in general. In these plays, *Dios* is translated as "God" and *teotl* as "deity." When *teotl* is used in an adjectival sense, it is translated as "holy." A related term, *teoyotica*, meaning "by means of holiness" or "through divinity," was used in colonial times to designate things that were connected to the Christian church, such as marriages performed by a priest. In the plays, this term is translated as "religious" or "in a religious way." *Tlacatecolotl*, the Nahuatl word used for devils, is translated as "demon"; the Spanish word *diablo* is translated as "devil."

8. **Divine titles.** A few titles used for preconquest gods, especially the powerful Tezcatlipoca, that were considered appropriate for the Christian God appear in these plays: "lord of the near, lord of the close" (*tloque nahuaque*), "giver of life" (*ipalnemoani* or variants), and "lord of the sky (or heaven), lord of earth" (*ilhuicaque tlalticpaque*). The friars thought

these appropriately described God's power and omnipresence, but the terms also carried associations with indigenous concepts of divinity.

9. Names. The names of biblical figures, saints, devils, and allegorical figures are translated into English. For purely fictional characters, their Spanish or Nahuatl names are retained.

10. Heaven and hell. The Nahuatl term for heaven, *ilhuicac*, means "in the sky." The term for the underworld, *mictlan*, "place of the dead," was adopted for hell. The translations use the more familiar English terms. In preconquest religion, the underworld was not a place of punishment. Most people's spirit or life force went there. Unweaned babies, warriors killed in battle or sacrifice, and women who died in childbirth went to different parts of the heavens.

11. Spirit and soul. The Spanish word *ánima* was introduced for the Christian concept of the soul. This word was often paired with *teyolia*, a Nahuatl term for a heart-based life force. This latter term is translated as "spirit."

12. Tlatoani. The word for the ruler of a preconquest altepetl is *tlatoani*, which literally means "speaker"; the Aztec emperor was the *huey tlatoani*, "great speaker." In colonial times, when altepetl were ruled by an elected governor and other officials, tlatoani came to be applied more loosely to high-ranking nobles, a practice that can be seen in these plays.

13. Precious and admired. Speaking in respectful tones, characters often address one another or refer to other people as "precious" or "precious and admired." The first term, *tlazo(tli)*, something valuable or precious, is related to the verb for "to love" (*tlazotla*) and can also be translated as "beloved." The second, *mahuiz(tic)*, means admired, honored, revered, splendid, or marvelous.

14. Added text. In the translations, words in brackets [ ] are added to clarify unclear wording or to supply text that seems to be missing.

Some other features of Nahuatl style cannot be shown very easily in translation. One of these is the reverential system. This grammatical program adds extra prefixes and suffixes to verbs and a respectful suffix to nouns. Showing all this in English becomes excessively clumsy: "The honored noblewoman causes herself to eat her honored tortillas." Therefore, although reverential nouns and verbs are very common in the Nahuatl plays, they are not systematically shown in the translations.

Also lost in translation are compound words. Nahuatl allows words to be joined together, the first term(s) modifying the last. For example, "my precious and admired mother" (or "child," "teacher," and so on) is one word. The longest word in these six plays is uttered by the servant of the Three Kings. Bubbling over with excitement after his first look at the baby Jesus, he describes "his precious, admired, totally precious, admired, good, and shimmering face." This makes a twenty-four-syllable word: *itlazomahuizcenquizcatlazomahuizqualtilizpepetlaquilizxayacatzin*. Even if "precious, admired" is repeated by accident, this is quite a mouthful.

Notes

1. Garibay 1978, 115–16.
2. See Karttunen and Lockhart 1987, 43–45.

PRONUNCIATION GUIDE
AND GLOSSARY

If you know Spanish, you can approximate correct pronunciation of Nahuatl by saying the words as if they were in Spanish. English speakers should pronounce *o* long, as in "note," and *a* as in "father." Also note the following:

1. Pronounce *x* like English *sh*.
2. Pronounce *z* like *s*.
3. Always place the accent on the second-last syllable.
4. The *tl* combination is voiced at the beginning of a word or syllable. Try saying "tra-la-la" and then change the *r* to an *l*. Then try "tla-tla-tla."
5. At the end of a word, *tl* is unvoiced, almost whispered. It is not like the *–tle* in "bottle." Instead, try saying "bought" with a little, whispered *l* at the end, still pronouncing the word as one syllable: "bought(l)."
6. The *tz* combination is similar to the *ts* in "nuts" or "itsy-bitsy."

Nahuatl also uses glottal stops and long and short vowels. Usually these features are not shown in colonial texts. To keep the terms more accessible, typical colonial spelling is used in this book. Some glottal stops are shown with an *h* in the glossary's pronunciation guide.

altepetl (al-TE-petl) corporate community, town, city
amatl (A-matl) paper

Chichimeca (chee-chee-MAY-kah) nomadic peoples of northern Mexico

cihuateteo (see-wa-te-TAY-oh) goddesses associated with women who died in childbirth

cihuatl (SEE-watl) woman

Colhua (KOL-wah) Nahua ethnic group

Cuauhtemoc (kwau-TAY-mok) Mexica ruler who led the final defense against Cortés.

Cuauhtitlan (kwau-TEE-tlan) Nahua altepetl, home of Juan Diego in the Guadalupe story

ichpochtli (eech-POCH-tlee) girl, young woman, maiden, virgin

ixehua (eesh-AY-wa) to put on an act, play in a farce

macehualli (ma-say-WAL-lee) commoner, vassal, "Indian"

machiyotl (ma-CHEE-yotl) symbol or sign

Malintzin (ma-LEEN-tseen) woman's name, from Spanish Marina

Mexica (me-SHEEH-kah) Nahua ethnic group, dominant Aztec power

mictlan (MEEK-tlan) place of the dead, underworld, hell

Motecuhzoma (mo-tek-SO-ma) Mexica ruler at time of Cortés' arrival

Motolinia (mo-to-lee-NEE-a) poor, afflicted; name taken by fray Toribio de Benavente

Nahua (NA-wah) collective term for speakers of Nahuatl, inhabitants of Central Mexico

nahualli (na-WAL-lee) a shaman or sorcerer able to change into an animal alter-ego

Nahuatl (NA-watl) Uto-Aztecan language widely spoken across Central Mexico and beyond

neixcuitilli (nay-eesh-kwee-TEEL-lee) example, play, moral tale

Nezahualcoyotl (nay-sa-wal-KO-yotl) fifteenth-century ruler of Tetzcoco

Nican mopohua (NEE-kan mo-PO-wa) "here it is told," Nahuatl version of the Guadalupe story

pilli (PEEL-lee) noble, person of the upper class

Quetzalcoatl (kay-tsal-KO-atl) "Quetzal Snake," preconquest deity associated with rulership, the priesthood, the wind, and the planet Venus, later associated with Christianity

Tenochtitlan (te-noch-TEE-tlan) Mexica altepetl, capital city of the Aztec empire, Mexico City

teopantlaca (tay-o-pan-TLA-kah) "church people," native religious officials

Tepeyacac (te-pe-YA-kak) site north of Tenochtitlan, location of Guadalupe shrine

Tetzcoco (tetz-KO-ko) second most powerful altepetl in the Aztec Empire

Tezcatlipoca (tez-ka-tlee-PO-ka) "Smoking Mirror," powerful preconquest deity, compared to both God and the devil

tilmatli (teel-MAH-tlee) rectangular cloth worn as a cloak

Tizoc (TEE-sok) unsuccessful Aztec emperor; character in *The Animal Prophet and the Fortunate Patricide*

tlacatecolotl (tla-ka-tay-KO-lotl) sorcerer, demon, devil

tlamahuizolli (tla-ma-wee-SOL-lee) miracle, wonder

tlapechtli (tla-PECH-tlee) platform, stage, bed

Tlatelolco (tla-te-LOL-ko) sister city to Tenochtitlan, northern part of Mexico City

tlatlacolli (tlah-tla-KOL-lee) sin, or a wider sense of damage or decay

tlatoani (tlah-to-WA-nee) ruler of an altepetl; in colonial usage sometimes high-ranking nobles more generally

Toci (TO-seeh) "Our Grandmother," preconquest deity

The Nobleman and His Barren Wife

This morality play bears no information about its date or place of origin. The script probably dates to around 1700 or shortly after: the manuscript is bound together with another play that is dated 1717, and the scribe used the letter "s" (rather than "ç" or "z"), a practice that began around 1700. It may be a copy of a play that was originally composed at a much earlier time. The surviving copy is in Mexico's National Library of Anthropology and History.[1]

This play inscribes its moral lesson into the simple dichotomy of a married couple, who do not even receive personal names: they are just "Nobleman" (*pilli*) and "Woman" (*cihuatl*). The husband is good and the wife is bad. The husband dies and goes to heaven; the wife dies and goes to hell. The specific ways in which the wife is bad are not quite so straightforward, however, and her story makes for an interesting drama about marital relations as well as demonic temptation and damnation.

As is true of several other morality plays, this text was intended to support the Catholic sacrament of penitence. Specifically, it stresses how important it is to confess one's sins to a priest annually during Lent and also when one is close to death. It is not enough simply to confess some sins. All must be told, with nothing held back out of shame. Otherwise one will be condemned to hell and tormented by demons for all eternity. In this sense, the wife's particular sins are beside the point: the fact that she never made a complete confession suffices to condemn her to hell.

While this is a general pattern in these plays, the specific sins committed by the bad people differ. Thus, the plays tell different stories and offer Nahua actors and audience members different models of bad behavior to contemplate. Often the sins are egregious, and Nahuas would have considered them immoral even without any Christian influence: a man who murders his wife, a wife who chases after other men, a boy who shows cruelty to his grandfather, a merchant who cheats people out of their property or offers a loan in return for sexual favors.

So what are the sins of the wife in this play? She has no children, nor does she want to have any. She is concerned about the expense. She also worries about losing her looks, and having to go around with messy hair or in clothes stained by an infant's urine or feces. These are sins of greed and pride, which number among the Catholic church's seven mortal sins. The fondness Nahua noblewomen felt toward fancy clothes and elaborate hairstyles attracted criticism from Christian writers, as in a song in Sahagún's *Psalmodia christiana* that contrasts these stylish noblewomen with Saint Clare, the first Franciscan nun.[2]

Wishful thinking does not prevent pregnancy. This couple has been married for twenty-two years, and the husband has longed all this time to become a father. The wife's failure to give birth may indicate something other than greed and pride. This is where the demons come in.

The play features four demon characters who, as in other morality plays, try to corrupt the characters' morals and keep them from purifying themselves through confession. In this play, the demons sometimes appear as humans and pass themselves off as friendly townspeople. For the scene where they meet to discuss their nasty plot, the actors might don devil costumes or reveal the horns or tails they cover up in the other scenes.

The demons are named Lucifer, Satan, Temptation, and, simply, Demon, the Spanish word *demonio*. In Christianity, Lucifer and Satan are two names for the same personage, the leader of all the devils. Using these names for two different creatures suggests native authorship.

It is Temptation who is most involved with the childless woman. The Christian concept of temptation (toward sin) was translated into Nahuatl with the word *teneyeyecoliztli*. It means "getting people to try things" and derives from the same verb used for rehearsing a play. The word does not carry any particular allure of the morally forbidden.

Temptation specializes in reproductive problems. He causes fetuses to die in the womb and also causes women to die in childbirth. He makes women squander their money, so they do not have enough for their

Nahua noblewomen in fancy skirts and blouses. Illustration from the *Florentine Codex*, Book Eight, f. 31r. (Reprinted with permission from fray Bernardino de Sahagún, *Historia general de las cosas de Nueva España, Códice florentino*. Facsimile of the *Codex Florentinus* of the Biblioteca Medicea Laurenziana, published by the Archivo General de la Nación, 1979.)

other obligations. The play does not refer explicitly to abortion, but a demon who gets women to spend money so that their fetuses die might well be one who tempts women toward that practice. Abortion would have been too sensitive a subject to broach openly in a community performance, but women in the audience would understand these references. Nahua traditional medicine included knowledge of abortifacients. This was one of the reasons priests disapproved of traditional healers. So, the childless noblewoman could be seen as someone who has had abortions, who has gone to traditional medical specialists behind her husband's back and in violation of Catholic teachings. If this is the case, it is no wonder she is afraid to tell the priest everything she has done and, thus, receives such terrible punishment.

The husband, in contrast, is presented as the good guy. An early scene establishes his goodness: when Jesus Christ, disguised as a priest, tests his faith by dropping in for a visit, the nobleman invites him in, treats him graciously, and serves him food and drink. Still hoping to father a child, the nobleman decides to give all his property to the church and to the poor, in order to gain more merit with God. His determination to give away all his money leads his wife to commit another questionable act: she takes some of the money and gives it to her friend Lucía to hide. For this to be a sin, though, the wife must have no rights of her own to the couple's property and must owe her husband complete obedience in economic matters.

This is not the way things always were for Nahua women. The early colonial era saw a decline in women's status. Under the influence of Spanish legal and religious institutions, the gender complementarity that characterized Nahua society at the time of the conquest gave way to a more patriarchal social order. Women came to exert less control over property and its inheritance.[3]

The woman in the play is contesting her secondary economic status at the same time as she is asserting reproductive choice. Women in the audience (and some men too) may well have sympathized with her plight, on either or both issues. Who would want to be married—or otherwise related—to a man who gives all his money away and leaves his wife and other kin no inheritance whatsoever? Certainly the church should receive a donation, but should it receive everything? Is the priest, who so quickly takes control of all the husband's goods, not himself a greedy interloper? This woman, unlike a wife murderer or a grandfather abuser, might not be someone the entire community can easily unite against. The play points to sources of tension in male–female relations, and in relations between native people and the priests who meddled in their moral and economic affairs.

The husband and wife contrast in the moral quality not only of their lives but also of their deaths. The husband falls ill but has time to confess. In the presence of witnesses, he disposes of his property as he sees fit. This is a good death.[4] Even though demons are present at the deathbed (and demons were believed to be drawn to these scenes), angels are on guard, and the demons are unable to corrupt the proceedings. In contrast, the wife's sinful status seems to invite her sudden demise—a bad death. Death itself, represented by an actor (probably with bones painted on his costume), comes for her in the night, and she dies with no opportunity to make that much needed confession.

The condemned woman returns to haunt the priest and lament her failure to live as a proper woman. As a childless woman, she could at least have been a godmother to other people's children, or pledged service to a saint. The graphic punishments inflicted on her body are very similar to those of Lucía in the play *Final Judgment* and reflect Catholic churchmen's views of feminine vanity.

When the demon Temptation speaks of death in childbirth, he uses the term that sixteenth-century Nahuas used when women died in their first childbirth, with the fetus still in the womb (*cihuaquetza*, "she rises as a woman"). These women became deities of the western sky and accompanied the sun from the zenith to the horizon.[5] However, these failed mothers were not benign: on their five festival days they descended to earth and caused illnesses and deformities in any children left exposed to their wrath. In the play, the childless woman who returns from the afterworld might for Nahua audiences have something of this character. This would make her scary and dangerous, but not necessarily an object lesson for one's own moral behavior.

Interestingly, the play ends on a note of gender harmony, with a male figure politely obeying a female's demand. These are Jesus Christ and the Virgin Mary. The Virgin secures Nobleman's entry into heaven. Popular belief in the Virgin's influence over her son, in New Spain as in Europe, elevated her to a near divine status. Here Nahuas could find something more like the gender complementarity of their own traditional social relations and religious beliefs. It is no wonder they found Mary a very appealing figure, however they might feel about women like the wife in this play.

Notes

1. Biblioteca Nacional de Antropología e Historia, Archivo Histórico, Colección Antigua, vol. 872.

2. Sahagún 1993, 240–41.

3. Kellogg (1995, 1997, 1998) documents this decline in women's status.

4. See Eire (1995) on Spanish beliefs about death and the afterlife.

5. On these beliefs, see Sullivan 1966; Sahagún 1950–1982, 4:41, 107, and 6:161–65.

THE NOBLEMAN AND HIS BARREN WIFE

Cast of characters in order of appearance

Nobleman
Angel
Woman (*Nobleman's wife, later* Barren One)
First Page
Second Page
Christ
Lucifer
First Demon
Satan
Devil (*named* Temptation)
Lucía
First Uncle
First Relative
Second Relative
Death
Priest
Saint Mary

Here is an exemplary model that tells about a ruler who loved our lord God very much. But his wife was trying to make him stop. She did not want him to make offerings. And our lord God despised her. She became barren.

(Here Nobleman enters along with an angel. Then he prays, kneeling down.)

NOBLEMAN: You who are my completely good angel, you who are my guardian,[1] you're the one our lord God commanded to protect me. And now I pray to you and I bow humbly before you, because I am your charge, our lord God left me to you, so that you would look after me. And now I beg of you, protect me, so I don't fall into some offense to the deity we share, God. And inspire me with your power. Stay with me until my life on earth comes to an end, then take me to heaven, where you live, along with the other angels and saints.

ANGEL: Don't worry, O my earthly master, you who are my charge, for I maintain complete confidence in the true judge, my ruler, God. He is watching over your entire life on earth, and I pray to him on your behalf. Live always and forever according to the commands of our mother holy church and the ten holy commands of the only deity, God. Pray to him and keep offering yourself to him. You people who live on earth, offer yourselves before our lord.

NOBLEMAN: O our lord, O God, you saved me with your precious blood, which you spilled for my sake. But help me. I think they are calling me now and declaring something to me. But I must do it and carry it out before our lord God. *(At that point two servants of his enter, along with his wife, who is carrying offerings.)* O my precious children, O my servants, here they are. Follow me. Give the gifts to the preacher, the speaker of the holy words. And with great humility, reverence, and devotion give them to [God] on our behalf. May he accept them, so that I may give him my soul. But he already knows it. Please go, O my children.

ANGEL: O master, O ruler, let's go to the church. Let's go and give [the offering] to God's precious ones, the precious priests.

(Wind instruments[2] are played. Then [the servants] go to the church. At that point the ruler and his wife remain. They speak with one another.)

---

1. Guardian angels are common figures in morality plays. Sometimes they try to reform the immoral characters and give up when their efforts are ignored. In this play, the wife's guardian angel does not even show up.

2. Flutes or trumpets.

NOBLEMAN: Please listen, O noblewoman. Fortunate are they who are willing to endure poverty for our lord God's sake, for rulership on earth will be their possession, will belong to them. Fortunate are they who live calmly and peacefully, for theirs will be, they will take possession of, the land, that is to say, the joys of heaven.[3]

WOMAN: As to what you're saying, who can know how it will turn out tomorrow or the next day, O my precious husband?

(At that point two pages enter.)

SECOND PAGE: May it comfort you to know that we went and left the offering at the church. God's precious ones, the precious priests, accepted it.

NOBLEMAN: That's good, O my children. It's late now. Go and rest.

(He exits. Christ enters, along with two angels, and he acts the part of a priest. He puts a white cloak over his head and knocks at the door.)

CHRIST: I love you very much, O my precious children. Are you there? Have mercy.

FIRST PAGE: May our lord God give you good health, O my precious priest. Come here.[4]

CHRIST: O my precious child, tell me, will the high-ranking nobleman perhaps permit us to stay and rest here in his entryway? The boys are very tired from carrying the crates, since it's still a long way to the church and it's quite dark.

(Then he goes to call him. Nobleman enters.)

NOBLEMAN: May God the Holy Spirit himself lead you here, O God's precious one, O my precious priest. In no way shall you just sleep in the doorway. Come in! It's not my home; it's God's home, where I'm waiting for his orders, whatever his face and heart may desire, tomorrow or the next day.

CHRIST: May it be as you wish, O my precious child. You remember all your promises,[5] since I am a traveler and far from my home.

(Then his servants set things up. They put down a table and the pages serve food. Christ sits down.)

---

3. Nobleman loosely translates the Beatitudes: "Blessed are the poor in spirit, for theirs is the kingdom of heaven," and "Blessed are the meek, for they shall inherit the earth" (Matthew 5:3, 5). The script refers to rulership on earth, rather than in heaven.

4. Repeated below, a traditional way to say "welcome, greetings."

5. The Works of Mercy, taught in the catechism, include sheltering travelers and feeding the hungry.

NOBLEMAN: I am a very poor man, O my precious priest. You must have a little bite of food, and here's a little something to drink, an offering.

CHRIST: Your charity and diligence are revealed in that, O my precious child. You have been sent here in penitence. But now, O my precious child, I must be going. I am very grateful to you. Take your rest.

NOBLEMAN: May God the Holy Spirit guide you along your way, O my precious and admired father.

(At that point Christ exits and the ruler [remains]. At that point his wife enters.)

NOBLEMAN: Now, O my precious wife, O noblewoman, take notice of my sadness and my anxiety. And may the Holy Spirit send you his good grace. How wretched we are! We have now been married for twenty-two years. The master, the ruler, our lord God has not given us a single one of his creations. May he grant us one of his jewels, his quetzal plumes.[6] All this time we've kept on praying to him. And we would acknowledge that we caused him much offense, that we are grave sinners four hundred times over. And what's worrying me, O noblewoman, is if tomorrow or the next day God were to send his justice, his staff-bearer, death, since we are just waiting for him to come and take us. And all our goods and possessions are not our goods and possessions. They are our lord God's goods and possessions. And we too are in his keeping. Let us return them to him. We've already sponsored all the Masses in the church. And now let the priests be called. Let's entreat them to have habits purchased and then let the poor sick people divide up the [remaining] money. This that you are hearing, O my precious wife, is what's troubling me today.

WOMAN: I've heard every word you've declared. And here is how I reply to your precious words. We have but a little bit of health left on earth. When some sickness comes over us, let there be money to give to people. Won't we be very poor, if it is distributed to people now? If we die, will we still think it's good? And if we did have a child it would have given us a great many worries, whether it were a boy or a girl. And wouldn't you have kept the money? Wouldn't it have been used up? And little children are very bothersome, O my precious husband.

---

6. Metaphors for children.

NOBLEMAN: What are you saying, O noblewoman? Listen to what our preachers tell us. It is true that deadly sin, which is called "mortal sin,"[7] that these deadly sins are how we break our lord God's commands, whether with our thoughts, or with our words, or with our deeds. And they are called deadly sins because they kill our souls and our bodies. Therefore anyone who does these things will suffer in hell forever if they are not destroyed here on earth through penance, which is the true life of our souls. And through them we lose eternal bliss. Don't take what I want away from me. Let it be done.

WOMAN: Let your wishes be carried out in this way. Let's go collect and see to the money.

NOBLEMAN: Let your wishes be carried out in this way. When I heard you talk like this, O noblewoman, it was a great comfort to me. Let's go. *(Then Nobleman [and his wife] exit. Lucifer, Demon, Satan, and Temptation enter, four of them.)*

LUCIFER: Please come, you servants of mine, you hands of mine, to whom I have given dominion. You, Demon, and you who are called Satan, and you who are called Temptation, what are you up to? What are you doing? Aren't some of the little people of the earth escaping from our hands? They are confessing. They fortify themselves with their guardian angels.

FIRST DEMON:[8] O ruler, O lord of hell, O Lucifer, don't worry. As for the little people of earth, the things we do to confuse people are not few in number. They cannot be measured. We always seize your vassals during the night. All of them will go to your home in the abyss of hell. You'll see them all, O ruler.

SATAN: And as for me, I who am called Satan, I do a great many things. I go into the churches everywhere. I close up their ears and put them to sleep so they can't hear the teachings that their preacher recounts to them. Even though they are attending Mass, they are thinking there about their lustfulness, their pleasures, their adulteries, their slanders, and they are thinking even more about how they will mock people, they will lend money to people at interest, and they will cheat people out of their goods and possessions. This indeed is how I do my work, O ruler, O Lucifer.

---

7. The phrase is in Spanish.
8. Demon is called this even though there is no "second" demon.

DEVIL: As for me, I who am called Temptation, know, O ruler, O Lucifer, that I am strong. The work with which I serve you is that I go in and immerse myself among the people everywhere, so that I make them confused about any sensible speech that I hear from them. I don't do just the one job. I also devote myself to making little children who are still in someone's belly die inside their rotten mother, so she dies in childbirth, or so she becomes barren. Thus she squanders things and has nothing with which to pay her debts here on earth. And now I've stayed for a long time on account of a certain ruler, who has a great many goods and possessions. He and his wife have been married for twenty-two years but have no children. His wife has become barren. Little children really disgust her. And she is firmly in my possession. In her whole life she hasn't made an honest confession. She just omits her sins out of shame. This indeed is how I go about my work, O ruler, O Lucifer.

LUCIFER: Your work that you all tell of makes me very happy and it's a great comfort to me to hear it. You are strong. Put a lot of effort into it! I'm very strong also. I'll wait on the stone steps [of the church], on Sunday when the palm fronds are blessed,[9] for anyone who hasn't confessed yet, who's just going [to church] in his or her sins. They won't belong to the true judge. They belong to me! They'll become my goods and possessions because they consigned themselves to me, they made themselves my servants. But now don't let go of the little barren one who has become your captive. Don't let her out of your hands! Watch out for her angels!

(Then they all exit. Woman, Nobleman, and a demon enter. A snake is tied around her neck. Lucía enters through another door. Another devil approaches them.)

WOMAN: O my precious daughter, where are you going? Why is the day so very hot? Just put your cloak over your head, O my daughter.

LUCÍA: Please come here, O my precious older sister. What you say is true—the sun is really burning. But won't we go behind them to go and make offerings, as was our thought? But I'm just on my way to see you, for I dreamed about you during the night. It was like I was seeing you. You were really crying, you were sad. And the ruler, your precious husband, was scolding you. I saw you.

9. Palm Sunday. People were supposed to have gone to confession during Lent.

WOMAN: Thank you for asking, O my precious younger sister, O my daughter. What you dreamed about me is true. I'm in a lot of trouble right now.

LUCÍA: I know it. That's what I'm saying. Let me ask myself, is there any end to weariness?[10] I haven't seen you for a week. But what are you troubled about, O my precious daughter?

WOMAN: O my precious younger sister, what your son is upset about is that God hasn't given us even a single child. It's been in vain that he's put offerings in the churches everywhere. And now I think he's getting desperate. He wants to give all the money we have to the sick because he sees he has no child. But you know, O my daughter, even if a little child comes to be born—well, they are really disgraceful, annoying, dirtying, and corrupting, the way they cry and the way they pee in front of people. So, what am I to think, on my own? Whatever my heart wants, won't this happen? Is what I'm saying bad, O my precious daughter, O noblewoman?

LUCÍA: Yes, what you're saying is true. You've had a good time. What do you think? How do you feel about it? You're living in a good place. And we certainly put on good clothes to cover our earth, our mud,[11] so that we go around looking beautiful. But would you look at the people who have children! Are they still clean enough to touch? They go around with their hair in a big mess and they go around with their children's pee on them. They go around all weak and dried up. And little children really make people waste away, O my daughter.

WOMAN: That's what I think and feel, what you're saying, O my precious daughter. But now he's sending me to summon our relatives. The dispersal of the money will take place in their presence. And tomorrow morning they're going to summon the priests. And he tells me we're going to confess and prepare ourselves so the money will be put into the church. How can it happen? Please give me your consideration!

WOMAN:[12] Yes. Let me rush off now. I've stayed a long time, O my precious daughter.

(Then the noblewoman leaves. Lucía stays there. Nobleman enters and Lucía approaches him.)

10. In other words, "life is tough."

11. A diphrase referring to the human body.

12. The copyist, turning to a new page, forgot to include Lucía's reply, in which she presumably offers to hide money for Woman. Later, Woman says that Lucía has done this.

LUCÍA: May our lord God grant you health, O master, O ruler, O my precious son. How is the precious day that your precious and admired father, our lord God, is giving you?

NOBLEMAN: Please come here, O lady, O noblewoman. Thank you; our lord God caused me to rise with a little bit [of good health]. But recently my earth, my mud has begun to feel very afflicted. But my spirit, my soul is alert,[13] O noblewoman. Thank you.

LUCÍA: You are suffering, O my precious son. Is there any end to weariness? But the noblewoman also came by. I was on my way to see her.

NOBLEMAN: O noblewoman, here are our relatives whom I sent her to go and call. Wait here a little while. Stay at rest, O noblewoman.

LUCÍA: So be it, O my precious son. Let me wait here a bit.

(Then two relatives enter, led by the noblewoman. Two demons, disguised as people, come to meet them.)

FIRST UNCLE: Let's hurry along, O my younger brother. I think that here come our dear friends. You are friends with them.

FIRST DEMON: And where are you going? We're on our way to see you, O honored people!

FIRST RELATIVE: O our dear friends, here we've come upon the very person who is having us summoned!

SATAN: It's very good that you're going to see him. Maybe you'll inherit something. But if you want, let us go with you so we can consider together what we're going to inherit.

FIRST UNCLE: [to Nobleman] O my child, O my son-in-law! [to the demons] O honored people, my sons, you say that it might be done like this, that we will go along with them.

WOMAN: So be it. What my precious sons are saying is very precious. I don't know you at all. Let me be deserving of you[r friendship].

FIRST DEMON: O precious noblewoman, don't worry. Whatever your heart desires, we will make it all come true. Let's go.

(Then they go. They all call to Nobleman.)

WOMAN: O my precious son, our relatives whom you're looking for have come.

NOBLEMAN: Please come here, O my uncles. As to why I've called you: go and summon the priest for me, for my earth, my mud, is now growing very weak, and my sins are a very great worry to me.

---

13. He is of sound mind, despite his poor health, and thus competent to dispose of his property.

FIRST UNCLE: What are you saying, O my son-in-law? Are you already sick in bed, that the priest is to be summoned? Do you have a fever? Come on out, O my precious son-in-law.

WOMAN: What are you saying to our uncles? Are you sick? I left just a while ago, O my precious husband.

FIRST DEMON: Please get up, my ruler, and stay awake for a little while longer. Let them call the priest immediately. First of all, consider what you are going to give your precious wife, the noblewoman. She's not going to be poor, is she?

NOBLEMAN: The priest will hear my confession, so that I'll be able to lay out my sins in front of him.

SECOND RELATIVE: So be it. Let me summon the priest. *(Then he goes into the church. Then he goes to call Priest, who comes to interrogate Nobleman.)* The poor sick person is lying here, O my precious priest.

PRIEST: May God grant you health, O my precious child. What's troubling you? Do you need to confess? Will you prepare yourself [for death]?

NOBLEMAN: Please come here, O my precious priest. Yes indeed, you will help me to prepare myself and confess.

(At that point he confesses. Then two angels enter and come to stand by the sick person, who makes his confession.)

PRIEST: O my precious child, you might be forgetting something. Search your conscience thoroughly. And do you totally reject the demon's pride, and all the ways he traps people? And do you totally reject all his deeds, with which he beguiles, confuses, and deceives people, O my child?

NOBLEMAN: O my precious father, I totally reject all of them, and I have said every single one of my sins. O my precious father, may our lord God truly pardon me.

PRIEST: O my precious child, our lord God has now pardoned you. I have now cleansed you. He has pardoned you for all your sins and now you belong to the holy church of our lord God, three persons but just one true deity. May he bless us. In the name of God the father, and God the child, and God the Holy Spirit, may it so be done. Now I'm going to go, O my precious child. If you die, I'll carry out everything you said, O my child.

(Then Priest leaves. Wind instruments are played. Then everyone exits [except Nobleman and First Uncle].)

FIRST UNCLE: O ruler, go inside. You're already very short of breath. Get some rest.

NOBLEMAN: So be it, O my precious children.

(At that point [Nobleman and First Uncle exit and] Death enters.)

DEATH: For it is by order of the true judge and sentencer, the eternal ruler, our lord God [that I have come]. But his wife is a great miser and a barren wretch, so I am going to seize her. She will die. I'm just going to destroy her in her sleep,[14] since our lord God has already passed judgment on her in anger. Know, O people of earth, that I am God's messenger. I am your end, I am your death. O people of earth, be sensible! Pray to our lord God, the true judge, your sentencer.

(At that point he shoots arrows. And when Death is finished, then he exits. The relatives enter hurriedly.)

FIRST UNCLE: What's happened to us? Our lord God has now destroyed our late son-in-law. He just died in his sleep. Don't let his wife know, since she is very sick, and if she finds out, won't she die immediately? O my younger brothers, what's to be done?

SECOND RELATIVE: That's what I'm about to tell you, O my younger brother. Let's tell the priest right away, the one who came to see him yesterday when he was still all right. Do let's hurry, for it's a long way to the church. When will we get there? When will he be buried?

(Then they exit, calling to someone. At that point Priest enters.)

FIRST RELATIVE: O my precious father, what's happened to us? Know that the ruler whom you came to see and give confession to yesterday has died during the night in his sleep. Death came suddenly and killed him, O my precious father.

PRIEST: O my children, the ruler's possessions are locked up. He gave them to me. Let us go and see him, O my precious children. *(Then they go to the home of the deceased. Priest cries out at the entrance:)* Jesus, Jesus, Jesus! O my precious children, what happened? You must bury him quickly.

SECOND RELATIVE: So be it, O my precious priest. Let's bury him quickly.

(Then the responsory for the dead is chanted. When it is finished they exit. And the condemned one cries out from the entrance to hell. At that point Priest enters.)

PRIEST: Now I must wait for whoever is coming here. It seems to me that it's gotten very dark. That is very frightening for priests. Why is a soul coming? (At that point the wicked ones bring the condemned woman out of hell. A snake is lying on her head, fire lizards are sucking on her, fire*

---

14. Thus, she will have no opportunity to call a priest and confess her sins.

dogs are biting her feet and she has fire butterflies on her blouse. And fire arrows are coming out of her ears.) Jesus, Jesus, Jesus! May the precious and admired name of the most holy trinity be exalted! And by its authority, speak to me, whoever you are who has been brought here [by] the fire dogs. Whether you are a man or a woman, explain to me in what sins you passed away. Speak to me, in the name of God the father, God the child, and God the Holy Spirit. Speak to me!

BARREN ONE: O priest, it's me. My husband, the ruler, died recently, leaving his money to the church. But I hid some of it. I entrusted it to a certain friend of mine, named Lucía. And you have found out that I passed away in my sins. I was buried a week ago, O priest.

PRIEST: But tell me, how is it that you were condemned, O my child? Speak, before me.

BARREN ONE: O God's precious one, it's because I was barren. And I used to receive communion while I was concealing a sin from my confessors because of shame.

PRIEST: What does the snake that lies on your head mean, as well as what's coming out of your ears, the snake from hell that's tied around your neck, and the blouse you're wearing, and the way you're belted, and what's tied to your feet?

BARREN ONE: Know, O God's precious one, that what lies on my head is how I used to tie my magnificent hair, and I used to bind up the ends of my hair. And the fire lizards emerging from my ears are like my splendid earrings used to be. And what lies around my neck stands for the precious necklaces and pearls I used to put on. And the blouse of fire that you see me wearing, which is very frightening, stands for the splendid clothing I used to wear. The fire butterflies that suck my breasts also stand for how I never suckled anyone here on earth. I used to really hate little children, so I was barren, I was barren. But I wasn't born to be barren. But here on earth our lord God scorned me. When I would hear my husband's words, "May God give us one of his creations, a child of our own," I used to get angry, even if it was just to be my godchild. In short, I didn't want any [children] at all on earth. That's why fire lizards suck on me now. And the fire dogs that come at my feet stand for how I would never set my feet on the ground.[15] Now you know all this. O God's precious one, teach this

---

15. Perhaps with the sense of "I would never get my feet dirty," referring to fastidiousness and laziness.

to others, so that no one does the same thing. Let my neighbors learn a lesson from me, the wicked women who are here, so they don't do the same thing.

PRIEST: And what else were you condemned for, O my precious child? I will pray for you to our lord Jesus Christ, and I will perform a Mass for you.

BARREN ONE: O God's precious one, what's the use? Your prayers won't do any good. They won't affect me. They won't do any good. If I had sponsored someone's baptism, or had them receive confirmation, or if they'd become my godchild [by my giving them] a scapular, as I was sent to earth for, so that I would have instructed them about the holy commands of the only deity, God, the ten commandments, or if I had devoted myself to some male or female saint and placed myself in their hands, thus I might have received help. But as it is, I've already been condemned, O my priest.

PRIEST: May our lord God help you and may his help save you, O my precious child!

BARREN ONE: Ay ay ay! I am four hundred times wretched! Would that I hadn't been born, that I hadn't enjoyed the earth, or that my mother had just smothered me in her sleep! What was the use of me being born? Ay ay ay! I am four hundred times wretched! Curse the earth! Ay ay ay!

SATAN: Were you just crying out to someone? They're not there anymore. Just hurry along now. You've already kept us waiting a long time. Just get going now, O wicked one.

FIRST DEMON: O wicked one, what in the world are you still wailing for? Will we ever let you go? You belong to us now; you're our possession now. Now you'll see there [in hell] how you failed to appreciate the earth. Get going, O my friend.

(They exit. Then heaven opens. Our precious mother speaks and the souls in purgatory[16] reach for her.)

SAINT MARY: O my precious and admired child, remember how you commanded children to obey their fathers and mothers. O my precious child, I beseech you, obey me, for the sake of your saved one

---

16. Nahuas were taught the Catholic belief that souls who can be saved but are not pure enough for heaven go to purgatory, a part of hell, where they are purified by fire until they can enter heaven. Here, some part of the stage set must represent purgatory, with actors impersonating imprisoned souls.

whom you saw here on earth.[17] And now he has complied with and carried out all his commands, as he went around serving you. And remember that he was always crying out to me. He used to say the Hail Mary nine times.[18] Now he is crying out in the place where people are purified by fire, purgatory.[19] O my precious child, help him, just at my command, you who are my precious child.

CHRIST: O my precious mother, it is true that I must obey you, for you are my precious mother. Don't be very concerned, for his soul will receive favor. In just a little while he will come forth from the place where people are purified by fire, purgatory. And now, take him, O my precious mother.

SAINT MARY: You have shown favor to the sinner, who is your creation. Receive him, O my precious child.

17. Saint Mary refers to Christ's earlier visit to Nobleman's home.
18. Popular belief held that the Virgin was kind to people who recited this well-known prayer.
19. The text pairs a Nahuatl term with the Spanish *purgatorio*.

Final Judgment

This play follows the basic story line of a Nahuatl morality play: someone commits a lot of sins and fails to confess them properly; smug devils carry the person off to hell. But it sets this scenario into a larger drama about the end of the world, or the Judgment Day envisioned in Christian tradition. The Articles of Faith and the Apostle's Creed, two texts in the basic catechism taught to Nahuas, say that Jesus Christ will return when the world ends and will judge the living and the dead, sending good people to eternal reward in heaven and bad people to be tormented in hell. Indigenous artists created scenes of this final judgment on a number of early colonial religious buildings.

Apocalyptic ideas captivated many Europeans' imaginations during the sixteenth century. The discovery of the Americas seemed like the sort of momentous event that could herald an approaching end-time. Many people hoped that Christian forces would conquer Jerusalem, which was controlled by the Ottoman Turks. This victory would bring about Jesus Christ's return to earth. Christopher Columbus sailed for Asia not only in search of a new trade route. He imagined that Asians would convert to Christianity and help to capture the Holy Land, invading it from the east. So it is not strange that Europeans would see the establishment of the Christian church in Mexico as part of a process leading to the end of the world. The Franciscans in particular were inclined to believe in prophetic and apocalyptic visions of the future.

A native artist's relief sculpture of the Final Judgment. Chapel at the Franciscan church in San Andrés Calpan, Puebla. Christ sits in judgment with the Virgin Mary, John the Baptist, and angels. The dead rise from their graves. (Photo by the author.)

Nahuas at the time of the Spanish invasion saw world history in terms of separate suns or ages of creation. They thought that they were inhabiting the last one, which would someday end in earthquakes. Like Europeans, they believed in various sorts of divination and prophecy. The conquest did not end their world, but it did bring drastic transformations. They adapted or invented prophecies to help make sense of these changes, sometimes merging their own traditions with apocalyptic scenarios brought by their Franciscan teachers.

Nahuatl chronicles tell of an early play about the end of the world that was staged in Tlatelolco—in 1533, according to one account. Spaniards also wrote about productions on this theme. According to fray Gerónimo de Mendieta, his fellow Franciscan Andrés de Olmos composed a play with this topic that was performed in Mexico City in front of New Spain's first viceroy, don Antonio de Mendoza, and the first archbishop, fray

Juan de Zumárraga. For both those men to be present, the production must have occurred between 1535 and 1548. Fray Bartolomé de Las Casas witnessed an early play on the same theme. It was in Mexico City, but he gives no date. He recalled a cast of eight hundred Indians, each with a different part to play.[1]

It is unclear whether these accounts describe the same event, with some imprecision in dates and locations, or two or three different performances. It is also unclear whether they bear any connection with the surviving play. This script, bound together with two other plays, is housed in the Library of Congress in Washington, D.C. One of the other plays carries the date 1687. The Final Judgment play may have been written around the same time, although it was probably copied from an earlier version. With only nineteen speaking roles, it could hardly be the same play Las Casas saw, even allowing for exaggeration.

One feature of Olmos's play offers a possible connection. Mendieta claims that the performance had a particular effect on many wayward women (*mujeres erradas*), who, in fear and remorse, turned to God. So, like the surviving play, it may have shown a woman being punished for sexual sins, in a graphic and frightening manner. Olmos's play may have lived on as a source or model for later plays on the same theme.

The surviving play is unusual in its use of allegorical figures: Time, Holy Church, Penance, and Sweeping. At the beginning of the play these characters speak of how time is running out for sinful humanity, although people could reform and find mercy if they wanted to. The figure called Sweeping embodies a devotional and purifying practice important to Nahuas before and after the conquest. Death also appears in this scene, but he can be found in other Nahuatl dramas, including *The Nobleman and His Barren Wife*.

Soon, though, action turns to a more human domain, as Lucía, the sinful woman, tries to confess to a priest before it is too late. The play differs from other morality plays in that Lucía is isolated from any community or domestic setting. The only other ordinary folks who appear in this play are two other living people whom Jesus Christ interviews after he has come down to judge the living and the dead.

Holy Church introduces the topic of marriage, the seventh of the church's seven sacraments, or special rituals that affect a person's moral or spiritual condition.[2] Although, like bad people in other morality plays, Lucía has failed to confess properly, the script describes her particular predicament as a failure to get married. Being single is not a sin, but the references to lust (made by Penance, Death, and Jesus Christ) indicate that Lucía has been engaging in premarital relations, to an extent that scandalizes the priest who agrees to hear her confession. She should have married her lover (or one of them). With the end of the world at hand, she cannot complete her confession and penance. Therefore, she will be among those consigned permanently to hell.

Nahuas appreciated sexual pleasure and the procreation of children, but they feared excessive sexual activity, whether within or outside of marriage. This was part of a general distrust of disorderly behaviors that could threaten personal equilibrium, public decorum, or cosmic order. Men who had too much intercourse would waste away. Women might die in childbirth, the fetus glued to the uterus by excess semen.

Fidelity within marriage was valued; adultery was considered a very serious breach of moral order. Virginity may have been expected of brides who belonged to the nobility, but otherwise some sexual activity between unmarried partners was accepted (and Lucía is not described as a noblewoman). Informal unions, known as "tying" oneself to someone, were not generally considered sinful or illegitimate. In preconquest times a group of women, known as "they who go around having a good time," acted as casual companions to the young warriors. Europeans saw these women as "prostitutes," but indigenous attitudes seem to have been less derogatory.

Roman Catholic priests and other colonial authorities sought to police indigenous people's domestic lives by insisting that couples formalize their unions with the Christian sacrament. Polygyny, common among the preconquest nobility, was suppressed; men with multiple wives were pressured to marry one of them in church and break off ties with the others. Priests tried to persuade Nahuas that any sexual activity outside of church-consecrated marriage was a deadly sin. However, they could not completely change native people's attitudes and behavior. Fray Juan Bautista, in 1600, observed that young couples preparing for church marriage routinely were already having sex and did not see themselves as committing a sin.[3] People sometimes lived in long-term unions, considering themselves husband and wife, without actually marrying in church.

The play gives no details about Lucía's previous behavior. She seems easily led astray, for when the Antichrist appears (an event that would precede Christ's return, according to apocalyptic narratives), she takes him for the real Christ. Audience members might see the priest's reaction to Lucía's confession as a realistic depiction, or perhaps a comic caricature, of Catholic priests' attitude toward sex. Some people might see Lucía as a woman who had simply enjoyed a few love affairs and was now a victim of priestly intolerance. Others might assume her behavior was outrageous enough to exceed what either Nahuas or priests would consider acceptable. Still others might have come to agree with the notion that all premarital sexual activity was immoral.

The graphic punishment that the demons inflict on Lucía reflects Catholic churchmen's misogynistic views of female vanity. Lucía artificially enhanced her beauty to attract men, and thus lure them into sin. So the demons replace her earthly necklaces and earrings with a snake and butterflies of flame. Her punishment resembles that of the wife in *The Nobleman and His Barren Wife*, who also failed to live up to Spanish churchmen's standards of female domesticity and obedience.

The judgment scene follows European narrative and artistic imaginings of the event. Angels, led by Saint Michael, would blow trumpets to awaken the dead, who would rise from their graves and return to a living, fleshly state. They, and the living people, would gather to be judged. Jesus Christ would descend from heaven and sit in glory, passing sentence on every human being in turn. The good would be placed to his right and the bad to his left. The good would ascend to heavenly bliss among the saints and angels; the bad would accompany the devils back to hell.

The playwright(s) imagined how Jesus Christ would interview different people. Believing in him and being sorry are not enough. He shows no mercy to anyone who carries a burden of sin. Other morality plays present a similar scenario: Jesus Christ, accompanied by Saint Michael or the Virgin Mary, reviews the moral status of recently dead characters. In these other plays the people do not speak for themselves. Rather, demons report on their bad behavior, sometimes explaining how the immoral person broke every single commandment. Jesus Christ then allows the devils to take the sinner away.[4]

In these judgment scenes, devils act as part of the moral order. Jesus Christ, after all, relies on them to carry out the sentences he imposes on the damned. The devils, in turn, relish the opportunity to inflict elaborate torments on the hapless sinners, sometimes thanking Christ for sending people to hell. Sacred powers, whether from the sky or the underworld, work in concert to sort people into their proper places. In contrast to indigenous visions of a world destroyed forever by earthquakes, with no future, *Final Judgment* presents a scenario of enduring spatial and moral stability.

Notes

1. Mendieta 1980, 648; Horcasitas 1974, 563; Las Casas 1967, 1:334.

2. The others are baptism, confirmation, confession (or penitence), communion, ordination, and extreme unction (or last rites).

3. Bautista 1600, 7r–v.

4. See *How to Live on Earth, Souls and Testamentary Executors,* and *The Life of Don Sebastián,* in *Nahuatl Theater,* vol. 1.

FINAL JUDGMENT

Cast of characters in order of appearance

Saint Michael
Penance
Time
Holy Church
Sweeping
Death
Lucía (*also* Second Living Person)
Priest
Antichrist
First Living Person
Christ
First Angel
Second Angel
First Dead Person
Second Dead Person
Third Living Person
Second Demon
Satan
First Demon

Exemplary model called Final Judgment

(*Wind instruments*[1] *are played. Heaven opens. Saint Michael comes down.*[2])

SAINT MICHAEL: O creations of God! Know, and indeed you already do know, for it is in our lord God's holy commands, that he will finish off, he will destroy the world that his precious and admired father, God, made. He will destroy, he will finish off everything he made: the various birds, the various living creatures, along with you. He will destroy you, you people of the world. But be assured that the dead will revive. As for the good and proper ones who served the just judge, the sentencer, God: he will take them to his royal home, the place of eternal and perfect bliss, glory, the place of perfect bliss of all the male and female saints. But as for the bad ones who did not serve our lord God, let them be certain that they'll get suffering in hell. So then, weep and remember it. Fear it, be scared to death, for the day of judgment will happen to you. It is very frightening, very shocking. It scares people to death, it makes people faint with fright. So then, fix your lives! The day of judgment is about to happen to you. It is the time, it is the moment, now!

(*Wind instruments are played. Saint Michael goes up. Penance enters, and Time, Holy Church, Sweeping, and Death.*)

PENANCE: It's impossible to say, to describe, how confused all the people of the world are. They're completely dizzy in the head from the various sins. What's wrong with them, what's the matter with them, that they can't give up their shocking sins, their hard-heartedness, their blindness? They are four hundred times unfortunate! Truly, some will die in their sins. The stubborn, the deaf, the blind, the careless: it can truly be said that they've destroyed people's eyes with sin. They've considered sin quite sweet, they've considered it pleasing to the nose. It's like they built a house out of lust and put it on for clothing. It's just like they think it's their food and drink. And as for their deity, their ruler, God: they've already forgotten him. They are four hundred times unfortunate! For their life on earth is about to end.

TIME: I am time. I am the time given daily to holy words. Our lord God gave me the task and put me in charge of guarding them every day, of taking care of them, calling out to them, reminding them of

---

1. Flutes or trumpets.
2. Stage directions later in the play refer to the use of a ladder.

things day and night. I don't shut my mouth for a moment. I'm yelling into their ears, so that they'll think of their creator, their maker, the deity, the ruler, God. I try to get them to cry out to him, to praise him, to serve him, to do as our lord God wants. I yell at them that they should go to his home to praise him, to ask him to give them his precious grace. But they just waste my life and my work. Even so, I say, I've fulfilled my obligations toward them. They won't defend themselves with anything about me, when they're each called and examined before God. They know what answers they'll be giving. And as for me: I will give an accounting to God the father, the all-powerful one, who created us. So then, they won't excuse themselves for anything by blaming me. It's time for them to be called.

HOLY CHURCH: I am the merciful mother of my precious son, Jesus Christ, who assigned me to be always weeping here, for the sake of the people of earth. Especially when any of them die, I shed my tears for their sake. I beseech my precious mother, holy fountain of perfect happiness,[3] to have mercy on them, to give light to his creations. May the seventh sacrament, which I'm keeping for them, not be wasted. Sometimes it seems like they will long for it and hunger for it. I'll feed them, I'll give them drink if they're thirsty. But now I'm waiting for them. I'm sad for them. Let them come and fix their lives. Let them pray. They'll receive mercy. And let them weep and be sad because of their sins, their defects.

SWEEPING: You who are people's mother, perfect and whole in your faith, everything you say is correct. They don't remember what doesn't please them. They just want to go on sinning. Don't I try as hard as I can? I'm always yelling at them. I try every day to get them to sweep things, to keep vigil, to get up in the morning, to do penance, to suffer cold: that is, to sweep their spirits, their souls in a religious way, to fast, to abstain from food so that they will receive mercy and pardon. And otherwise, there is no way at all that they'll be able to enter our lord God's royal home. They won't be able to gain pardon if they don't do penance first. This instrument of penance I'm carrying[4] does them good, for it is considered the ladder to heaven, by which they'll be able to enter heaven. For it won't be long until they're called before our lord

3. The Virgin Mary, another maternal figure.
4. A broom.

God, so that each of them will give him an accounting of how they lived on earth. They mustn't use us to defend themselves before God.

DEATH: I am the constable, I am the appointee, I am the messenger of the all-powerful one who sits in authority in heaven and here on earth. He is sending out sunbeams, filling up every place in heaven and every place in the world. And let the people of the earth know for sure that, tomorrow, the day after,[5] God's precious child will come down. He is coming to judge the living and the dead. And as for the good ones: he'll take them to his royal home in heaven. But as for the bad ones, who did not serve him here on earth: he'll throw them into the depths of hell. And let the people of the earth know for sure that the day of judgment will happen to them. What will happen to them is very frightening. And so, let them fix their lives because it is time, it is the moment when they will be judged, when they will be examined as to how they served our lord God.

HOLY CHURCH: What you've declared, what you've spoken is quite correct. For you all are the servants, you are the workers of my precious consolation and only child, Jesus Christ, who is my precious husband in a religious way. He appointed you so that you would yell at the sinners of the earth and bring to their attention that, through sin, they've thoroughly covered their spirits, their souls, with earth and dust. They've filled them with mud. And now let's go, let's go yell at them so they'll come to prepare themselves in a religious way, with weeping, with tears. And as for me, I'm waiting for them in order to purify them, to bathe them. I will purify them in a religious way with the seventh sacrament, marriage, which I'm keeping for them.

TIME: I'm going right now. I'll yell at them. I'll remind them every hour to remember what they must do so they won't squander and waste the lifetimes that our lord God entrusted to me. *(Time exits alone.)*

HOLY CHURCH: I am the holy light of the only faith. I illuminate all Christians. I shed light for them in a religious way, so that they will come and I will purify them. They're very dizzy in the head with sins. If they will weep and be sad my precious son, Jesus Christ, will pardon them and give them the kingdom of heaven. *(Holy Church exits alone.)*

DEATH: The people of the earth are really pitiful. They are blind. They don't keep in mind that one day, sometime, they will be judged. It's

5. Soon, in the near future.

just lust. They dirty their souls with sin. But I say the people of the earth, the blind ones, the careless ones, know that they've really masturbated themselves black in the face with sin. And their spirits, their souls don't concern them. Let them scrub and bathe themselves with the holy light of goodness. When the day of judgment happens to them, will they remember then? Will they weep then? It's true, it's correct that there's no longer any way for them to receive mercy. The people of the earth are four hundred times unfortunate! For the day of judgment will happen to them tomorrow. It is time, it is the moment! *(Wind instruments are played. Death and Sweeping exit. Lucía enters. She comes worried.)*

LUCÍA: Oh! O my deity, O my ruler, Jesus Christ! How unfortunate I am! What's happening to me now? It's like my soul is being squeezed to death. It's like it's going in among clouds. And what am I to do now? Let me go and confess. Maybe my soul will be a bit calmed by that. Let me go look for my confessor. For my face, my heart are really aching! *(Lucía goes and knocks on a door. Priest enters.)* May our lord God be with you lovingly, O my precious father. *(Priest speaks.)*

PRIEST: May our lord God guide you, O my precious child. Come here. What do you want?

LUCÍA: Know, O my precious father, what I've come for. Don't let me anger you with it, O my precious father.

PRIEST: What do you want, O my precious child? Say it. For our lord God appointed us to give confession to you people of the world.

LUCÍA: O my precious father, I want to confess before our lord God and you, O my precious father.

PRIEST: O my precious child, what I hear pleases me greatly. Your sins worry you, they oppress you. Let's go into our lord God's temple-home. *(Then Lucía confesses. And while she is confessing, Priest stands up. He is very frightened.)* Jesus! Jesus! What are you saying? What have you done? Aren't you a Christian? Don't you know that you've committed great sins four hundred times? You are four hundred times unfortunate! If only you had saved, if only you had cleansed your soul! Why didn't you ever receive the sacrament of marriage? Just to the devil you sent the seventh holy sacrament, holy matrimony. You are four hundred times unfortunate! Now you never wanted to get married on earth. But know for sure that you're going to get married down in the depths of hell! Your reward will be suffering in hell. And now, what accounting will you give to your deity, your ruler? For there's no way you can help yourself now, because it's already time. God's judgment has already arrived. Now you will marvel at how God's precious child will come down. He's coming to judge the living and the dead, such that they each will give an accounting to their maker, God. And you, too, will appear before the just judge, God's precious child, Jesus Christ.

(Priest exits. Lucía remains.)

LUCÍA: Oh! How terrible! O God! I am four hundred times greatly unfortunate on earth! What did I hear? What did God's precious one say to me? How very frightening and worrying it is, what God's precious one says. If only I'd listened, if only I'd believed what my God was commanding me, along with my father, my mother, and all my neighbors. All of this, which they used to harangue me about, would just turn into my indignation. I used to just scoff at the holy sacrament, holy matrimony. I am four hundred times unfortunate now! Let insolence be despised! What have I done? What good did insolence do me? May the earth and time be despised! Now the world's about to come to an end, about to be finished off. I am four hundred times unfortunate! I am a great sinner!

(Wind instruments are played. The living enter. They sit on the ground, along with Lucía. Their chins hang down. The Antichrist enters. On the inside he wears a cloak of wickedness;[6] on top he wears a tunic. He raises the fingers of his left hand. There are fireworks as he enters.)

ANTICHRIST: O my precious children, don't you know me? It's me, who endured pains on earth on your behalf, who suffered on your behalf. And now, know for sure that I will finish off, I will destroy the earth. Believe in me, O my creations, for I will pardon you your sins, your defects. Believe in me. Look at my precious blood, and my precious body.

FIRST LIVING PERSON: You're not the one we're waiting for. Our deity, our ruler will come. He's the one who suffered and died on our behalf. Because of our four hundred great sins they stretched him by the arms on the cross.

LUCÍA: Yes, you're the one we're waiting for, O my deity, O my ruler. Pardon us our sins.

---

6. Designs to show "wickedness" might be devils, or skulls and bones.

ANTICHRIST: Yes, I'll help you. Don't you know that I'm all-powerful in the world?

("Christ became"[7] is raised in song. Heaven opens.[8] Christ enters. He leads out Saint Michael, who brings scales.[9] And Christ brings out a cross. He stands at the edge of heaven. And the Antichrist quickly exits. There are fireworks.)

CHRIST: Come, you who are my war leader, Saint Michael. Here in heaven it's now time for me to bring time to an end, to destroy it. It is called "Final Judgment,"[10] the day of judgment. As I put down in my holy commands, I will sweep things, I will purify heaven and earth. The people of earth, the living and the dead, have made things very dirty because of their bad lives. And now, awaken them, the living and the dead, the good and the bad. And to the good ones I will give their heavenly flowery riches, heavenly jades and garments, heavenly palm fronds. But as for the bad, let them know for sure that the house of hell and the sufferings of hell will belong to them, because they couldn't keep my holy commands. *(Christ comes down, and Saint Michael. Christ sits down.)* I've already given you orders as to what you will do, you who are my war leader.

SAINT MICHAEL: Very well, O my precious teacher. Let the dead come to life, let the living rouse themselves. Let them take their bones and gather them together. And let them take hold of their earth, their mud.[11] Give them reviving, through the Holy Spirit, along with their souls, so they'll be able to answer you, so they'll say what they did that was good and what they did that was bad, their deeds.

CHRIST: Through my power they will revive, they will come to life. I give them reviving, as I revived on the third day. In just the same way let my creations revive![12]

(Wind instruments are played. Christ exits by another door; he will not go back up to heaven. Then Saint Michael plays a wind instrument.)

FIRST ANGEL: Rouse yourselves, you living ones! By God's orders, take your bodies!

---

7. *Christus factus est*, a Latin chant from the liturgy for Holy Week: "Christ became for us obedient even unto death."

8. A curtain might be opened in front of a raised space.

9. To weigh people's souls, to determine whether they were good or bad.

10. This phrase is in Spanish.

11. Their bodies.

12. The Nahuatl verb used for resurrection means to revive, rouse oneself, or come to one's senses. It does not imply a return from the dead.

(Saint Michael plays a wind instrument again. He cries out to where the dead will be.)

SECOND ANGEL: "Arise, O dead, and come to judgment."[13] Revive, you dead ones! Come out, you who are underground! Take your bodies, by our lord God's orders!

(At this point the dead enter, fully fleshed. Saint Michael plays a wind instrument again.)

SAINT MICHAEL: Now you have revived. Gather yourselves together. Now you will make an accounting before the just sentencer, the judge. Don't anyone be confused. Wait for your deity, your creator, God.

(Wind instruments are played. Saint Michael exits. The Antichrist enters. He comes jeering at the living and the dead. In a little while, Christ enters.)

ANTICHRIST: Now I have come. Fulfill my precious words.

("We Praise You as God"[14] is raised in song. The Antichrist quickly exits. There are fireworks. Then Christ enters. First Angel and Second Angel enter. Saint Michael leads the way.)

CHRIST: Come, you pearl of heaven, you who are Saint Michael the Archangel! Summon the living and those who were dead. Let them gather together here in front of me so that I will make an accounting of them, of when they still lived on earth.

SAINT MICHAEL: So be it, O my precious teacher. Let me cry out to them.

(Saint Michael plays a wind instrument. Then they each go before Christ. He sits down. And the angel weighs things on the scale. First Dead Person kneels.)

CHRIST: Come, you! Did you carry out my commands while you were still living and flying about on earth? Speak. Answer me, the way you used to talk on earth. Speak in the same way now.

FIRST DEAD PERSON: O my deity, O my ruler, I carried out, I worked at, I fulfilled your holy commands. I carried out your orders. Ask my angel,[15] O my precious teacher.

CHRIST: Thank you. You will be perfectly happy in heaven. You will prosper. Your joyfulness will never be finished or come to an end.

(He blesses him. Saint Michael pushes him to Christ's right-hand side.)

CHRIST: Come, you living one. Whom did you honor on earth, and whom did you love?

13. This statement is in Latin.
14. *Te Deum laudamus*, a Latin hymn.
15. This refers to the person's guardian angel.

FIRST LIVING PERSON: You, you who are my deity, you who are my ruler.

CHRIST: If it's true that I am your deity, I am your ruler, did you carry out my holy commands? Did you fulfill them?

FIRST LIVING PERSON: I didn't do it, O my deity. Pardon me. I am a sinner.

CHRIST: Today pardon doesn't exist anymore. Go! *(Saint Michael pushes First Living Person to the other side. Then Second Dead Person kneels before Christ.)* Come, you who were dead. What did you do while you still lived on earth? Did you work for me? Did you serve me on earth? Answer me!

SECOND DEAD PERSON: Not at all. Pardon me, O my ruler, O my teacher, O God!

CHRIST: Today, in the time of judgment, pardon doesn't exist anymore. Go! *(Saint Michael pushes Second Dead Person away. And the demons drag him off. They lay him on the other side. Second Living Person, Lucía, kneels.)* Come, you living person! Did you carry out my holy commands, the ten of them? Did you love your neighbors, and your father and your mother?

SECOND LIVING PERSON, LUCÍA: Yes. It is you, O my deity, O my ruler, whom I loved first, then my father and my mother.

CHRIST: If it's true that I am your deity and you loved me first, and then your father and your mother, did you carry out my command, and the command of my precious and admired mother, in the seventh sacrament, holy matrimony? Were you chaste when you lived on earth? What have you accomplished?

LUCÍA: No. I didn't work for you and I didn't recognize your precious mother. Pardon me, O my deity, O my ruler!

CHRIST: Now, since your heart never spoke to us on earth, it was only your lust that you used to work at. Go, do it. Maybe you're forgetting something of your lust. Work at it. You can be sure that you can't hope for anything in heaven. How unfortunate you are now, that you never wanted to get married on earth. You have gained the house of hell. You have earned it. Go see the ones you served. I don't know you. *(He pushes her toward the demons.)* Come, you who were a living person on earth. What's giving your heart such pain? Is it my holy words? Did you cry out to me when you were sleeping and when you were walking around?

THIRD LIVING PERSON: I never, ever, forgot you, when I was eating, when I was drinking, when I was walking around, or when I was sleeping, O my precious teacher.

CHRIST: Thank you, O my creation. It's just the same with me: I was always going around thinking of you. And I'm keeping your flowery necklace for you. *(Saint Michael pushes him among the good people.)* Come, you inhabitants of hell! Take your servants to the depths of hell. And as for the wicked woman, take her into the sweat bath of fire. Torment her miserably there!

SECOND DEMON: O our lord, we're grateful to you. We know well that we've just been waiting around for your coming. We are fortunate! Your precious heart has been very generous. Let us be deserving of your creations. You all, grab up the fiery chains and the fiery metal rod with which we will beat them. And tell our ruler, Lucifer, that we're taking his servants over there. Have him send the fiery metal warping frame[16] right away to where we're going to take his servants. *(Satan[17] enters. He goes grasping the fiery metal warping frame.)*

SATAN: I'm bringing everything right here that we'll tie them up with, so not one will escape from our hands. Now we have our drink and our food, there in the depths of hell. We tried our hardest, so our servants fell into our hands.

(All of them say, "O our lord, help us!")

CHRIST: Never again will you have any hope! Know for sure that they'll torment you miserably forever, eternally, there in the depths of hell! *(Again they all say "O our lord, O God, just save us sinners!" Then they take them away. There are fireworks. They yell as they go. And the good people put on flowery crowns of palm fronds. Christ goes up. In the middle of the ladder he says to them:)* O my servants, come on up! Come and get your riches, which I have in store for you, which will never be finished, which will never come to an end!

(Wind instruments are played. The angels, Christ, and the good people go up. Then they bring out Lucía. Fire butterflies are her earrings, a snake her necklace, and they tie one around her waist. She comes yelling. The demons answer her:)

---

16. A device to prepare yarn for weaving, reimagined as a red-hot torture implement made of metal.

17. As in *The Nobleman and His Barren Wife*, Satan and Lucifer are imagined as two different beings.

FIRST DEMON: Get moving, O wicked one! Don't you remember what you did on earth? Now we'll pay you back in the depths of hell. Get moving! Run along!

LUCÍA: I am four hundred times unfortunate! I am a great sinner! Oh, I have earned the house of hell!

SATAN: You don't yell until now, you wicked one? Now we'll make you happy in the depths of hell. Now we'll get you married, over in our palace, because you never got married on earth. Run along! Get moving! Our ruler, Lucifer, is waiting for you!

LUCÍA: Oh! Oh! How unfortunate I am! I am a sinner. I have earned torment in hell. If only I hadn't been born on earth! Oh! Oh! Curse the earth, and the time in which I was born. Curse my mother too, who made me! Oh! Curse the breast milk with which I was nurtured! Curse what I used to eat and drink on earth! Oh! Curse the ground I used to kick, and the rags I used to wear, for they've all turned into fire! Oh! They burn me terribly, the fire butterflies that come hanging here from my ears. They stand for how I used to beautify myself with my earrings. And here, wound around my neck, is a very frightening fire serpent. It stands for my necklaces that I used to put on. And here I come belted with a very frightening fire snake, the heart of the house of hell. It stands for how I used to enjoy myself on earth. Oh! Oh! If only I'd gotten married! Oh! How unfortunate I am!

FIRST DEMON: Now you'll pay the penalty. You'll pay for everything. You had no esteem for your neighbors on earth.

(They beat her.)

SATAN: Get moving, O wicked one! You don't remember until now that you should have gotten married? How come you didn't remember it while you were still living on earth? But now you'll pay for all your wickedness. Run along! Get moving!

(They beat her. Just thus they make her go in. There are fireworks. The demons play wind instruments. Then Priest enters.)

PRIEST: O my precious children, O Christians, O creations of God! Now you have seen an ominous marvel! It's true. It's written in the holy book. Be sensible! Rouse yourselves, look at yourselves in the mirror, how it happened to your neighbor. And don't let the same thing happen to you. It is a model, a measuring stick,[18] which our lord God gives us.

---

18. The audience members should see themselves reflected in the play, and learn good behavior.

Tomorrow, the next day, the day of judgment is going to happen. Just pray to our lord, Jesus Christ, and to the noblewoman, Saint Mary, so that she will pray to her precious and admired child, Jesus Christ, so that afterwards you will earn, you will obtain joyfulness in heaven, glory. Let it be done in this way.

Hail Mary.[19]

19. Apparently the Hail Mary prayer was to be recited here, an activity in which the entire audience might participate. Even people with only the most basic knowledge of Christianity would know this prayer by heart.

The Three Kings

The story of the Three Kings or Three Wise Men (or Magi) derives from the Gospel of Matthew (2:1–12). These Bible verses tell of wise men who came to Jerusalem from the east, asking, "Where is he who has been born king of the Jews? For we have seen his star in the East, and have come to worship him." King Herod, the Jewish ruler of Judea under Roman colonial authority, consults the priests and scribes. They tell him that Christ was to be born in Bethlehem. Herod asks the wise men when the star appeared, and then he sends them to Bethlehem to search for the child. He asks them to report back to him, "so that I too may come and worship him." The star leads the wise men to a house, where they see Mary and Jesus. They present Jesus with gifts of gold, frankincense, and myrrh. Warned in a dream that they should not return to Herod, the wise men take a different route back to their own country.

Because the gifts numbered three, early Christian interpreters numbered the givers at three as well, and they were later given the names Casper (in Spanish, Gaspar), Melchior (Melchor), and Balthasar (Baltasar). They also became associated with different ages: Casper with old age, Melchior with middle age, and Balthasar with youth. Beginning in the fifteenth century, Balthasar was depicted as an African man.[1] The visit to Jesus, assigned to the date January 6 and called the Feast of Epiphany, is celebrated as Día de los Reyes, "Day of the Kings," in Spanish-speaking cultures.

The Three Kings were the first gentiles, or non-Jews, to worship Jesus. Therefore they symbolize and foreshadow the Christianization of the world's pagan peoples. For colonial Nahuas, a story about pagan kings being led to Jesus by a prophecy and a star could sound like their own history. Having at least partially accepted Christianity, Nahuas retained respectful memories of the early colonial leaders who had welcomed the friars and built the first churches, sometimes downplaying the violence that accompanied subjugation to Spanish rule. Their histories told of miraculous comets, fires, and other prophetic signs that preceded the arrival of the Spanish. Thus, they could see in the Three Kings a likeness of their own ancestors who first participated in Christian worship.

Some people of native or mixed descent projected Christian elements even into the preconquest past. For example, the deity Quetzalcoatl struck some (including certain Spanish priests) as a possible Christian apostle, perhaps Saint Thomas. The historian don Fernando de Alva Ixtlilxochitl claimed that his famous ancestor Nezahualcoyotl, who ruled Tetzcoco for much of the fifteenth century, believed in a single god, a heaven for good people, and a hell for bad people.[2] Such ideas, circulating in the colony, might make people receptive to images of Nahua or Nahua-like rulers who accepted monotheism early on. In the play, the Three Kings are monotheists even before they come to Bethlehem, while their servant, a lower-ranking man, believes in multiple gods.

Colonial scripts survive for two Nahuatl Epiphany dramas. The one included here is held by the William L. Clements Library at the University of Michigan. Nowhere is there a date or any place or personal name. The script is bound together with two other plays. One of these ends with a statement that says it was copied in 1760 from a text prepared in 1678. Some of the content of the Epiphany drama ties it to a sixteenth-century text (see below). This may indicate an early origin, but the text was passed along and recopied.[3]

Motolinia, a Franciscan priest who came to Mexico in 1524 and adopted this Nahuatl name, which means "poor" or "afflicted," described the special attachment that Nahuas felt for the Three Kings. Writing in 1540 or 1541, he said the January 6 celebration "seems to them like their own festival." The friar continues:

> And many times on this day they put on the play about the Kings' offering to the Child Jesus, and they bring the star from far away. . . . And in the church they have Our Lady with her precious Son in the manger, before whom, on that day, they offer wax candles, and some of their incense, and doves, and quail, and other birds that they seek

out for that day, and always up to the present time the devotion to this day is increasing in them.[4]

This passage shows that Epiphany plays were an established and cherished performance tradition within a decade of the first Nahuatl dramas.

Motolinia says that people set up nativity scenes inside their churches and then imitated the Three Kings' actions by laying offerings in front of the statues. This statement provides a helpful clue to understanding a feature of the play in this volume. The actors playing the Kings go right into the church building to see Jesus and offer their gifts. They speak to the Virgin Mary, as well as the infant Jesus, but Mary never says anything. Later, an angel speaks to Joseph, but he does not answer. So, in the play it seems that the actors were to walk in procession down the aisle of the church and then present their greetings to the *statues* of Mary and Jesus that were part of the community's manger scene. Similarly, the angel's speech at the very end would have been directed at the *statue* of Joseph. The stage directions refer to the Mass and the gospel readings, suggesting that the play was merged into services in the church, as well as its seasonal arrangement of holy images. In contrast, the other Nahuatl play on the same story has Mary reply eloquently to the Kings' greetings, so she is obviously played by a real person, and the stage directions do not indicate the use of the church building.

The play's author or authors definitely associated the Three Kings with Nahua lords of olden days. Throughout the play, the Kings are models of noble speech and good manners. Furthermore, when Casper talks to the baby Jesus, a portion of his greeting comes right from a speech that a high-ranking preconquest lord would have made to a new ruler, though altered to fit the Christian context.[5] Melchior, too, speaks lines adapted directly from this speech. Thus, these characters speak in the voice of ancestral Nahua lords and greet Jesus as if he is their new ruler. This maneuver makes the Nahuas' acceptance of Christianity seem legitimate: these noble ancestors seek out and worship Christ, so Nahuas watching the play could get the message that they should do the same. The text treats Christ as if he is a ruler like the Nahua rulers of old, with similar responsibilities toward his subjects. And it is to him—not to Spanish authority—that these well-spoken lords declare their loyalty.

The Three Kings contrast sharply with King Herod. Herod loses his temper, scolding and threatening the Jewish high priests. He fawns on the Kings, while secretly planning to kill the child who he fears will usurp his throne. In medieval European drama, actors playing Herod would rant and rave so much that Hamlet, in Shakespeare's play, says that an actor who overacts "out-Herods Herod."[6] So people in Europe were used to seeing Herod act like this and probably thought his over-the-top behavior was funny.

Yet in New Spain, Herod's position resembles that of the Aztec emperor Motecuhzoma when Cortés arrived. The Spaniards came from the east, across the Atlantic. They came from a mysterious world outside Mesoamerica, of which the Nahuas knew nothing. Cortés insisted that Motecuhzoma and other native rulers submit to a foreign power, the Spanish king, and to a new god.

In the play, Herod orders that the Three Kings be welcomed with flowers. He politely describes his seat of power as their "home." Motecuhzoma staged an elaborate welcome for Cortés on his first entry into Tenochtitlan, speaking as if Cortés had arrived in his own kingdom and presenting him with various flower wreaths and necklaces. The principal Nahuatl-language account of this meeting describes these flower gifts in detail.[7]

As native histories of the conquest developed in the decades following the Aztec defeat, Motecuhzoma came to be seen as a bad—or failed—ruler, who acts much like Herod does in the play. He gets angry when people tell him of troubling, prophetic dreams. He asks the keepers of the pictorial manuscripts to explain who the Spaniards are. He accuses his priests of lying to him and neglecting their duties. Motecuhzoma himself, in these portrayals, "out-Herods Herod."[8] His own name, which means "angry lord" or "he gets angry like a lord," supported this characterization.

Herod and the Three Kings have ambivalent characters: they can be seen in different ways. The Three Kings talk like Nahua rulers, but they come from far away in the East, riding horses, like the Spanish did, and they are called by the Spanish word for kings (*reyes*) as well as the Nahuatl term. Herod acts like Motecuhzoma, but he also uses Spanish words to insult his priests (*diablo*, or devil; *chicharrones*, pork rinds). His pride, anger, dishonesty, and threats of violence might seem like typical Spanish traits to the native people who were living under Spanish rule. Colonial texts often carry these sorts of double meanings, which allow people to construct their own interpretations. The texts rarely offer a direct criticism of colonial power structures.

The play ends with an angel warning about the slaughter of the innocents, Herod's execution of Jewish children in a futile attempt to kill the young Jesus.[9] The other Epiphany play, which is longer, extends its action to include the planning and execution of this massacre. In one scene, actors playing soldiers pretend to beat babies. This disturbing scene, and even the brief reference in the play presented here, might call up memories and oral traditions about the indiscriminate violence and widespread death that Nahuas suffered during the Spanish conquest. However, the play ends on a hopeful note, with the Holy Family about to escape the coming danger.

Notes

1. Farmer 1992, 312–13.
2. Alva Ixtlilxochitl 1975–1977, 1:447; he was an older brother of don Bartolomé de Alva, author of *The Animal Prophet and the Fortunate Patricide.* On Quetzalcoatl, see Carrasco 2001, Gillespie 1989, Nicholson 2001.
3. The plays from the William L. Clements Library are in *Nahuatl Theater,* vol. 1. The other Epiphany play is in *Nahuatl Theater,* 4:74–125; an earlier version, the manuscript for which is currently unknown, was published in Paso y Troncoso 1902 and Horcasitas 1974, 281–327.
4. Motolinia 1979, 55.
5. This speech is part of a collection compiled by the Franciscan Bernardino de Sahagún in the mid-sixteenth century (Sahagún 1950–1982, 6). See footnotes in the play for details on the relationship between these texts.
6. *Hamlet* III.ii.14.
7. Lockhart 1993, 114–16.
8. See, for example, Durán 1994, 491–94, 503–506. Gillespie (2008) shows how native texts depict Motecuhzoma as a failed ruler, responsible for the Aztec defeat. Horcasitas (1974, 254–55) also notes how Motecuhzoma's alleged behavior resembles Herod's in this play. See also Burkhart 2008.
9. Matthew 2:16.

THE THREE KINGS

Cast of characters in order of appearance

Casper
Melchior
Balthasar
Messenger (*servant of the Three Kings*)
Steward (*of Herod*)
Herod
First Priest
Second Priest
Third Priest
Angel

The life of the three rulers, kings,[1] *begins here, starts here: how they greeted the precious and admired holy child, the child of God, our lord Jesus Christ. They came from the East. And the exemplary model*[2] *begins here, is placed here: how it happened that the three rulers, kings, came from the East. Their messenger, their guide comes leading them. And the star goes a bit ahead. And when the three rulers, kings, are about to reach the flat area next to Herod's altepetl, the star will be hidden. And then Casper speaks.*

CASPER: I've been looking for a long time and I no longer see the wondrous star, our wondrous guide, that has been leading us up until now. It seems to me, what I think, is that we've reached the place where the wondrous child we're looking for was born. Truly indeed, here is the great altepetl of Jerusalem. I think we've now found what we're looking for. But come, servant of ours. Go forth, go into the great altepetl of Jerusalem. Tell [Herod], explain to him, that we came from the East and that we kiss his hands and his feet, four hundred times. Let him give us his royal permission for us to go and reveal our concerns to him. And here on the outskirts of his great altepetl of Jerusalem, here we await his royal permission so that we can go there, we can go reveal our concerns to him.

MESSENGER: Let me carry out your royal command, let me do what you command me, since I am your servant. *(The messenger goes to Herod's door. He greets the steward. He says to him:)* O ruler, may the deities give you health. Greetings. Know that I am the servant of three rulers, kings.

STEWARD: Welcome, O my friend. Your problem must be very serious, for it certainly can be seen on your face.

MESSENGER: O master, O ruler, may the deities give you health. Greetings. Know that I come from the East. And my home is over there in the place called Persia. And I have guided three rulers here. And I have arrived here in your great and royal land. And as to your great ruler, Herod: take me before him. By order of the rulers, the noblemen, I come to greet him.

STEWARD: Very well, O my friend. Wait for me here a little while. Let me see, let me tell the ruler, Herod. *(And then the steward goes up in front of Herod. He takes off his hat. He bends his knees three times, and kneels before him on one knee. And then he says:)* O our lord, O master, O ruler, O lord, in all places has your fame and your renown gone out,

---

1. The Spanish word *reyes*, paired with the Nahuatl word for rulers, *tlatoque*.
2. The play.

arrived, been declared, been pronounced. You are all-powerful. All the people of the world—nobles, rulers, lords—fear and respect you. But our deity, our ruler is performing a great wonder upon us today. Here to your palace, your royal home has come the messenger of three rulers, kings, who have come, who've traveled here from very far away. No one like this has ever come to your royal altepetl. His speech is quite different, and his face is very full-bodied. And I think he's a pagan. And he wants to speak to you. He's waiting for your royal command there in the doorway. Shall I call for him? Shall he enter? Shall he come and appear before you?

HEROD: What you're telling me is a great omen, a great wonder! Let him come in, let him appear before me so I can find out where he's from and what he wants.

(The steward bends his knees three times in front of Herod. He kisses his hands and his feet. Then he comes down and summons the messenger. He says:)

STEWARD: Do come in, O my friend. The ruler, Herod, is calling for you.

MESSENGER: Very well, O my friend. *(The messenger goes in front of Herod. He kneels.)* O master, O ruler, give me your hands and your feet, so that I, your servant, may kiss them. *(Herod stands up for this. He sits down again.)* Greetings, O nobleman, O ruler, you master, Herod! May the deities give you health! Know that three rulers, noblemen, have sent me as a messenger. They have arrived here in the open area next to your great altepetl. And they're waiting for me there. They came from the East, very far away. And they kiss your hands and your feet four hundred times. And they ask you very humbly, they beseech you to give them your royal permission to come appear before you, to reveal their concerns to you, O master, O ruler.

HEROD: O my friend, welcome! May our lord God give you health. You must tell your masters, your royal friends, your lords, that I thank them four hundred times for their royal and wondrous affection, with which they have come to honor my altepetl, my home, the inside of my house. Let them come here, let them come inside their royal home, let me be deserving of their wondrous faces, let me learn what they are concerned about. I await them.

MESSENGER: Very well, O ruler, O my nobleman.

(And then Herod summons and gives orders to his nobles.)

HEROD: And, you rulers, you nobles, you lords, go, meet them, greet them! Wind instruments will be played, and there will be dancing! Honor them, adorn them with flowers! I'll wait for them here.

(And then the messenger and Herod's nobles go to meet the others with flowers and wind instruments. The messenger goes first. He says:)

MESSENGER: I went where you sent me. I appeared before Herod, the great nobleman, the great ruler. And he is most grateful for your affection. He says: "Let them come in, let them come, let them rest inside their house. Anything I own, all my belongings, are their belongings. Everything will belong to them."

(The rulers move on a bit. They get down from their horses. And then wind instruments are played. [Herod's nobles] adorn them with flowers. And then Herod comes down, greeting them, going on bended knee before them. Herod says:)

HEROD: Greetings! You have arrived, you have come, you honorable men, you lords, you rulers! May the deity, the ruler, our lord God, give you health. Does the lord of the near, the lord of the close, God, give you a little health?

MELCHIOR: Do sit down, O master, O ruler, you who are Herod. We are amazed by your hospitality. Your heart has been generous. We are your servants, we are your vassals. We have indeed enjoyed a bit of health. We lavish kisses on your precious hands and your precious feet.

HEROD: Come up to your home, your altepetl. Come on in. You shall eat, since it's at your own home that you've arrived. *(The rulers enter. They rest. [Herod's nobles] treat them with great honor.)* Tell, you lords, you rulers, you honorable men, you noblemen, why you've come all this way. I want very much to honor your affection.

MELCHIOR: We've been very fortunate. You have shown us great favor, O master, O ruler, O Herod. Since you are a nobleman, you are a ruler, you honor your uncles. And know that our grandfathers long ago, the elders of long ago, had a prophecy that the great sages of ancient times handed down to them. And the prophet's name was Balaam. And he said that from father Jacob a wondrous star would be born, that from Israel a nobleman, a ruler would ascend, would arise, would grow, who would wound and punish the leaders of Moab, who would destroy the children of Sheth.[3] And the elders, our grandfathers, put such trust in this prophecy that they waited for the nobleman, the ruler, along

---

3. Balak, ruler of the Moabites, wanted the prophet Balaam to curse the Israelites, who were traveling through his land on their journey out of Egypt. But Balaam saw that the Israelites were blessed by God and he defied Balak. The prophecy recounted here is from Numbers 24:17: "I see him, but not now: I behold him, but not nigh: a star shall come forth out of Jacob, and a scepter shall rise out of Israel; it shall crush the forehead of Moab,

with his star, by which he would be known and marveled at when a sign, an omen, or a star would appear in the sky. Our grandfathers appointed twelve wise old men to stay always on a mountaintop in the East and watch for when the wondrous star would be observed. And it's now been sixteen hundred years that they've been waiting continuously for the star, in the observatory on the mountaintop. And now some days ago the giver of life, the lord of the near, the lord of the close, our lord, wanted it to happen, in the middle of the night, when people were asleep everywhere in the altepetl. And the twelve old men saw a very wondrous star. The star was shimmering more brightly than the sun. It was bright everywhere, full of rays. And it was a very great wonder that inside the star they saw a very wondrous, pure, very appealing little child, who was inside it. And then they rushed off and ran to my home. They went to wake me up. And the rulers, the noblemen who are here were with me, were visiting me. And then I called them, I woke them up. We looked at the star. And it seemed that the wondrous, holy child inspired us. Then we came to an agreement, we dined together, we put on our gear, and gathered our provisions. And then we took to the road in order to search for the child. And then the wondrous star led us in this direction. We came this way watching it. And we came here, we reached your altepetl of Jerusalem. We lost our wondrous guide. We don't see it any more. And therefore we now have realized that we might find what we're looking for here in your great altepetl. O four-hundred-times lord, O master, O Herod, we beseech you, tell us where the ruler of the Jews was born, where he lies. For we have truly seen his star in the East. And we've come to worship him, we've come to bow down before him, we've come to honor him.

HEROD: O ruler, are you confused? What are you talking about? Who is the ruler? Who is the ruler of the Jews if not me? The Emperor of Rome, Caesar Augustus, granted me the rulership. Isn't it my property? Isn't it my possession? Aren't I the ruler? Don't I rule? Have I perished already? Am I dead already? Have I been finished off already? Have I lost my wits? Aren't I Herod? Aren't I a nobleman anymore? Who will rule over me? Now: let them come quickly and explain it to me, my Jewish leaders, my priests, the sages, those who keep the books, the religious nobles, the religious leaders. Let them come and explain

---

and break down all the sons of Sheth." Christian interpreters thought this predicted Christ's coming.

to me what star, what child, what ruler the rulers are talking about. Quickly, for I'm about to die, I'm about to faint! Oh no! I am suffering! Ay! Ay! Ay!

STEWARD: Very well, O ruler. Let me call for them. Don't worry. *(Then the steward goes to summon the priests.)* They're coming now, O ruler. Let's not become confused, all of us, we servants of yours, we vassals of yours, we people of Jerusalem.

FIRST PRIEST: May the one true deity, the leader, God, give you health, O master, O ruler, O Herod. We gaze into your face, we servants of yours. We are very joyful, happy, and contented for it appears that our lord God gives you health. Give us your hands and your feet so we can kiss them. What do you want? Let us hear it, let us obey you.

HEROD: You Jews, you high priests, you sages, you who keep the books, you've confused people four hundred times. You go around mocking people, you go around deceiving people greatly. You don't know what truthful words are any more. You aren't worth mentioning any more. Aren't I constantly reminding you that I'm your ruler? You certainly love me. How well you lie! Three rulers have arrived. They came from the East. In their home over there they saw a star in the middle of the night. It's said that the star is the ruler of the Jews who has been born. Who is the child? Who is the ruler who will rule over me? Quickly, explain this to me! Didn't you see the new star? Are you asleep every night? Sleepyheads! Lazy bums! Pigs! Don't you recite prayers in the middle of the night? Rotten Jews, children of the devil, quickly, go find out, satisfy me, and I won't destroy you, O scoundrels!

SECOND PRIEST: Don't be angry, O our lord. What's the use? What's happening isn't our concern or our fault. You should know that our lord promised us that someday he'll give us God's precious child. He'll send him here to earth. He'll come to take on flesh for our sake. And if he has come, are we to tamper with his holy will? Our lord God declared and established the prophecy.

HEROD: Go look up, O scoundrels, in the holy book, where he will be born, the one who will be the ruler of all of you.

FIRST PRIEST: Go get the holy book. Let's look it up. May God reveal to us the one they're looking for, the little child, so that our great ruler, Herod, will calm down.

THIRD PRIEST: Here it is. Let's look it up. May the master reveal it to us.

(At that point the Jewish priests will search in the holy book.)

FIRST PRIEST: O master, O Herod, here the prophet Isaiah, chapter,[4] says: "From his root will emerge, will sprout, will grow, a certain royal child. And a wondrous flower will sprout, will blossom." By this it would appear that the nobleman, the ruler, will be born from, will belong to the lineage of David.

HEROD: I already know, O scoundrels, you pip-squeak, that he will belong to the lineage of David! Where will he be born? In what altepetl? Quickly, look it up, explain it to me, and I won't burn you, flay you, turn you into pork rinds,[5] rotten Jews!

THIRD PRIEST: May our lord God help us! Don't let the ruler torment us! He's really angry! Now he'll burn us, and turn us into pork rinds!

SECOND PRIEST: You wonderful ruler, you very appealing person, you who are Herod, here is what our lord God set down, which we're looking for. And you must know what the prophet, the seer Micah says, in one chapter: "And you, Bethlehem, you land of Judea, you are not small among the leaders and nobles of Judea. From you will come the leader, the governor, the ruler who in a religious way will govern the altepetl of Israel."[6] By this it would appear that the master, the ruler has been born over there in Bethlehem, in the land of Judea. Let them go look for him there, if you want.

HEROD: In Bethlehem! Go look it up, O scoundrels! Now I will burn you! How can it be that you never told me, O pigs, children of the devil? *(They open the holy book again. Then Herod chases the Jewish priests away.)* Leave me at once! Then I will consult with the rulers. *(The priests exit. And Herod turns toward the rulers. He is very humble.)* Pardon me, you very honorable lords and rulers. I got a tiny bit angry at my nobles in front of you because they didn't explain to me how wondrously it would happen. And now I beg of you, tell me how much time has passed since the star appeared, was seen, when you saw it over there in your home. Tell me, I beg of you!

---

4. No chapter number is given. The prophecy quoted is Isaiah 11:1–2: "There shall come forth a shoot from the stump of Jesse, and a branch shall grow out of his roots: And the Spirit of the Lord shall rest upon him." Christian interpreters thought this meant that Christ would come from the lineage of Jesse's son David.

5. The Spanish word *chicharrones* is used here.

6. Micah 5:2 reads "But you, O Bethlehem Ephrathah, who are little to be among the clans of Judah, from you shall come forth for me one who is to be ruler in Israel." See also Matthew 2:5–6.

CASPER: O ruler, O my nobleman, you honorable man, you ruler, you who are Herod, you shall know it. Don't let us make you angry. We're not angry at you. For we've been impressed by your hospitality. And we won't lie to you. You are very honorable, you are a ruler. Know that it has been thirteen days since we saw a wondrous star over there in the East. It wasn't long ago that we came along watching it. But this morning we lost our wondrous guide here at the entrance to your altepetl of Jerusalem, O four-hundred-times lord, O Herod.

HEROD: Thank you, you lords, you rulers. Your hearts have been generous. Now, go to the great altepetl of Bethlehem. It's not far. It's right here, close to Jerusalem. I hope things are very well with the child. And when you've seen him, come by and tell me so that I too can go and greet and worship the deity, the ruler, so that I can go and take him as a ruler. Go there.

BALTHASAR: May peace be with your precious self, and may the lord of the near, the lord of the close, the giver of life, our lord God, give you health, O my nobleman, O lord, O master, O ruler. We kiss your hands and your feet. Now we are going to go, O ruler, O my nobleman.

(Then Herod escorts the rulers down below, outside his house. And then they go, they exit. And in front of the church they discover the star under the arch. Then Balthasar speaks. He is quite astonished at the star. He says:)

BALTHASAR: O my precious friends, look! Our wondrous guide that led us this way, the wondrous star, is leading us again! Oh, do look, O my precious and admired friends!

MELCHIOR: We should be very happy about this, because we've found it! The lord of the near, the lord of the close, the giver of life has shown us how our wondrous guide came straight in this direction. It's stopping now, it's pausing now. It has stopped, it has paused—above a shack! It's drawn close to it. But what does it mean? Wouldn't it go up to a great palace, here at the entrance to the altepetl? Come, you who are our servant. Go in, go look, go find out what marvel our lord, our ruler is keeping there.

MESSENGER: Very well, O rulers. Let me go in, let me go look. *(At that point the messenger enters the church. He goes and looks. He comes out again. He gives a speech.)* You rulers, you kings, I did what you commanded me. I went and looked. And there's no way I can describe it, no way I can compare it with anything. I went in. I looked. It's very bright! It's like when the light, the sunlight, is about to rise, and is issuing forth in all directions. And I saw a precious, admired, and totally blessed maiden holding in her arms a precious, admired, and blessed little child. And there's a little old man sitting next to her. And all around them are precious and admired little children with wings. And there are two animals next to them.[7] And the heavenly precious noblewoman outdoes all the various precious flowers, ash-colored and yellow precious flowers, deep-purple-tinted ones, all the various precious flowers, like roseate spoonbills, that lie issuing forth there.[8] And the precious, admired, totally precious, admired, good, and shimmering face of the precious, admired, and blessed child is utterly pure. And his totally precious and admired hair is like gold, the way it shimmers, or like snow, it's so pure. And the precious and admired holy child was born in a totally good place, he was born in a hut. And, O rulers, let's go, let's go greet him, let's go honor him, let's go humble ourselves before him, let's bow before him, O rulers!

MELCHIOR: May our wondrous deity, our ruler, God, be forever praised! We've found what we're looking for. Let's go in, O rulers, O my friends! Let's go worship him! Let's go bow before him! Let's go make offerings to him!

(At that point the rulers get down from their horses. They enter the church. They humble themselves. They walk in a regal manner. They go and kneel at the foot of the altar where Mass is performed, and in the Gospel readings, when the Creed is finished,[9] they will greet the precious and admired holy child, one at a time, with orations. Casper begins:)

CASPER:[10] O master, O our lord, O precious jade, O quetzal feather, O fine turquoise, O bracelet! You have seated yourself here. Your precious father, God, has placed you here, O lord of the near, O lord of the close, O giver of life. It is true that your progenitors, your great-grandfathers, the prophets, the patriarchs have gone, have gone to lie down, and the

---

7. The messenger is referring to Joseph (often depicted as an old man), cherubs, and the donkey and ox that are typically included in nativity scenes.

8. Filling Christ's birthplace with flowers is an indigenous motif. The roseate spoonbill is a bird with pink feathers often invoked in Nahuatl songs.

9. These stage directions suggest that the drama is integrated into the church service.

10. Casper's speech, through the word "beheaded," closely parallels part of an oration for the installation of a new ruler, recorded in the sixteenth-century *Florentine Codex*. See Sahagún 1950–1982, 6:47. After greeting the new king, the speaker notes the passing of previous rulers and laments the sad condition of their subjects, who have no leader. The play replaces preconquest rulers with Old Testament leaders. The plight of the vassals becomes the plight of all humanity, awaiting Christ's arrival.

master, the ruler, David, and the master, the ruler, Abraham, who go along further back. They left behind, they set aside the carrying frame, the instrument of carrying, the instrument of bearing,[11] which is very heavy, which cannot be lifted, which is unbearable. Is it possible that they still come to know, that they still come to see what is behind them, in back of them? Is it possible that they come to frequent their water, their hill,[12] which lies now as in the beginning, which now is becoming like his desolate place? Is it possible that they still frequent some forest or grassland, where the instrument of carrying, the instrument of bearing lies scattered?[13] And truly the tail, the wing[14] no longer has a mother, no longer has a father. And truly it no longer has eyes, it no longer has ears.[15] It is as if it stands mute. It does not speak, it does not talk. It is as if it stands beheaded. No longer is there anyone who is its head, who goes in front of it.[16] Now, O my deity, O my ruler, precious and admired holy child, it is you who will grasp, in your embrace will remain the work for your precious and admired father, God. And I confess before you that up until now I was living in darkness, in gloom, since I did not know you. But now you have illuminated my spirit, my soul, along with all those who live in heaven, your creations, whom you have come to illuminate. And, O my deity, I beg of you, receive well my spirit, my soul, and my life, so that it may be done, so that I may make an offering to you of this copal, called "incense."[17] Receive it well, O my deity, O my ruler. *(At that point he goes about on his knees, he makes the offering, and he kisses the precious and admired holy child. He draws back again. He says:)* And, O my deity, O my ruler, I also confess before you that you are the true priest, you are the true clergyman. You will devote yourself to serving your precious father, God. And also, O my deity, you will make an offering of yourself on the cross in order to appease your precious father, God. And, O my ruler, O my deity, O lord of the near, O lord of the close, O giver of life, receive well my spirit, my soul, and my life.

11. Metaphor for government: rulers "carry" their people like a burden. See Sahagún 1950–1982, 6: 246; Karttunen and Lockhart 1987, 54.
12. Their altepetl: the word *altepetl* is a compound of water (*atl*) and hill (*tepetl*).
13. The leaderless community has reverted to a wild state.
14. The vassals or common people.
15. With no one to govern them, the people lack good judgment.
16. The people lack a leader.
17. Copal is the native incense, a fragrant tree resin. The text also gives the Spanish word *incienso*.

MELCHIOR: O my precious and admired deity, O my ruler, you who are truly a man, you who are truly a deity, I believe in you with all my heart. You made, you created heaven and earth, the seen and the unseen. You're the one to whom the rulership is delegated, so that you will govern the world, so that you will rule it. And as for all your creations, we've been waiting for you all this time, we've gone around sighing for you all this time. Now you have arrived, now you have come. Your precious and admired father, God, sent you. And the breath, the words of your precious and admired father, God, have gone upon you.[18] And you will get tired from the heavy load.[19] And you will go and put on the carrying frame, the burden. Truly, your progenitors, your great-grandfathers, the patriarchs, the prophets, the rulers and lords of Israel made you known. Those from whom you descended, who go along further back, made you known.[20] You will go and carry something, you will go and bear on your shoulders your cross, the instrument of salvation, which you will place on your back. And in your lap, in your backpack[21] your precious father, God, places the carrying of, the bearing of, the tails, the wings, who are to be saved. They're like a little child who has to be cajoled, who becomes angry, but only for a moment. In your own embrace you will go and place your water, your hill, our mother holy church. Soon you will go carry her in your arms, you will go lull her to sleep. The breath, the words of your precious father, God, the lord of the near, the lord of the close, have gone upon you. He has pointed his finger at you, he has encharged you. Perhaps you can still back out of it? No longer! And now, O my precious and admired deity, O my ruler, may your precious and admired name be utterly praised, you who are my ruler. I have benefited greatly from your wondrous love. And what will I do for you in return? I bow low before you, I worship you, I give myself entirely to you, I give entirely

18. God has, by the authority of his word, selected Christ for his duties on earth.

19. Beginning with this sentence and ending with the phrase "No longer," Melchior's speech resembles a later passage in the *Florentine Codex* oration that Casper's speech parallels. See Sahagún 1950–, 6:48–49. Melchior identifies past rulers with Old Testament figures and Christ's altepetl with the church. The cross is a burden that Christ must carry, and the humans he will save are like the vassals encharged to the care of a ruler, who cuddles them as if they are little children.

20. This refers to Old Testament texts that Christians interpreted as prophecies about Christ.

21. This refers to responsibility for governing or protecting others. See Karttunen and Lockhart 1987, 53.

to you my spirit, my soul, and my life. And this gold: receive it well, O my deity, O my ruler. Pardon me. Amen.

(At that point he gives a kiss and makes an offering. Melchior does not say anything more. And then at that point Balthasar speaks.)

BALTHASAR: O master, O ruler, you have in your keeping the sky and the earth, nobility and rulership. And it is really true that you are God, O lord of the near, O lord of the close, O giver of life. And I believe in you completely, with all my spirit, my soul, and my life. And you, for our sake, have left your precious and admired kingdom and your precious and admired royal seat. And now, for our sake, you will remain here on earth, you will teach people. And for our sake your enemies, the Jews, will tie you by the hands to a stone column and flog you. And for our sake they will shamefully stretch you by the arms on the cross. You will die. And it's just for the sake of the people of the world. And truly, since they are your creations, you will save them, by means of your death. And now, what, truly, will I give you? What, truly, have I come to offer to you? It's nothing at all. It's just this here that I offer to you, a very precious bitter potion, called "myrrh."[22] And when your precious and admired body is buried in the sepulcher, they will anoint it with this. And now, O my precious and admired deity, what, truly, have we come to offer to you? It is only our spirits, our souls, and our lives. Pardon us fully, O my precious and admired deity. *(At that point he gives a kiss, as Casper and Melchior did. He draws back again. He says:)* And you, O precious, admired, and blessed maiden, the beginning of sin never reached you.[23] And your precious and admired grace lies gathered all together there in heaven and everywhere in the world. Your queenly honor will never be finished, will never come to an end. And of what, truly, will I make an offering to you? What, truly, have we come to give you? It is nothing at all. It is only our spirits, our souls, and our lives. Pardon us fully, O my precious and admired mother. Now we are going to be on our way. May it so be done. Amen. Jesus, Mary, and Joseph.[24]

(Then at that point an angel appears. He gives instructions to the three rulers. He says:)

---

22. The Spanish word *mirra* is used.

23. This refers to the Virgin Mary's immaculate conception, or conception free from original sin.

24. This may be a formulaic blessing rather than a salutation of the three individuals named.

ANGEL: You rulers, you kings, you are most generous, you have shown favor to the precious, admired, and blessed maiden and her precious, admired, shimmering, perfect, and only child, since you came, you came to greet him, you came to make offerings to him. But I beg of you, don't go back the way you came. Take a different road, so that you don't go and fall into the hands of Herod, the great scoundrel. For he just lied to you when he said: "I too will go, I will go to worship him." And he is very angry. He wants to sentence him to death. But in no way is it time yet for him to die. Who will save the people of the world? *(When Mass is over, at that point the angel cries out to Saint Joseph, giving him instructions. He says:)* O Joseph! O Joseph! O Joseph! Flee with the precious and admired holy child! For Herod, the scoundrel, is coming. He is looking all over for him. Take him to Egypt! Hide him under a big palm frond, so that he won't sentence him to death! He's coming to kill all the little children! Go quickly, O Saint Joseph!

The Tepaltzingo Passion Play

Nahuas practiced various devotions during Holy Week, the days from Palm Sunday to Easter Sunday. Holy Week provided opportunities to hold large-scale ceremonies and to engage in penitential practices that were not entirely different from the fasting and bloodletting common in preconquest rites. Spanish priests were impressed by the Nahuas' enthusiasm for self-flagellation, a penance imitating the flogging that Jesus received. This was performed especially on Fridays during Lent, the forty-day period leading up to Easter.

Religious confraternities dedicated to Passion-related themes such as the True Cross, or Our Lady of Solitude,[1] organized Holy Week processions. Especially on Holy Thursday, people would march through the streets, often carrying crosses, torches, or images of Jesus and Mary, and often whipping themselves. Mexico City processions featured thousands of marchers. Such large assemblies of indigenous people made the Spaniards nervous: every year rumors spread that the natives were plotting a revolt. To commemorate the Last Supper, when Jesus fed his twelve disciples and washed their feet, native nobles provided a feast for poor people after the Holy Thursday procession. At the feast, twelve disabled people enjoyed a foot-washing and gifts of new clothing.[2]

In the 1590s fray Francisco de Gamboa began to have people act out scenes from Christ's crucifixion during Friday sermons during Lent, at San José de los Naturales, the main Nahua church in Mexico City. The earliest surviving Nahuatl play script, dating to around 1590, expands

A Franciscan friar preaches about the Crucifixion. The native artist depicts Nahua listeners as if they are part of the scene. Sixteenth-century drawing in fray Gerónimo de Mendieta's *Historia eclésiastica indiana*. JGI 1120, Joaquín García Icazbalceta Manuscript Collection. (Courtesy of the Nettie Lee Benson Latin American Collection, University of Texas Libraries, The University of Texas at Austin.)

just one Holy Week event, the farewell dialogue between Christ and Mary, into a complete play. This farewell, called the *despedimiento* in Spanish, is not in the Bible. It derives from a thirteenth-century Latin text written by an Italian Franciscan, Giovanni da Cauli, directed at the popular devotional practice of meditating upon the various sufferings that Jesus and Mary endured.[3]

It is not clear when longer plays in Nahuatl presenting the whole story of Christ's Passion, or torture and death, were first performed. The Nahua historian Chimalpahin dates the first performance of the Passion in Coyoacan, a lakeside altepetl now part of Mexico City, to 1587.[4] Other communities might have begun this tradition earlier.

Nahuas came to see Passion performances as an activity that supported the political and religious legitimacy of the hosting altepetl. A Nahuatl document from Cuernavaca, written in the late seventeenth or perhaps early eighteenth century but purporting to describe sixteenth-century history, presents the first Passion play as one of that colonial altepetl's foundational events. Without giving any precise date, the document says, "This is when it begins, how the Passion of our deity was performed, not just a frivolous thing, how they seized him. . . . And so we are to remember how our deity died. That is how it will go on being done in his memory." Whether Cuernavaca sponsored early Nahuatl Passion plays is not known, but some of its leaders chose to claim that it had.[5]

Six (if not more) long Nahuatl Passion play scripts date to the eighteenth century. One of these, an incomplete script missing both its beginning and its end, still resides in a local archive, in San Simón Tlatlauhquitepec, Tlaxcala.[6] The others, now in Mexican and U.S. archives, might have been removed from their communities when church and Inquisition officials cracked down on these performances in the mid-eighteenth century (see the introduction). These six plays constitute the largest related group of Nahuatl dramas. They share many features, with two or more plays paralleling one another nearly word for word in some sections. The relationships among them have yet to be worked out in detail. However, the shared content proves that texts were passed around and copied by people in different communities, and that individual scripts were sometimes pieced together from multiple sources or models.

The play presented here is from the altepetl of Tepaltzingo, in the state of Morelos, south of Mexico City. The location of the original colonial script is unknown, but the Latin American Library at Tulane University holds a clear photostatic reproduction. Although the script does not include a date, someone who wrote a note on the front of this text did the same with a play from nearby Axochiapan, which is dated 1732. This suggests that both plays might have been collected or confiscated at the same time, in 1732 or later.

The people of Tepaltzingo felt a particular attachment to the Passion of Christ. Sometime before 1681, the local indigenous people (who included both Nahuas and Otomis) started a confraternity dedicated to Jesus of Nazareth. The confraternity possessed a statue of Jesus on the way to be crucified, kneeling with the cross over his back and shoulder. By the early eighteenth century, this statue had gained a reputation for working miracles. Many people made pilgrimages to Tepaltzingo to pray before the image. Seeking to monopolize the profitable trade with these visitors, local Spaniards, with the archbishop's support, seized control of the confraternity in 1724. This archbishop banned the confraternity's Holy Week procession and warned the natives not to interfere in matters beyond their understanding. The indigenous people protested. A later archbishop in 1743 upheld Spanish control but did, at least, insist that three of the confraternity's officers had to be native people. To shelter the famous statue and its visitors, Tepaltzingo built an elaborate shrine during the second half of the eighteenth century, with scenes from the Passion sculpted on its façade. However, the arguments over who controlled the confraternity lasted until the organization was dissolved in the mid-nineteenth century.[7]

Tepaltzingo's Passion play was probably sponsored by this disputed confraternity, its audience swelled by pilgrims. When the indigenous people put on this elaborate Nahuatl-language production, they cast one of their own men in a role shared with the miraculous statue and pretended to crucify him as if he were Jesus himself. Doing so, they commented on the local power relations, asserting their right to represent the story of the Passion in their own terms.

The play covers events from Palm Sunday, when Jesus rides a donkey into Jerusalem, through his death on the cross on Friday. A note at the very beginning suggests that the play was performed on Palm Sunday. It seems likely that parts of it were performed on different days of Holy Week, so that the crucifixion would actually be staged on Good Friday. However, the script itself presents no further instructions of this kind.

The Passion story told here derives from the four Gospel accounts, enhanced by elements that were added to the story in ancient and medieval times. One of these is the proclamation of Jesus' death sentence. Catholic priests might have provided one or more model plays or narratives, imported from Spain or put together in Mexico, which were later shared between communities to make new variations and combinations. Some curious motifs may be local innovations: the Jerusalem authorities run away from words Christ writes on the ground; the men who come to arrest him fall down twice, rather than once; multiple men try to stab him but are unable to hit their target.

One alteration of the Gospel story occurs when Jesus takes a valuable ointment that he and the apostles possess and rubs it on Mary Magdalene's head. In the Gospel versions a woman (Mary Magdalene according to John 12:3) brings ointment to Jesus and anoints his head or feet. In the Bible this act foreshadows the later scene in which women bring ointment to anoint Christ's dead body on Easter morning, only to find his tomb empty. An ambiguity in Nahuatl grammar might account for the shift: there is no difference between "he anointed her" and "she anointed him." But the change also fits with the respectful treatment that Christ's female followers receive in this play. All the women, even the former sinners, express sincere and constant devotion. For Jesus to "waste" something that belongs to him and the apostles, rather than to Mary Magdalene, also gives Judas more cause to be angry with him and thus proceed with his betrayal.

Judas is a villain in the play, but he does not embody pure evil. He agonizes over a decision that is motivated by his own and his family's poverty, and he regrets his action as soon as he sees Jesus being abused by his captors. The highest authorities, Roman Pontius Pilate and Jewish King Herod, pass the buck, displaying an indifference that colonized Nahuas might associate with their own distant overlords. The Jewish authorities of Jerusalem, symbols of political authority at a more local level, are the most villainous characters, though even some members of the Jewish council—Joseph and Nicodemus—recognize Jesus as the Messiah.

Characters actually labeled as "Jew" or "Jews" (Spanish *judio*) always behave badly in Nahuatl theater and other Christian texts in Nahuatl. Jesus, Mary, and the apostles never receive this label, even though they were Jewish. In this way, the vicious anti-Semitism prevalent in Christian Europe at this time spread into Nahua consciousness. In 1492 all of Spain's Jews had been forced to convert to Christianity or else leave the country. Some nominally converted but practiced Jewish customs in secret. In the colonies as in Spain, the Inquisition persecuted suspected

"Judaizers," sometimes burning them at the stake in big public spectacles. Nahuas in Mexico City occasionally saw public humiliations and executions of people who had been convicted for Jewish practices.[8]

The story of Christ's death and resurrection is Christianity's most important narrative. Appropriating it, Nahuas identified with its hero and his friends and could view Christ's tormentors as embodiments of their own enemies. Since they associated Christ with the sun, they also enacted a drama of cosmic destruction, preceding the renewal on Easter morning. Easter generally falls soon after the spring equinox, as days become longer than nights. In Central Mexico, the greenness of the annual rains is still some time away, but the sun is shifting toward the summer growing season. The god dies but will return to life, as will the dry-season landscape of the Nahua altepetl.[9]

Notes

1. The Virgin Mary when she is grieving over Christ's death.

2. Information on flagellation, confraternities, and processions is from Grijalva 1624, 72v, 74r; Motolinia 1979, 55–56; Mendieta 1980, 420–21, 435–37; and Torquemada 1975–1983, 5:337, 340–41. In a 1572 letter, Viceroy Martín de Enríquez told the king that for at least the past thirty years rumors circulated about the Holy Thursday processions, and an armed guard patrolled the streets before and during the procession. *Cartas de Indias* 1970, 1:283–84.

3. On the Friday performances, see Torquemada 1975–1983, 6:395; Vetancurt 1971, part 4, 42. On the play, see Burkhart 1996. On da Cauli, see Peck 1980, 40–41.

4. Chimalpahin 1965, 291.

5. Horcasitas (1974, 251, 335–36) reproduces the Nahuatl. The document, a primordial title, is called the *Códice municipal de Cuernavaca*. I thank Robert Haskett (personal communication, February 4, 2010) for his insight into the significance of this text. See also Haskett 2005.

6. See *Nahuatl Theater*, vol. 4.

7. Reyes Valerio 1960.

8. Chimalpahin (2006) mentions several occasions when people were burned or displayed before the public as Jews.

9. On solar associations with Christ's Passion in a twentieth-century Nahua community, see Reyes García 1960.

THE TEPALTZINGO
PASSION PLAY

Cast of characters in order of appearance

Christ
Saint Peter
Saint John
The (other) Apostles
Malchus
The Jews
Caiaphas
Magdalene
Martha
Woman (*accused of adultery*)
Simon
Judas
Mary
Eleazar
Joseph
Nicodemus
First Jew
Annas
Jew with a Long Beard
Notary
John Mark

Angel
Majordomo
Samuel
Leader (*of the Jewish soldiers*)
First Witness
Second Witness
Orobeo
Pilate
Third Witness
Fourth Witness
Fifth Witness
Herod
Simeon
Veronica
Centurion
Second Jew
Longinus

It begins on Palm Sunday.

CHRIST: O my children, go to Jerusalem. A little donkey is standing there, with its colt standing next to it. When you see it, you are to bring it here with a bridle. If someone says to you, "What are you doing? Where are you taking the donkey?" you'll tell him, "The ruler needs it." If they bother you, just put up with it.

SAINT PETER AND SAINT JOHN SPEAK: Very well, O our teacher. Let's go get it.

(Saint Peter leads and Saint John follows.)

SAINT PETER: What the teacher sent us for is standing here, O my friend.

SAINT JOHN: O my friend, let's take it. That's it, now we've seen the sign. *(Saint John pulls it along and Saint Peter goes behind. Then a Jew named Malchus[1] comes chasing them.)*

MALCHUS: Where are you taking the donkey you're hauling?

SAINT PETER: What you're asking about, O my nobleman—the ruler needs it. *[to Christ]* We've brought the little donkey, O our teacher.

CHRIST: O my precious children, put the saddle on it.

SAINT PETER: We've put the saddle on it, O our teacher.

CHRIST: O my children, take hold of it for me, let me sit on it. Let us go to Jerusalem. And this very day I'll begin my teachings, with which I will instruct the Jews.

(Then all the apostles leave, some going behind and some in front.)

THE JEWS SAY: It's him, the teacher Jesus Christ!

(Then they leave. The children of the Jews go to meet him. They sing in praise "Blessed is he who comes in the name of the Lord, hosanna in the highest."[2] Some of them bring flowers in their hands, others fronds; they wave them at Christ. The rulers and priests of Jerusalem speak.)

CAIAPHAS: O rulers, who comes there? A great many commoners[3] come leading him this way. What's happening? The ground is rumbling.

ALL THE JEWS SAY: O high priest,[4] I think it's the one they call Jesus of Nazareth.

CAIAPHAS: Who are you, coming from over there, fancying yourself such a very great personage? A great many of the commoners come leading you here. Don't you hear the little children calling you, imploring you,

1. In the Bible, Malchus is a slave of the Jewish high priest (John 18:10).
2. This line, from Matthew 21:9, is in Latin.
3. *Macehualli*, meaning commoner, acquired the colonial meaning "Indian" as well.
4. Literally, "priest-ruler," used for bishops and other high church officials.

saying to you, "Here you come, you who are very good and proper, you who are the child of God"? Be kind to them. Don't you hear it? Make them stop!

CHRIST: Why should I stop them? Don't you priests see the Book of David anywhere, the word of God anywhere? From the mouths of little children, God will be addressed and prayed to.[5] If the children didn't say it, who would say it? Because although I may live as a commoner, as man and deity everything belongs to me and everything is my creation, heaven and earth and hell. *(Then all the rulers and priests sit down in their temple.)* You, Jerusalem: if you knew what I know, you'd cry and feel sad, like I cry and feel sad. I gaze at you, O you unfortunate Jerusalem. In just forty years it will be time for you, altepetl, to be cast down and abandoned.[6] *(Then Christ enters the temple. He admonishes them.)* What are you doing here in the temple? Don't you see the Book of David anywhere in my father's home? People ought to enter with weeping and sadness. But all of you act like you think it's just a marketplace, where you buy and sell things, where you make fun of people. Aren't you ashamed? Get out, scoundrels! *(Then he beats them. They go out the door. Then he sits down and preaches.)* Listen, you nobles of Jerusalem. Although I have come here into your altepetl, I am very angry at you here. Many children of yours led me here. They will all be precious to me, for that is the will of my precious father, God, who sits in heaven. He sent me from there, such that I came to appear as a commoner here on earth. I will establish, make a beginning, of hardship. I will die, and with my death I will open heaven, so that those who are precious to me, those who serve me and follow my commands, will go there. But wretched are those who disregard and belittle my words and teachings. They will pay the penalty in hell, where they will burn forever. And wretched are those who are big hypocrites and snobs. They will burn forever. At that time they'll say, "We wish we hadn't been born! We're so wretched!" *[to Mary Magdalene]* Especially you, who've come here into the home of my precious father who sits in heaven. It's just for the sake of your bragging and your pleasures on earth that you begin and end your day, thinking no longer of your deity and ruler. It's truly on account of you that I'll be stretched by

---

5. "Out of the mouths of babes and sucklings thou hast brought perfect praise" (Matthew 21:16); the line refers back to Psalm 8:2 (attributed to David).

6. An allusion to Rome's destruction of Jerusalem in 70 A.D.

the arms[7] on the cross. What's become of you? You don't see any more. It would be better if you hadn't been born. Listen well to what I say now. If you don't change your life and cut off your sins, and if your dirty life doesn't make you weep and worry, you'll never go to my home inside heaven and you'll never see my face again, for I will abandon you in the great houses of hell. You'll be locked up forever there, to suffer the penalty for your pleasures on earth. Your beauty and good looks with which you fix yourself up will all turn into red-hot coals in hell. How wretched you are, you woman!

MAGDALENE: Oh! Oh! O my God! That's it! I am dying now. My finery is burning me so very much! How much more will it be in hell, for it will torture me with burning pain.[8] You finery of mine, I despise you now! I have no more use for you. You really burn. Drop down over there! You really made me suffer. Oh! O my God, how wretched I am! *(She falls down and lies face down, and two women—Martha and the adulteress—come and take her away.)*

SIMON: O ruler, O teacher, I am very thankful that you worked so hard to teach all of us. Do rest a bit. Come into your home and have a bite to eat, and your students, too.

(All the Jews exit.)

CHRIST: O Simon, I'm very grateful that you will take us to your home. Let's go.

(Simon sets the table. Then Christ sits down along with the apostles. At that point Magdalene enters. She speaks.)

MAGDALENE: O my dear young man, which one is the ruler, the teacher?

SIMON: O noblewoman, it's the one who is here in the middle.

MAGDALENE: I beg of you, tell him for me that I want to see him.

SIMON: Very well, O noblewoman, let me see him. *[to Christ]* O our teacher, a dear woman has come who wants to see you.

(Christ stands up. He walks around a bit and the apostles go to meet Magdalene.)

CHRIST: O dear woman, why do you want to see me?

(Magdalene kneels before Christ. She stands up.)

MAGDALENE: Oh! O my deity, O my ruler, only you are perfectly exalted. Do not despise me. Pardon me, your creation, for I have come

---

7. This is how crucifixion was expressed in Nahuatl.

8. In *Final Judgment* and *The Nobleman and His Barren Wife*, the demons dress the condemned woman in flaming finery. Magdalene here throws off her jewelry or other adornments.

here before you to cry and to kiss your precious princely feet. I don't bring anything to present to you, only my tears. Let me just sprinkle them on your feet. Let me also clean them for you with my hair. O my deity, may your heart be compassionate, O my ruler.

CHRIST: O John, bring here the precious ointment you have in your hands.

SAINT JOHN: O my precious teacher, here it is.

CHRIST: O dear woman, you have said you are turning yourself over to me and that you despise earthly joys. And for as long as you live here on earth you are to always give torment to your earthly body.[9] Now I will give you a precious liquid, which is not liquid of the earth here. Bend down and let me spread the precious ointment on your head. O dear woman, with that you will be happy. It will become your good fortune in heaven. Arise and go to your home. (Then he blesses Magdalene.)

JUDAS: God knows, but why is Christ wasting what he spread on this woman's head? Wasn't it just wasted? And why do such a thing? Truly indeed, if the ointment had been sold it might have fetched three hundred pesos, which we could have used for a long time, or poor people struggling on the brink of danger could have been shown mercy.

CHRIST: What are you saying? Even though I spread the precious ointment on the head of the noblewoman, what she did is very good. She washed my feet with her tears. And you, you say you would have shown mercy to the poor and miserable. But I am about to abandon you; I am about to go away. The poor will be living here with you. When I'm gone you will show them mercy. But I won't be living with you for much longer. Why do you say this? Truly indeed I say to you that what this noblewoman did will be praised. The Christians of the world will hear of it.

(Christ exits along with all the apostles. Judas just goes to the edge of the doorway. He returns and speaks.)

JUDAS: O teacher, why did you want to waste a very good ointment? I think you'll just give me problems. But you'll pay the price of it. And if not, may my name not be Judas Iscariot!

(Judas exits. Christ enters along with the apostles. They sit down. He teaches.)

CHRIST: Now listen, you nobles and commoners of Jerusalem. Do not be confused about me. I am the one you've been awaiting for a long

---

9. According to legend, Mary Magdalene had been a lascivious woman but led a very ascetic life after Jesus' death.

time. Now I've come to tell you my breath, my words.[10] Change your lives! You must not go to the place of great affliction, to hell. It would be better for you to go to my home in heaven, a place of great joy.

CAIAPHAS: O ruler, what is the troublemaker saying? He really embarrasses people and he's really about to crack my skull. Let him give a talking to that woman who's in jail, for she is a sinner.[11] Have them go get her, have them bring her here before me.

JEWS: What a splendid idea you have, O high priest. Let him give her advice, for what she did is worthy of death. Let's go get her. *[to the adulteress]* Come out here, O wicked woman! Now you'll see! We'll take you before the troublemaker, your lover. He'll pass judgment on you. Get a move on, O wicked woman! *(They all speak in front of Christ.)* O rulers, we've brought this woman here.

CAIAPHAS: O my nobleman, what do you want? Here is a miserable little woman, who sinned, who committed mortal sins. She committed adultery, taking a lover. Our grandfathers and grandmothers left orders that anyone who takes a lover will be stoned. Now then, what do you want? Pass judgment on her.

(Christ comes down and writes something on the ground.[12] Caiaphas and the Jews all stand up and read what is written on the ground. They all exit quickly, running. Only Woman remains.)

CHRIST: O dear woman, which of these nobles who were here brought you here before me?

WOMAN: O ruler, O teacher, they've already gone. They hurried away after they saw you write something on the ground.

CHRIST: O dear woman, go to your home. Take comfort, for you will be precious to me. Don't sin any more. Go. *(Then Woman exits. All the Jews enter along with the priests. Then Christ teaches.)* Now listen, you nobles of Jerusalem, and you commoners, you Jews. Don't be confused. I came down from heaven. My precious father, God, sent me from there, so I came to take flesh inside my precious mother. I'm the one who will save people. I will die. But even though I will die, I'll revive in three days. I'll ascend to heaven, to go sit at the right hand of my precious father, God. Later on I'll come from there to judge the

---

10. My important message.

11. This is the woman caught in adultery, in John 8:3–11. Earlier in the play, she helped Mary Magdalene off the ground.

12. In John 8:7, Jesus also says, "Let him who is without sin among you be the first to throw a stone at her." Then the Pharisees walk off one by one.

lives of the living and the dead. But as for you: how wretched you are! Even though you're about to knock me down as if I were a house, I'll soon raise myself up and come back to life. In just three days my body will arise. It will be very pure, it will be very good. And at that time you will say, "That is the child of the virgin."[13] For it is I who made heaven and earth and hell. Everything is my creation, everything you see and don't see.

MALCHUS: We're asking you questions now. How many more years will you treat us like this, will you keep going around mistreating and tormenting us so? What are you saying to us today? Who are you? Where did you come from? Who sent you here? What are you saying to us? Who told you the things we're hearing? Who taught you, you troublemaker? Don't crack our skulls! Don't you know we're nobles?

CHRIST: You are not sensible, you don't see, you don't believe. Truly I say to you, you will believe when I, the child of the virgin, come back to life and arise. It will be me.

MALCHUS: O rulers, he's really cracking your skulls. You should leave. Let the troublemaker go and yell over there. Let's go.

(All the Jews exit.)

CHRIST: O my precious children, come and listen. I know well that in just two days the festival of Passover[14] will take place. That is when the child of the virgin will be made known to people and betrayed, so that I will save people on the cross. I will suffer and be tormented so that I can open up heaven for those whom I'll take there, my vassals, those who are good and proper.

(Christ and the apostles exit. The farewell.[15] Saint Mary and Christ enter from either side. "The Passion of Our Lord according to Matthew"[16] is chanted.)

CHRIST: You supreme noblewoman, you who are Saint Mary, you who were chosen by the Most Holy Trinity, you who surpass all women, you who are very humble, you utterly good virgin whom no one can

---

13. *Ichpochtli*, meaning girl or young woman, was used for the Virgin Mary and the concept of virginity. Repeated emphasis probably added connotations of sexual innocence to the term, but it also retained its more general meaning.

14. Nahuas also heard this Spanish word, *pascua*, as a term for Easter and other major Christian festivals, such as Christmas.

15. The Spanish word *despedimiento* is used here.

16. This phrase, in Latin, probably refers to a Latin chant composed in 1585 by Tomás Luis de Victoria, Spain's most famous Renaissance composer. The chant consists of lines selected from chapters 26 and 27 of the Gospel of Matthew, all of them words spoken to or about Jesus.

equal, you are God the father's precious daughter. May the peace of
the deity Holy Spirit be with you. But know now, O my precious
mother, that it is time, the time has come, we have now reached the
time when I will die, and with my suffering, my creations will be saved,
those who are proper and good and those who are bad. That is why I
came to be born from your belly, so that I would die on behalf of my
vassals, the people of the world, so that they would be saved. And
now, O my precious mother, take comfort. Let your precious soul be
calm. Don't be sad. I must die. And what my precious prophets said,
that I will die, must come to pass. O my precious and admired mother,
rejoice and take comfort. My suffering and my death will become the
joy of the good people of the world. But now I am going to Jerusalem.

MARY: You who are my consolation and precious child, who emerged
from my womb, as you came to become a man, what are you saying?
You are my one and only precious child. And I know well that your
torment and death, by which you came to save us, are what you came
here to earth for. But now, O my precious child, with all your power you
could save people, even if you didn't die. Let the price for destroying
the sins of the world be your health, and let it also be your blood that
was spilled when you were still a little child and they cut your flesh
from you.[17] Let the price also be the way you fasted everywhere in
the wilderness. Let it also be the pain and suffering of your heart when
you instructed people in the altepetl. Let that be the price paid for
the sins of the world. It will be possible if this is how you want it to
be, you who are my precious child.

CHRIST: O you who are my precious and admired mother, what you
are saying can no longer be done. I must die on account of the sins in
the world.

MARY: O my lord, O my child, if you please, have mercy on me. If this
is what you want, let it be done in this way. But my heart suffers
great pain and torment. Have mercy on me!

CHRIST: O my precious mother, truly indeed I must obey you, for you
are my precious mother. But on the other hand I must obey my precious father, God, more. He wants me to go to Jerusalem.

MARY: O my precious child, remember for me how you ordered and
advised children to obey their fathers and their mothers. And now, O
my precious child, I implore you, do not go to Jerusalem.

17. This refers to Jesus' circumcision.

CHRIST: O my precious and admired mother, I really must die, for I'm about to be late for my death. And the first fathers,[18] our relatives, the prophets, who are in limbo, are very discontented. They've been waiting for me a long time, as has my predecessor, Saint John the Baptist, who went to comfort them and tell them that I'd go and save them soon. And now I really must go to die in Jerusalem.

MARY: O my precious and admired child, that is the will of your precious father, God, to whom you owe great obedience. But let it be when you are mature and old that you die, you who are my only child.

CHRIST: O my precious and admired mother, we have already reached the time when I shall die. It also says in the holy words that I am to die now. Even if the earth were destroyed, that wouldn't delay my dying. And now, O my precious mother, remember that when you went to make an offering of me before Saint Simeon, he told you of your suffering, that your face, your heart would suffer great pain.[19]

MARY: O my precious and admired child, wait for me, until I die. Don't let me witness your death. Don't let it happen in front of me.

CHRIST: Oh! O my precious and admired mother, it's no longer possible for what you're saying to be done. The people of the world would perish, just from the sins that have been done. But now I will pay for them, so that they will come back to life. Because when they sinned, they sinned in public, therefore I will die [in public]. That will be the price. Someone has to die and it has to be very painful and shameful. And Adam [and Eve] stretched out their arms to the fruit tree as they sinned. In that way they betrayed their children. And I must be stretched by my arms on the cross, so that I may save the children of Adam and [Eve[20]] from the hands of the demon.

MAGDALENE: O my lord, O my ruler, what are you saying? Your precious mother is dying. O my lord, O my ruler, if you please, have mercy on her! (Then Magdalene talks to Saint Mary.) O noblewoman, O my dear child, what's happening to you, O you completely humble person, you who are Saint Mary? (Then Magdalene cries out and calls to Martha.) O noblewoman, O my older sister, bring a little something to drink. Let's give it to the noblewoman. It might revive her a bit. Hurry!

18. Adam, Eve, and other Old Testament personages, who await Christ's descent to limbo, a part of hell, on Holy Saturday to release them and bring them to heaven.

19. This refers to Simeon's words to Mary during her ritual purification, "and a sword will pierce through your own soul also," in Luke 2:35.

20. Plural forms suggest that Eve's name was accidentally omitted.

(Then Martha enters, bringing a little water. They will give it to Saint Mary to drink.)

MARTHA: You utterly great noblewoman, you who are Saint Mary, you who are the mother of God, what's happening to you? Be strong, and drink a little water, O noblewoman, O my dear child.

(Then they give her a little water to drink. Christ is sad.)

CHRIST: O my precious and admired mother, perk up. Don't die of sadness. O my precious and admired mother, calm down and be strong, for truly I say to you that there's no one who will die the way I will die. It will be very painful and shameful, because my suffering will last a long time. My heart, my body, and my face will suffer great pain and torment. My enemies the Jews will mockingly dress me in a cloak. They'll spit on me. Their fingers will be full of my hair and they will lay on top of my head, with metal, a twisted rope, a circlet of thorns.[21] And they'll strike my hands and feet with metal and they'll stab my heart with a metal staff. And they'll beat my body everywhere, 6,606 times, so that what the prophets left said will be verified, will come true. They left it said that his body would suffer everywhere: on his head, his hands, and his feet. And now, O my precious mother, calm down, be strong, try your hardest not to be sad. Pay close attention. You have no child, you are alone, you are just a poor little thing. What's to be done? You must realize it, O noblewoman, O my mother.

(Then two apostles, Saint Peter and Saint John, enter.)

SAINT PETER: O our lord, O our teacher, why are the dear women crying, as if you're making them worry? Comfort them.

(Then Magdalene goes to meet them, clasping her hands.)

MAGDALENE: Both of you, implore him also, for we've been pleading with him all this time but he no longer wants or accepts our words and entreaties. Now then, plead with him, both of you, also. Maybe he'll obey and accept what you say.

SAINT JOHN: O my teacher, you mustn't want to go to Jerusalem, for you already know that the people there hate you very much and want to kill you. Spend Passover right here.

---

21. The crown of thorns, forced onto Christ's head with metal staves. Repeated references to metal (staves, nails, and lance) suggest "Spanishness," since the Spaniards introduced iron and steel to Mexico. Spanish armor made a big impression on the Nahuas at their first sight of it. See, for example, Lockhart 1993, 80.

CHRIST: O my precious children, it's not possible any more, it no longer can be done, for my precious father, God, wants me to go to Jerusalem and spend Passover there.

MARY: Oh! O my precious child, you speak in such a way that my heart suffers terribly. I can't go on, O my child, for the time has come when I'm about to die.

CHRIST: O my precious and admired mother, that is all. I must leave you. But let it be with your permission. Bless me, O my precious and admired mother, O noblewoman.

(Then they bless Christ.)

MARY: May he bless you, blessed young man and my only child, in the precious and admired name of God the father, and you, and God the Holy Spirit. You mustn't take off yet. Hug me again, for I have blessed you.

(Then he embraces his mother.)

CHRIST: O my precious and admired mother, don't be anxious because I'm going to die, for that's what my precious father, God, wants. Everyone in the world has been pushed around by death. My death [will save them]. And now, O my precious mother, I say to you that even though I will die, I will revive again on the third day and you will see me again. My body will be pure through and through. I'll never die again. Then you'll be happy, O precious noblewoman, O my mother.

MARY: O my precious child, O my consolation, O my joy, it's what your precious father, God, wants. If you want it, let it be done in this way, you who are my only child.

CHRIST: O my blessed mother, what deathly sadness you suffer on my account. You mustn't fall, O my precious mother. O Magdalene, take hold of her, and don't let her fall down anywhere. *(Then Magdalene and Martha and Saint Mary all exit.)* You who are my precious children, my students: let your hearts be satisfied, for we'll be going on to the altepetl of Jerusalem. I will spend Passover there, and we'll be there for three days. Let's go. Get a move on!

([Christ and the apostles exit.] Then Caiaphas and all the Jews enter and hold a town council meeting.)

CAIAPHAS, HIGH PRIEST: Now that I've gathered you very honored people together, you rulers: you already know that Christ, the child of Mary, is stirring people up, deceiving them, and confusing the commoners. They all follow along after him. They go around saying and testifying that he is the Messiah. But we know he's just a poor wretch, a little commoner. And they no longer have regard for our very splendid altepetl, because he is spoken of as if he's really great, and so he confuses people. He really deserves death. Tell me: what on earth shall we do? If we just leave things the way they are, he'll become ruler and make all our vassals his vassals. And as for the people of Rome: won't they come to destroy us? They'll say: perhaps this is another time for us to take their kingdom from them. Won't they come to lay siege to our altepetl? And as for our very splendid temple and the commands of God: won't everything perish if all the commoners obey Christ's teachings?[22] You already see that our fathers took great care of the laws, because he[23] left them as a gift. Even though we might destroy them ourselves, aren't we also very wise? If he truly were the Messiah whom we await, would he be afraid of death? You see that no one's showing up here in our altepetl today because of how we tried to stone him on Sunday. That's why he went to hide.

ELEAZAR: O ruler, what you're saying—that Christ die—is very splendid, for it shows you love your vassals very much and you perform your duties honestly.

(At that point Joseph makes a complaint.)

JOSEPH:[24] O my nobleman, you very honored people who have gathered here, why do you say that Christ stirs people up and mocks them? Whoever says that just speaks from envy. Don't you know that he is virtuous and humble, and doesn't everyone esteem him for his humility? If the prophecies are genuinely true, that the Messiah will come here to the altepetl, he has already reached us. Please tell me: is there anyone like him anywhere, have you seen anyone like Christ anywhere, who appears so splendid? He is very virtuous, very humble; his good deeds are very great. He cures all the sick and he performed a great miracle, in that he brought Lazarus back to life after six days, who lay festering for four days in a tomb. And the miracle happened right in front of me. Why do you now say that this Christ stirs people up and goes around deceiving them?

CAIAPHAS: Joseph, everything you're saying is very bad. You used to think that you should lead us, that we'd take you and your white beard

---

22. Caiaphas's words are ironic. Many Christians saw Rome's destruction of Jerusalem in 70 A.D. as a punishment for Christ's torture and death.

23. God, or Moses.

24. This is the Bible's Joseph of Arimathea.

as our mirror, our model.[25] But it starts with you, that you're defending the troublemaker, Christ. Don't you have any regard for all the elders? Are we the only ones saying that Christ is a troublemaker? Aren't all the commoners in agreement?

NICODEMUS:[26] But why are you responding to Joseph with anger, O ruler? Everything in what we say is all true. Truly indeed, Christ is the Messiah himself, who has come. You all see all the holy miracles he performs. He cures your sick, and brings your dead back to life. But you pay him back by hating him and speaking ill of him.

CAIAPHAS: Move them right this instant! Move them over there to the door! They mustn't sit where the rulers are gathered together, because they are stupid. Have them leave immediately! *(Right then Caiaphas strikes the table. They make Joseph and Nicodemus go out the door.)* Listen, O you honored people, to the true words I say. One person must die on the festival, so that the whole world won't perish. Now then, it's not anyone. So that the various people will be saved, I order, and it is my will, that it be proclaimed everywhere in the altepetl that when anyone sees Christ, they must take him into custody right away and bring him here before us. If he defends himself, then let them kill him immediately, let him die at their hands.

(All the Jews rejoice.)

JEWS: May your will be done in this way, O high priest. Let the town crier proclaim it!

TOWN CRIER: [blank space]

FIRST JEW: We have already gone and carried out your command, O my nobleman.[27] O very honored one, O high priest, it's very good that you say that Christ shall die. Let him pay for his sins. But you say it's to be proclaimed publicly. It mustn't be done that way. Let's be sensible about this. As you know, each and every resident of the altepetl loves him. Won't they come to his aid? Let's just seize him in secret.

CAIAPHAS: What you're saying is true and correct. Let it be done this way. And here's what I say to you. As you know, the troublemaker

---

25. Our good example.

26. A Pharisee, mentioned in the Gospel of John.

27. In some Passion plays, the town crier makes a proclamation threatening the citizens of Jerusalem with death if they offer shelter or friendship to Jesus. In this play, it seems, the copyist started to include this material and then decided to have the Jews keep their agreement a secret. He may have been working from more than one earlier script.

revived Lazarus a few days ago. And that's what the people of the altepetl praise him about so much. That one really worries me, for he falsely
thinks of surpassing us. As you know, Lazarus is a lord. He mustn't help
[Christ]. We'd better kill him too. He mustn't help the troublemaker
who will take our kingdom from us. We who have homes here will no
longer be esteemed. Lazarus must be killed in secret, O rulers.

JEWS: What you're saying is very splendid, O ruler. May your will be
done in this way.

CAIAPHAS: Now you see that Jesus no longer has any shame or regard
for others, for he wants to destroy our altepetl. Now he's subverting
the commoners. But he's a poor little wretch. Now he wants to destroy
us and destroy our altepetl, which God greatly esteems.

ANNAS: Don't you know that he's just a crazy person?

CAIAPHAS: O rulers, let's not just talk. Let's put our hearts at ease concerning Christ. We've been negligent and now he's about to surpass
us. Anyone who isn't angry is to speak up! Even though he's a healer,
the commoners show him great obedience. Furthermore, he really
bothers me. When he entered the altepetl on Sunday they ushered
him in with palm fronds in their hands. And all the people of the
altepetl met him and praised him in song. I heard them say, "Blessed
is he who comes in the name of the Lord. Hosanna in the highest."[28]
What are those words? That's the very thing that sets my soul on fire.
He's really gotten them all worked up. I want to crush him right away.
I really want to put my heart at ease. Tell me: where were we? We
should have taken him into custody then. Moreover, he used to come
out in front of us every day. Every one of the commoners believes his
teachings, and the people of the altepetl follow him now. Will he
destroy us? Do we no longer get any respect? He must die quickly.
First, I order you, and second, I implore you.

JEWS: We agree, O high priest.

JEW WITH A LONG BEARD: O rulers, listen to me a bit, and with your
permission I say before you, the high priest, that your command that
Christ die is very good. However, you already see that sudden actions
can sometimes lead to bad results. I'm not saying that the rotten
scoundrel shouldn't die. But you see that we are already in Passover
and all sorts of people from all over are all coming to gather together

28. This is in Latin.

here. They all know Christ. Let's not inflame the commoners. Let Passover take place first. When it's over, then the troublemaker should be seized and taken into custody.

CAIAPHAS: What you are saying is very true. He shouldn't be sentenced to death during Passover.

(Judas enters. He bends his knees a bit in front of Caiaphas.)

JUDAS: O my nobleman, greetings! I've come to you today for you truly serve and slave away, favoring our lord, O my nobleman. Today you all suffer pain and anguish in your hearts and your bodies. You're looking around for Jesus, wanting to arrest him. You try many times, but it can't be done. But now, if you want, I will deliver him into your hands. Think about it. And that is what I've come for, poor wretch that I am.

CAIAPHAS: Thank you very much. So be it. Very well, sit down and tell us how we can do it, O my friend.

JUDAS: O very honored rulers, when you've heard what I have to say, take my teacher into custody right away. Don't be afraid because all the various people worship him and his power is very great. Look to what you will give me and I will deliver him into your hands so that you can take him into custody.

CAIAPHAS: But, O my friend, O Judas, what you say is very great, but I don't believe you because, as the saying goes, "he who tells people a great many things is giving them absolutely nothing."[29]

JUDAS: O my nobleman, is what I'm saying so difficult? He will be brought before all of you in custody. I will give you Christ. Know that I didn't come here just to be spying. For right now I say that I despise Christ and all his teachings. May I not die a good death if I ever go back to him. You said that once Passover is over, you will take him into custody. It would be better right now. Don't put off the death sentence to be imposed on him. If he finds out that you don't dare to take him into custody here, it will be delayed for a long time. If you kill him now, then all his students will forget him. May God not want me to be a two-faced liar in matters concerning the altepetl, and before the officers of the law. Therefore I will kill Christ. Give the orders quickly. You already see that a great many of the commoners love him. Nevertheless, I know that I will put an end to all your problems. However, you shall give me thirty pieces [of money]. Moreover, you're to give me a document too, to make sure that what you say will be carried out.

---

29. In other words, "talk is cheap."

(Caiaphas stands up quickly. He embraces Judas and all the Jews stand up and bend their knees a bit in front of Judas.)

CAIAPHAS: God bless you, you splendid fellow, because you speak on behalf of God's commands and you save all of us. O my friend, O Judas, you are a very, very sensible person. God certainly knows that I'd be happy to give you something that would be equal to my kingdom. But in any case you will see my loving charity sometime. Now then, as to the document you want, we'll make it right here in order to give you the thirty coins,[30] because you don't want to get tired of waiting. Come, O notary, make the document and give it to the young man.

NOTARY: Very well, O ruler.

(Then he writes. They give the document to Judas. After they give it to him he takes his leave.)

JUDAS: O rulers, let me leave you for now. Be of good cheer, for in any case I will come speak to you again. Wait for me.

(Wind instruments are played. The Jews exit. Christ and the apostles enter, speaking.)

SAINT PETER: O our teacher, where do you want us to go to make preparations for you to celebrate Passover? Because you don't want us to be here. Perhaps you want us to go into the great altepetl of Jerusalem?

CHRIST: Come, O my younger brothers. Go into the great altepetl of Jerusalem. On the road you will see a water carrier. You're to follow him. Wherever he goes indoors, you go in. You will say to the owner of the house, "Our teacher has sent us here to you. He's coming to honor you here in your home and to celebrate Passover." And that person will show you a fine little house.

(Then the apostles bow before Christ.)

SAINT PETER: Very well, O teacher, let us be on our way to carry out your command.

(Wind instruments are played. Christ and the apostles exit. Then Saint Peter and Saint John come back toward the outside of a house. Then the water carrier enters. They follow after him where he enters into the home of John Mark.[31] At that point John Mark reveals himself in the doorway.)

---

30. Nahuas borrowed the word *tomin*, Spanish for an eighth of a peso, to mean both that specific value and money in general.

31. The host of the Last Supper is not named in the Bible. John Mark is mentioned in the Acts of the Apostles and is often identified with Mark the Evangelist. Farmer 1992, 322.

SAINT PETER: May peace be with you! Know that our teacher has sent us here, for it's here in your home that he will celebrate Passover. It's just for this reason that he's sent us two here. Give us something to do. *(John Mark joins his hands together and gazes upward.)*

JOHN MARK: Let the teacher come! How very fortunate and favored I am that he will enter my home, I his vassal, who will serve him poorly. Let his will be done. Here is the house, along with me, a creation of his. I'll do whatever is of service to him. If it isn't so, he will pardon me. Give him my leave to do this.

SAINT PETER: Very well, O ruler. Let us go and report to the teacher. *(Then wind instruments are played. The Jews enter. Then the apostles exit. Then Judas rushes in. He addresses them.)*

JUDAS: O priests, I would be happy just to come here calmly to greet you and we would all be content. But I've come in a hurry to tell you about where the Messiah will celebrate Passover this evening. Know that two of his students came to this altepetl. He sent them here. He didn't tell them directly but just gave them a sign—when they meet a water carrier, "Wherever he goes indoors, you go in." They were to tell the homeowner that Christ would be coming in. After I heard this, I secretly followed the messengers. I also saw them go into the home of John Mark. I know for sure that Christ will come there. That's where he'll eat the lamb. I came rushing from there in order to speak to you. Think about how it will be done, and pick out the strong soldiers that I'll take along. *(Judas sits down.)*

ANNAS: O soldiers, put your war gear on right away! Let there be a watch placed on when Christ arrives, because that's when he'll be taken into custody, along with his students, so we can take them to the jail.

JUDAS: O rulers, please listen for a bit. We mustn't rouse up the commoners with whom Christ dined, along with his students. I know for sure that he won't sleep there. Rather, he'll go to the garden where he always prays. The soldiers must go there in order to arrest him. *(Then Caiaphas stands up. They bow before Judas.)*

CAIAPHAS: What excellent good sense you have. Let it be done as you say.

JUDAS: O my nobleman, think about what is to be done and wait for me here. Tonight I'll come to tell you and advise you when it's time. *(Wind instruments are played. All the members of the town council exit. Christ enters. Saint Peter and Saint John, who were sent as messengers, enter from another place and go to meet Christ. Judas enters again, along with the other apostles.)*

SAINT PETER: O our teacher, everything is ready where you will celebrate Passover. Your vassal is waiting for you. We're waiting too, for anything that you want.

CHRIST: Let's go, O my children. Get moving. Let's go.

SAINT JAMES: Very well. Take to your feet, O our teacher.

(John Mark meets up with him, kneels before him, and joins his hands together.)

JOHN MARK: O teacher, I don't merit or deserve for you to enter my home. It's only what you want, to honor me and your house here. I am very thankful and grateful for it. I humbly beg you to bless me, along with all your servants here, so that they will genuinely work for you here on earth and, afterward, enjoy your kingdom in heaven.

(He blesses John Mark. Then they go to the table.)

CHRIST: O my younger brothers, do sit down. *(Then they sit down. Everyone eats. Then "As they were eating"*[32] *is sung.)* O my younger brothers, for a long time it's been my wish and desire to eat with you and celebrate Passover, before the torment is done to me. I tell you truly that this is the only time I will eat with you, until it is in the kingdom of my precious father, God. Now then, do eat, O my younger brothers.

O my children, this tortilla is my body; the tortilla is filled with [my body], which will be stretched by the arms upon the cross for your sakes. Eat it, O my children.

O my precious children, this wine is my blood; the wine is filled with [my blood], which will be spilled on the cross for your sakes, in order to strengthen the new way of living. Drink it, drink it all up, O my children.

O my precious children, even though you are eating with me here and enjoying yourselves, I tell you truly that here at the table with me is the one who will sell me, who has betrayed me to those scoundrels the Jews. Yet he is unfortunate! It would be better if he hadn't been born. But what lies written in the books of the prophets must happen to the virgin's child.

SAINT JOHN: O my teacher, if you please, tell me who has done such a thing.

---

32. A Latin chant from the liturgy, quoting Matthew 26:26: "Now as they were eating, Jesus took bread, blessed and broke it, and gave it to his disciples."

CHRIST: O John, yes, I'll tell you. You'll see in just this way: it's the one to whom I'll give the tortilla that's moistened [with sauce]. That's the one who has done this thing.

THEN EACH ONE OF THE APOSTLES SAYS: Is it me, O our teacher?

CHRIST: No. Sit down.

JUDAS: Is it me, O teacher?

CHRIST: You're the one who said it. Bring it to an end.

(Then he washes the others' feet.)

SAINT PETER: No, O my nobleman, O ruler. You who are my ruler are going to wash my feet? I can't possibly permit it, O ruler.

CHRIST: You don't yet understand what I'm doing now.

SAINT PETER: In all the world I can't possibly allow you to wash my feet, for you are my lord, you are my ruler.

CHRIST: Please listen, you who are Peter: if I don't wash your feet, you won't go and enjoy yourself with me in heaven.

SAINT PETER: O my lord, O my precious father, don't just wash my feet. Wash my head as well!

CHRIST: Please listen, you who are Peter: one who is already clean doesn't need to bathe, but only to wash his feet. And you are clean here, you aren't dirty and muddy. And not all of you are clean. *(When it is finished, Christ sits down. "On Easter he arose"*[33] *is said.)* O my precious children, you have seen what I have done for your sakes. I have showed you my love here. Please listen. You call me your teacher. What you are saying is true: I am your teacher, I am your ruler. But today I bowed down at your feet, I washed your feet. And in the same fashion you are to wash one another's feet. I have set down a model, a sign, for you. As I have done, you will do likewise. I tell you truly, because the holy words of the prophets that lie written in their books must come true, that someone who drinks with me and eats with me is the same one who will kick me and offend me. And as for all of you, don't go forgetting what I have said, for I am about to leave you. And here is a new command I order you to obey, and with which I dress you and which I twist tightly upon you. Love one another as I have loved you all this time. And if you love one another, that is how the people of earth will recognize that you are truly my students. And if the people of earth scorn you, you're not to despair over it. Remember that they scorned and hated me first, and I am your teacher. Pain and affliction must happen to you now. I

33. Which Latin chant this refers to is unclear.

tell you truly that you will cry and feel sad. But as for the people of earth, they will go about enjoying themselves and having a good time. But your crying and your sadness will turn into great happiness, which will never be finished, never disappear or come to an end. And as for you, O Simon Peter, please listen. Don't despair, don't grow faint over anything. I tell you truly that the demon is asking for you all, in order to scatter and disperse you like wheat. But I prayed to my precious father, God, on all your behalf, to keep your ardent faith from disappearing. Pay attention to these good words of mine. Encourage your younger brothers, give them strength. And so, let's go to my grandfather David's garden. Get up; let us go.

SAINT PETER: O my precious teacher, I owe you thanks. I, Peter, a little old man, am very grateful for all your words, with which you strengthen my heart for me. The only thing I'm worried about is, where you are going? It seems that you're about to leave me.

CHRIST: Where I am going you can't go yet. Someday you will go there.

SAINT PETER: Why can't I go there, O my teacher?

(Christ and the others walk around a bit.)

CHRIST: O my precious students, listen. At that time, all of you will leave me all alone. But I won't be alone, for my precious father, God, will be with me. You will suffer torments on earth. You mustn't grow faint because of that. Let your faces, your hearts, be sure of that. As for me, I came to go beyond the earth. And tonight all of you will be confused about me. As it lies written in the holy words, "I will beat, I will torment the shepherd, at which time the sheep will be scattered." But I will revive in three days. I'll lead you to Galilee, where you will see me.[34]

SAINT PETER: O my teacher, truly I say that even if my younger brothers become confused, I won't be confused. I will be strong.

CHRIST: O Peter, I tell you truly that tonight before the turkey cries out, you'll deny me three times, you won't acknowledge me.

SAINT PETER: Truly I say that I won't leave you, even if you're taken into custody. What happens to you I will suffer along with you. And even if I must die along with you, I won't leave you.

(Wind instruments are played. Christ exits along with all the apostles. Judas turns right back at the door, moving around while speaking.)

34. See Matthew 26:31–32: "You will all fall away because of me this night; for it is written, 'I will strike the shepherd, and the sheep of the flock will be scattered.' But after I am raised up, I will go before you to Galilee."

JUDAS: Now that's all, that's fine. I'll sell him. I'll do it, since I've already said so, I already made a judgment. And as for him, he knows that I've already left him. But I'm really pondering, in my heart I'm thinking, and I see how the teacher picks me out, as though he no longer wants to acknowledge me. And my face, my heart, are in great pain and torment. But how can I do it? For a little while I was satisfied. He pressured me to bring it to a conclusion, to do it. But here is what I say: maybe that's it, maybe I am a wretch, maybe I am a great sinner on earth. My teacher wore himself out to leave me a word or two of his teachings, which are very agreeable. My teacher loved me. He assigned his love to me. And now I'm about to sell him. What's he taken from me? What's he afflicted me with? He's shown me a great deal of favor. Oh dear, what am I about to do? Oh dear, what am I about to undertake? Is it just a joke? I've never taken on a task like what I've thought of today, like what I'm about to do. Will I do it? What will I get if I sell him? I know well that my reward will be suffering in hell. Shall I just quit it? Is it still going to be like this? Let me consult well with my face, my heart. What's bothering me? He is a great teacher and a benefactor of the Jews. He gave life to the dead and he healed the sick. And I will betray him to the Jews. Won't the commoners get him out right away and speak up for him? Moreover, what will the rulers do to him? Won't it just be a few days that he's imprisoned? Won't they get him out? And isn't he all-powerful, such that God will save him? Perhaps I'll just go give it a try. How will I betray him to them, especially since I'm stalling now? What in the world am I thinking? By this my heart will be content and satisfied. For all this time I've been suffering pain, hurt, and affliction. I serve him. He sends me on errands. I don't cast any of his words aside; I obey all of them. I don't earn anything there; I go around in rags. The cold comes right in on me, and there is great misery on earth. And my wife and my children have nothing coming to them; they go around in worn-out clothes. I can't provide their dinner, their breakfast.[35] And the people of my household have no rest and no happiness. Their faces, their hearts suffer pain and anguish. I support myself with great affliction and anguish. I am homeless! Who will offer me relief? What will happen to me? Who am I waiting for on earth? But will I just quit like this? What's scaring me? What's holding me back? What's

35. Their daily meals.

intimidating me? I think that if I betray him to the rulers, lords, Jews, and pontiffs, they'll esteem me very much for it, they'll show me much favor. But as for him, what does he give me? What do I gain from him? He just keeps me in more of the suffering and torment that I've been enduring. Is that how I serve him? What in the world am I saying? My teacher, my ruler, will show me favor; I'll get better through him. But I can't do it anymore. Here is what is very distressing: that fine and precious ointment that he spread on a wretched little woman's head was just wasted. If it had been sold, it would have fetched a price of perhaps three hundred pesos. But it all spilled onto the ground. He should have said, "My children are poor. Let something be bought with it so that they have clothes to wear." But why would I still have confidence in the teacher? Why would I still love him? Whatever will happen to me, however I am to perish, it is because I dare to betray my teacher. I can't hold out any longer. The time has truly arrived. Let me go see the Jews, the rulers, the pontiffs, the priests. Let me give it a try. Let me go notify the elders and the soldiers.

(Judas exits. Wind instruments are played. Christ enters along with three apostles and "O Good Jesus"[36] *is said.)*

CHRIST: O my precious children, my heart and my soul are very troubled. Wait for me here. Pray to God, so that you will not fall into temptation. *(Then the apostles sit down and go to sleep. Christ goes to where Angel is. These words are said three times:)* O my precious and admired father, I wish you didn't want me to die. But you are my precious father. It's not what I want that will be done, but rather your will that will be done. *(Then he goes to wake up the apostles. The words are said three more times.)* What's the matter with you, O my precious children? You haven't stayed awake and kept vigil for even a little while yet, even though it's just one hour. Get up! Pray to my precious father, God, so that you don't fall into badness and wrong. Don't let the demon lead you into sin. *(They do not answer him but just keep sleeping. Christ kneels three times before Angel and tries to wake up the apostles three more times.)*

ANGEL: Try your hardest, O my lord, O my precious father, breathe your hardest! Don't feel faint! O Jesus Christ, please listen now. Before your precious father, God, ruler everywhere in the world, I am placing

36. Latin chant from the liturgy for the festival of Mary Magdalene: "O good Jesus, praise to you! You pardoned the many sins of the sinful woman, because she loved you very much."

your prayers, with which you humbly prayed to him. And I am placing before him your blood, your red dye, from when you sweated blood.[37] And finally, all of us who live in heaven humbly begged him not to let you suffer and die, but to save you instead. But he spoke firmly to us. He said, "My precious child, Jesus Christ, knows well that the people of the world will be saved by means of his blood, his earth,[38] and his death. Therefore my precious child wants to die, as is necessary for the sake of the souls of the people of earth." And now, O my precious father, what do you want?

CHRIST: I greatly desire the salvation of all the people of the earth. For the sake of their souls, death is what I strive and long for. With my death I will save the people of the earth. May the will of my precious father, God, so be done.

ANGEL: O my precious father, you know you must be strong. You are great and valiant. The torment that you are about to suffer is also great. Be strong-hearted, for it will not last long; the torment will pass quickly. And after it has passed, then you will reach a place of great joy. And as for your precious father, he won't abandon you, he will always be with you; he has said so. And he'll look after your precious mother and your students. What will happen to them? You will see just how they are.

(Then the Jews come sit down in order to hold a town council meeting. They approach Judas, where they will count out the coins for him. Christ will just remain kneeling.)

JUDAS: O rulers, we're dawdling. Let's go quickly. And give me my pay, for I fulfilled my pledge, and I'm very tired. Also, give me the strong soldiers.

CAIAPHAS: Very well, O young man, now we will give you your pay. O majordomo, count out the silver[39] for the young man.

MAJORDOMO: Very well, O ruler. Come, O young man, here is your pay. Wrap it up in your cloak.

JUDAS: Very well, O ruler. *(Then they count out the coins for him. When they have counted them out for him, Judas moves some distance away.)* There are

37. Red dye or paint is a metaphor for blood. According to the Bible, Jesus sweated blood while praying in the Garden of Gethsemane (Luke 39:44). The actor playing Christ would somehow pretend to do this.

38. His earthly body.

39. The Nahuatl can refer to silver or gold. In the Bible, Judas is paid thirty pieces of silver (Matthew 26:15).

the thirty pieces of silver they came to give me. Please let my heart be content with it. Please let my heart be satisfied with it. Now I will have my goods and property. I'll buy a house and fields for myself, and I'll have things to drink and eat.

SAMUEL: And here are the strong soldiers. Speak to them. And as for you all, go following along after him. Don't get distracted; you're to do as he orders you. Haven't you brought the chains? You're to tie him with them right away. Don't let him run away.

LEADER: We hear what you say. Don't worry.

JUDAS: Please listen to what I say to you here. Don't turn back. Don't seize another student of his, who goes around with him, for they resemble one another. Now then, listen: I will kiss the one you are to seize. Have you paid close attention? Don't let him run away. If you make him run away, it won't be my fault any more, for I've already left him and betrayed him to you.

(Then the Jews go to where Christ is. Judas leads.)

CHRIST: O my precious children, stand up. Let's go, for here comes the one who will betray me.

JUDAS: Be of good cheer, O teacher. Say whether I come with wicked people.

CHRIST: O my friend, why do you come to betray the virgin's child with a kiss? *(Judas leaves right away.)* But as for all you, who are you looking for?

JEWS: Jesus of Nazareth.

CHRIST: I am Jesus of Nazareth. *(Then all the Jews fall down when they hear it.)* Stand up. Who are you looking for?

JEWS: Jesus of Nazareth.

CHRIST: I am Jesus of Nazareth. *(They fall down again.)* Stand up. Who are you looking for?

JEWS: Jesus of Nazareth.

CHRIST: And I've already told you, I'm him. If I'm the one you're looking for, if you've come to arrest me, arrest me! But leave my children be. You mustn't harm them.

LEADER: Arrest him, seize him, for he's the one we're looking for! Bring the chains and tie him up!

SAINT PETER: O our teacher, we're beating up the scoundrels!

MALCHUS: Get a good look at him! Find out which scoundrel cut off my ear!

CHRIST: O Peter, put your knife, your sword, in its place. Don't you want me to suffer the torments, like my precious father, God, wants?

Or how else is everything that lies written about me in the holy words going to come true? If I wanted to, wouldn't I appeal to my precious father, God? Wouldn't he send me all the angels, the soldiers who fill up all of heaven, who are more than 96,000 files of twenty, who would come to my aid so that I would not be betrayed to the Jews? Bring the poor man's ear. *(He sticks his ear on. The rulers come and sit down in their places.)* You have come here to arrest me as though I were a thief, bringing your swords. Haven't I gone about among you every day, and been with you in the temple? You should have seized me and arrested me then.

MALCHUS: Truly, will we let you go now? O soldiers, seize him, arrest him! *(He slaps Christ's face.)*

LEADER: Keep your eyes on the scoundrel, for we paid for that rotten trickster.

(Then they put a rope around his neck and tie his hands. Then they beat him to the ground and kick him. Some of them tear out his hair and slap him in the face.)

FIRST JEW: Please stand up. Stand up! Get up! O scoundrel, if you don't stand up, then we'll kill you.

(Then the apostles leave; they go along crying.)

LEADER: Let's take this scoundrel to the home of the great ruler Annas. Hurry up, O troublemaker! [*to Annas*] O ruler, greetings! Here's the scoundrel, the troublemaker and rotten trickster, that you're looking for. Take a look at him.

ANNAS: Come here, you who call yourself a teacher. What do you go around teaching, and riling people up with? And who are your students? Let me see them.

CHRIST: I used to teach people in the light of day, in front of everyone. When I'd gather the Jews together in their temple, I'd advise them that on earth there are no secrets, no hidden and dark places. That's what I told people. Why are you asking me? They know well what I taught them.

LEADER: Shut up, scoundrel! You really lie.

(They slap Christ in the face.)

CHRIST: If it's not true, you say what I couldn't say. But if what I said is good, why do you slap me in the face?

LEADER: Will we only slap you in the face, you scoundrel? We'll kill you, we'll destroy you, you'll die at our hands!

ANNAS: Take him to the home of the ruler and pontiff, Caiaphas.

LEADER: Very well, O ruler. Now we'll see about you, O scoundrel! Will you also talk the same way in front of the great ruler and priest Caiaphas, like you've got no respect? Hurry up, get a move on, O scoundrel! *[to Caiaphas]* O ruler, this is the scoundrel, the trouble-maker, who goes about riling up the commoners and trying to destroy all your honor, and the honor of Jerusalem. Sentence him, as is necessary, to death!

CAIAPHAS: Truly indeed, we are hearing a great many bad and improper things about him. Let the inquiry[40] be carried out. Let the witnesses get started, let them verify it. Now then, that is all.

FIRST WITNESS: O ruler, listen. This is how this scoundrel stirs people up in regard to the tribute that's owed to the ruler and emperor who sits in Rome.

SECOND WITNESS: O my nobleman, O ruler, as to this scoundrel here, we've heard indeed that he goes around saying he could knock down your temple, which you built with your own hands, and build it again in just three days, much more magnificent and much finer. That one is a real troublemaker!

CAIAPHAS: What? You don't give any response to everything that's said to you here, with which you are accused? I order you, by the authority of God, who is our lord forever, tell me, is it true? Are you Christ? Are you the child of God? Tell me, quickly!

CHRIST: It's you who said that I'm the child of God. I tell you all truly, it won't be long before you see the virgin's child sitting at the right hand of all-powerful God.

(Then Caiaphas tears his cloak. They slap Christ in the face.)

CAIAPHAS: Why are we still looking for witnesses? You've all now heard his blasphemies that belittle and slander God. And as for that business of fancying himself a deity, how do you see it?

THE JEWS ALL CRY OUT: He really must die, for he deserves death!

CAIAPHAS: We don't have the power to pass sentence on him, for it's not our job. Tomorrow let's take him before the ruler President Pontius Pilate, so that he will pass a just sentence on him. But for now, guard him for a while in the jail. Do not fail to keep an eye on him.

(They take him to jail, where they make fun of him. They blindfold Christ.)

---

40. The play uses various Spanish legal terms, linking the treatment of Jesus to proceedings of the colonial courts: inquiry (*información*), witnesses (*testigos*), blasphemies (*blasfemias*), oath (*juramento*), evidence or proof (*probanzas*), actions (*causas*), and sentence (*sentencia*).

LEADER: Very well, O ruler. Take him straight to jail. That's where he'll be.

FIRST JEW: If it's true that you're the child of God, tell us, who slapped you in the face?

JEW WITH A LONG BEARD: If it's true that you're the child of God, who spit in your face? Just like that you're the child of God. Tell us!

(After they have taken him to jail, Saint John enters. He sees that Christ is some distance away. Then Saint Mary enters.)

SAINT JOHN: Forgive me, O my mother, O noblewoman.

SAINT MARY: O my child, O my nephew, where did you go and leave my joy, my precious child? You are also my child's own messenger. Tell me, what of your teacher, who so especially loved you? Where did you go and leave him?

SAINT JOHN: O noblewoman, please listen for a bit. Your precious son, our precious teacher, our fortitude, has been sold by that scoundrel Judas Iscariot. He betrayed him to those scoundrels the Pharisees and the lordly rulers in Jerusalem. They paid him thirty pieces of silver for him.

(Then Magdalene and Martha enter. They weep.)

SAINT MARY: O my children, O my daughters, your teacher has been sold. A price has been put on him. Thirty pieces of silver were his price.

MAGDALENE: Oh! How very tearful and grievous is what you are saying. You just deprived us of our consoling happiness.

MARTHA: Oh! How very heartbreaking, that such a thing is happening to our benefactor, our treasure. Where will we be able to see him? Tell us, O my child.

SAINT JOHN: O my precious mother, please listen, since you all are asking me how it happened. Our savior and all of us celebrated Passover over on Mount Zion, in the home of a person dear to your precious child. And he said a great many extremely comforting words to us there. And when it was all over, then he went along with us to the bottom of the hill, to his garden. Our precious savior went there to pray to his precious father, on your behalf and on our behalf. He sweated blood there. His precious blood poured right onto the ground because of his fear. When he was done praying to his precious father, then Judas Iscariot came in. A great many of the nobles of Jerusalem accompanied him, fitted out and prepared for war. And once they'd gone there, then they arrested him. They didn't treat him at all kindly. They didn't treat him with any respect. Then they tied his hands, put a rope on his neck, and knocked him to the ground. Right then they plucked out his beard. They kept shoving him, and they kept kicking him. They took him, bound, to Jerusalem. And now, O noblewoman, I came quickly to tell you the distressing news, that you will see your precious child with sadness. Pay close attention. Please get going and hurry along to Jerusalem.

(Saint Mary kneels.)

SAINT MARY: Oh! O you who are perfectly splendid, you who are completely merciful, O compassionate one, I leave my precious and admired child in your hands, to you. Don't make him suffer, for he is a kind and merciful person. Everyone loves him. O my lord, don't let my precious child, Jesus, die. Don't do anything bad to him, O my lord. But if it's what you want, I beg of you: let the people of the world be saved, but let them be saved by some other means, for you are all-powerful. Don't let my child die. Rescue him from the hands of the sinners. Give him to me! *(Then Magdalene embraces her.)* O my daughters, come with me to Jerusalem. Let's go see my precious child.

SAINT JOHN: Go along with God's precious mother. As for me, let me set off and go to see your teacher. So I'll hurry off. Give encouragement to your precious mother. Go along with her to Jerusalem in a calm and peaceful way.

(Then he exits. The Marys follow.)

SAINT MARY: Let's go, O my daughters. Let's go seek out my precious child, my fortitude. Let's go die with him. Let's get going.

MARTHA: O my precious friend, you have seen that our precious and admired mother is very upset. Let's go follow her to Jerusalem.

(Then they all exit. Saint Peter warms himself by a fire. Three Jews go there: Orobeo, Malchus, and First Jew.)

FIRST JEW: Seems you're warming yourself by the fire here. Aren't you also a student of Christ's?

SAINT PETER: Maybe you're mistaken. I don't know him. I don't know the one you're looking for and talking about. Please, let me just go somewhere else, in peace. Don't let anything bad happen to me here.

(Saint Peter moves some distance away.)

MALCHUS: Why don't you acknowledge him, admit you know him? Didn't we see you over there in the garden? Weren't you also with him when he was seized and arrested?

SAINT PETER: Garden where? O my nobleman, who was I with sometime? You all are just making it up, making accusations. Leave me be! It wasn't me!

OROBEO: We're not making our words up for fun. O scoundrel, are you lying? Isn't it true that you're also a student of the one who was seized and arrested? Don't you also speak the Galilee language?

SAINT PETER: God knows! May he destroy me, may he kill me right here if I'm lying. Truly, I don't know the one you're talking about. It is the very truth. Here is the oath: I don't know him! *(Right then the rooster[41] cries out three times.)* Oh! O our lord, O my precious father, O my teacher, I am a wretch, I am a rotten sinner! I didn't declare that you are my deity. I did what was bad and wrong in front of other people. And I denied you. Don't despise me, a rotten sinner, for it! Forgive me, O my deity, O my creator! *(Then Saint Peter exits.)*

ANNAS: Bring out the one you have in custody. Let's take him to the home of the ruler President Pontius Pilate. Have the witnesses go there.

LEADER: Very well, O my nobleman, O ruler. *(Then they bring Christ out.)* It will be today, O scoundrel, today that you'll pay the penalty for your wickedness. You'll go before the great judge, President Pontius Pilate. Come on, get moving.

(Then Judas enters.)

JUDAS: Let me wait for him a bit, let me be satisfied as to how they're treating the one I betrayed. Maybe they're doing something bad to him. Is he all right? They're bringing him out here now. *(He stares at him.)* Oh dear! How wretched I am! What will I do? I have sinned terribly. I think they're going to kill him! No one cares about him. Oh no! O our lord, truly I have sinned greatly. There's no way you'll be able to have pity on me or show me favor. I can no longer live as your vassal on earth. I must throw my wicked self off a cliff, or go hang myself somewhere. *(Judas flings the coins on the ground.)* O my lords, O rulers, I have sinned in that I have sold to you, betrayed to you, God's own blood, his red dye.[42] Here's your silver! Take it! And release my teacher, God's precious child!

FIRST JEW: What business are you of ours, you scoundrel? Did we go and arrest you? Did we make you come here on our account, come betray him to us? Do we know whether you sinned? Majordomo, you go pick up the silver. Don't put it back in the altepetl coffers, for

---

41. Here a Spanish loanword, *caxtil* (from "Castile") describes the calling bird, earlier labeled by the Nahuatl term for "turkey hen."

42. Metaphor for a child of noble lineage. Judas's use of this phrase expresses his newly recovered respect for Jesus.

we'll use it to buy something. Put it somewhere else. A field will be bought with it, where vagabonds who die here in Jerusalem will be buried. Take him, make him get a move on.

(Then they take Christ to Pilate's home.)

CAIAPHAS: O my nobleman, O ruler, greetings, you who are Pontius Pilate, for our teachers, the Jews, have arrived before you. They've brought someone to your presence. We beseech you to listen to what they say.

PILATE: Please come. Welcome. Let me hear your complaint.

FIRST JEW: O our lord, O ruler, we have brought a very great scoundrel before you. He confuses a great many people here in your home of Jerusalem. He has stirred up all our vassals, residents of the altepetl, the people of Jerusalem. So you must pass sentence on him.

PILATE: And which one have you thus come to accuse so severely? What harm did he do? Is there evidence, or perhaps witnesses who will verify what he did?

LEADER: There, O my nobleman, O ruler, are the witnesses you seek. There are a great many; look at them. And they will testify honestly. Here's one of them.

PILATE: You witnesses: don't tell any lies in front of me. Don't say anything hateful, but rather speak very honestly. It seems to me that he is without sin. Now then, say only what you know.

THIRD WITNESS: O my nobleman, we cannot lie to you. Here is what we witnesses have seen and heard regarding how very painfully he confuses people. He says to all the Jews, "I am Christ, I am the ruler. You don't need to give tribute and service to the emperor Caesar, who is ruler in Rome."

PILATE: O notary, write it out thus, set it down thus.

NOTARY: Very well, O my nobleman, O ruler.

LEADER: O ruler, here are the other witnesses.

FOURTH WITNESS: Here's what we know about the troublemaker. He fancies himself a ruler. He says to people, "I am a ruler, I am the ruler of the Jews." He thinks nothing of the religious rites in Jerusalem. He has no respect for you. He has no respect for the rulers, elders, priests, pontiffs, and ministers.

PILATE: O notary, write it out thus, set it down thus.

NOTARY: Very well, O my nobleman, O ruler.

FIFTH WITNESS: O my nobleman, you should know the lying words of this troublemaker. He fancies himself a deity. He says to people, "I am the child of God. And your temple, which you've adorned today, I could knock it down and build it again in just three days." This is what he greatly confuses people with everywhere. We're not just accusing him falsely. What we say in your presence is quite honest.

PILATE: O notary, write it out thus, set it down thus.

NOTARY: Very well, O my nobleman, O ruler.

LEADER: O ruler, now you are satisfied, for you've heard all his deeds and deceptions. And so we beseech you, pass sentence on him, for he must die.

PILATE: Please come, you poor wretch. Please tell me, are you the ruler of the Jews?

CHRIST: It is you who say that I am the ruler of the Jews.

LEADER: Take careful note of his wickedness, O ruler. Right in front of you he acknowledges his deceptions, that he goes around saying, "I am the ruler of the Jews." He's admitted to one thing. And as to something else, he likewise will admit that he fancies himself a deity. You must pass sentence on this scoundrel.

(They slap him in the face. Christ says nothing. He just puts up with it.)

PILATE: Respond to everything that's said about you here. Look, you've been charged with a great many things. Get yourself out of this mess. But I'm not the one who's doing it, for it was my priests and my vassals who came to deliver you into my hands. Say what you have done! *([Christ] says nothing.)* I see no sin in this one. But what am I to do to him?

LEADER: O ruler, why is he without sin? He really confused and tricked all our vassals. He began in his homeland of Galilee and got here to the altepetl of Jerusalem. If he were without sin, would we have brought him here before you?

PILATE: But as I understand it, he's from Galilee, which is governed by the ruler Herod.[43] He sits there as ruler. Take him before Herod and tell him that I beseech him to reprimand him and pass sentence on him. It would be better if he's his subject.

LEADER: Very well, O my nobleman, O ruler, let us go there. *(Then they take Christ to the home of Herod. Then Herod enters.)* Get over here, get moving, O troublemaker! *[to Herod]* O master, O ruler, we have brought this troublemaker before you. The ruler Pontius Pilate beseeches you, saying, "Here is a vassal and subject of his who was brought before me.

---

43. Herod Antipas, son of Herod the Great.

How he goes about stirring people up here in Jerusalem! Let him reprimand him, let him pass sentence on him."

HEROD: The ruler Pontius Pilate has shown me favor. Please come
here. Are you the one who calls yourself Christ, whom my father was
looking for long ago? Please answer me.

(Christ says nothing. They slap him in the face. He just puts up with it.)

LEADER: O scoundrel, answer the ruler! It seems you can't talk.

HEROD: Why don't you perform some miracle before me? I've been
hearing of your reputation, what people say, for a long time. I'll have
mercy on you if you perform some miraculous deed before me. *(Christ
says nothing.)* I think it's a crazy person that you've brought here. Make
fun of him over there, for he's really giving me a headache. *(Then they
shove Christ around.)* Dress him in a ruler's white cloak. Put it on him.

SAMUEL: It seems you've turned mute. O scoundrel, aren't you the
one who went around teaching five or ten days ago, all around the
temple? O ruler, here's what a ruler you are!

(Then they put the white tunic on him.)

HEROD: And now, take him before the ruler again. He[44] showed me
favor, but he[45] just turned mute before me. The ruler knows what to
do to him. Let him see to him.

LEADER: Very well, O ruler. Get a move on, O scoundrel. Now we'll
see to you! *[to Pilate]* O ruler, Herod says, "Take him before the ruler
Pontius Pilate again, for he doesn't give me any answer. Let him pass
sentence on him."

PILATE: What shall I do? You all, go seize him, and pass sentence on
him according to your laws.

SIMEON: We've brought him before you. He's in your hands now. He
must die. Work justice on him.

PILATE: Please come. What have you done wrong, that you've been
accused? Answer me! *(Christ says nothing.)* But listen, you Jews. I see
no sin in him. And I can't sentence him to die. But you will be satisfied
with this: I'll seize and arrest him. I won't just give him a talking to.
I'll flog him. His blood will really flow and his flesh will be ripped to
shreds, so that he won't rile people up about anything ever again.

LEADER: O ruler, if he doesn't die we won't be satisfied.

44. Pontius Pilate.
45. Jesus.

(And then they take him to jail, where they beat him. Then they bring him out. Christ comes bound up in a red cloak. Then they put him on a stone base, where they make fun of him. They place a crown of thorns on him and [in his hand] a reed stalk.)

MALCHUS: Greetings, you ruler of the Jews. *(He slaps him in the face.)*

FIRST JEW: Here's your kingdom, O ruler! *(Then he puts the crown of thorns on him.)*

JEW WITH A LONG BEARD: Here's your royal staff, O ruler, which makes you look like the ruler of the Jews. *(He gives him a reed stalk.)*

PILATE: Now I'm bringing him out in front of you. I flogged him, so you'll be satisfied that he is without sin. Take a good look at him. Here's the one you accuse.

ALL THE JEWS: Seize him! Stretch him by his arms on the cross!

PILATE: Impossible. You be the ones to seize him and stretch him by his arms. But as for me, I see no sin in him.

SAMUEL: His sins are very great! And it is written in our laws that he must die because he says he's the child of God.

PILATE: But why don't you answer me? Don't I have the power to stretch you by your arms and also the power to save you and have mercy on you?

CHRIST: As for you, you won't be able to do anything to me unless it's by order of our lord God, who sits in heaven. It's not you who's the big sinner here, but rather the greater sinner is he who delivered me into your hands.

PILATE: But I don't know what to do, for I've already punished him. Now I say that you always pardon someone on your festival of Passover. Barrabas, the murderer, lies in jail here. His sins are notorious; he has destroyed many people. Let him die. But as for Christ, let's have mercy on him. But what do you want? Say it.

JEWS: Impossible. We will have mercy on Barrabas! We demand him!

PILATE: But as for Jesus, who is called Christ, what am I to do to him?

THE JEWS WILL SAY THREE TIMES: Stretch him by his arms on the cross!

PILATE: I will not bear the shame of stretching your ruler by his arms.

LEADER: We have no other ruler! Our only ruler is the ruler Caesar! And if you won't pass judgment on him, you'll be in rebellion against Caesar. That way all those who pretend to be rulers will understand that they are enemies of the emperor.

PILATE: Very well. Listen, you Jews. It won't be my fault that the teacher, who is precious to God, will die. Look here. I wash my hands in front of you. It will be done the way you want.

SAMUEL: We thank you, O ruler. Don't let anything trouble or frighten you. We now bear it on our shoulders. It will be our sin. For anger and wrath will come onto us, all sorts of stones and sticks[46] will happen to us, because of his death. So here we appoint ourselves, and we appoint our children and our grandchildren, that we shall all pay the penalty.[47]

PILATE: O notary, read them the sentence. Let them all hear it so that they are satisfied.

(Then they read out the sentence.)

NOTARY: I, Pontius Pilate, president here in Jerusalem by order of my ruler Tiberius Caesar, August Superior. Before me have passed all the actions and evidence, the accusations and demands of the Jews, with which they have accused Jesus, who is called Christ, whom they have said is such a troublemaker in the altepetl of Jerusalem. And I have seen all the evidence that speaks to the complaints made against him. And by my order he was flogged and tortured. But they were not satisfied with that. They said again that he must die, so that many people will take him as an example. And I have accepted their demands. And I have left him in their hands for them to do to him as their hearts desire. This sentence was issued here in the altepetl of Jerusalem on the twenty-fifth day of the month of March.

(They bring Christ out. They take him to Calvary and they make him carry the cross on his neck and two thieves go along following him, tied up, and Veronica meets him on the road to Calvary. She cleans his face.)

VERONICA: They're bringing my precious teacher here. His face and head are just covered with dirt. Will I be so fortunate and favored as to get next to him to clean his face? *(She kneels and cleans his face.)* Oh! You who are my precious teacher, it seems it is true that you are all alone, you who are the holy royal prince. Endure your torment, which you suffer because of the sins in the world, since you are our lord, since that is why your precious father, God, sent you here. *(Saint Mary,*

---

46. Punishments.

47. This speech expands on the Bible's "His blood be on us and on our children" (Matthew 27:25). Christians who blamed the Jews for Christ's death used this passage to justify anti-Semitism.

Saint John, Martha, and Magdalene bow down. Veronica shows them his face [imprinted on her cloak].) You precious and utterly good noblewoman, you who are Saint Mary: please look at the precious and admired face of the precious and admired fruit of your splendid womb. How very heartrending it is, since by my hands and by means of a miracle it was copied onto the cloak.[48] And try to hold up and be strong, you noblewoman and virgin. *(Saint Mary kisses Christ's face [on the cloth]. Veronica shows it to people everywhere. She turns back upward.)* You people of the world, please see here how very tear-provoking, distressing, and heartrending is the precious gaze of the ruler of the world, the precious child of God the father. Let us thus be grateful for his compassion, since it is for our sakes, for us people of the world, that everything is done to him. His precious face and his precious body reveal that he is human. May you, my female friends, you the children of Jerusalem, encourage him. Let's all follow him, because of his precious suffering.

(Saint Mary meets up with her child.)

SAINT MARY: O my precious child, O my happiness, O my precious child, where are you going? Who will console me, your mother? Come, talk still to those of us who are going along here, your relatives. You who are my joy: how is it you go all alone? What of your students?

(Christ turns back.)

CHRIST: You children of Jerusalem, you dear women: don't cry for me. Don't spill your tears for me. Keep them. You'll spill them for your own sakes, when you are going to give birth. You'll say, "How very fortunate are the wombs that have not given birth to a child, the breasts that have not nursed a child, because they have not seen children of theirs." And I see all this punishment done to me, in respect to you, when the wood is green. How much more will the dry wood be punished! And at that time you who are barren, you who are childless will say, "May you, mountains, come crumbling down on top of us! May you, hills, come crumbling down on top of us! Cover us!"[49]

---

48. Veronica wipes Christ's face with her *tilmatli* (indigenous cloak) rather than the legendary veil. In the story of Our Lady of Guadalupe, the Virgin Mary's image is imprinted on a Nahua man's *tilmatli*.

49. Christ's speech is based on a Bible passage about the coming destruction of Jerusalem: "Daughters of Jerusalem, do not weep for me, but weep for yourselves and for your children. For behold, the days are coming when they will say, 'Blessed are the barren,

(And when they have reached Calvary, Pilate speaks. And when they have stretched out Christ by the arms on the cross, the Jews will distribute his shirt among themselves and gamble for it.[50])

PILATE: Come here, you Jews. Put this here at the top of the crossed pieces of wood, saying that he is the ruler of the Jews.[51]

LEADER: O ruler, I wish you hadn't placed that like that, for he's not our ruler. Our only ruler is Caesar, who sits in Rome. Come here, O soldiers. Place the crossed pieces of wood, the cross, on top of his arms.

(Then they stand the cross up. All the Jews make war whoops by hitting their mouths. They shout.)

CHRIST: O my precious father, I place my soul, my spirit, in your hands. And I beseech you to pardon those who are tormenting me here, for they do not know what they are doing.

CENTURION: It's true that this is the child of God, because he asks pardon for those who are tormenting him here.

CHRIST: Today you will rejoice with me in paradise.[52] *[to Mary]* O noblewoman, there is your child. O John, there is your mother. I'm very thirsty, I'm very thirsty.

(Then they give him bitter water and vinegar.)

FIRST JEW: You're very thirsty? Here it is. Drink it up. If you're so thirsty, some kind of a ruler you are.

CHRIST: O my precious and admired father, why have you delivered me into the hands of others?

(Then each of the Jews attempts to pierce him. They are unable to do it.)

FIRST JEW: He really is the child of God. I have done my job well.

SECOND JEW: There's still me. Bring him here. I'll do my job.

(They all say these words. And then they go and get hold of a blind man; he will do their job.)

CHRIST: O my precious and admired father, I place my soul entirely into your hands.

---

and the wombs that never bore, and the breasts that never gave suck!' Then they will begin to say to the mountains, 'Fall on us'; and to the hills, 'Cover us.' For if they do this when the wood is green, what will happen when it is dry?" (Luke 23:28–31).

50. The Spanish word for shirt, *camisa*, was adopted into Nahuatl to refer to the long white shirts that became a standard item of clothing for indigenous men.

51. The object referred to is the sign reading "Jesus of Nazareth, the King of the Jews," which Pilate puts on the cross (John 19:19).

52. In the Bible, this is what Jesus says to one of the thieves (Luke 23:43). The centurion speaks immediately after Jesus dies (Luke 23:47; see also Matthew 27:54, Mark 16:39).

LEADER: Come here, you, Longinus.[53] Do your job here. Give it a hard push.

(Let the motet "O Lord Jesus Christ"[54] be spoken.)

LONGINUS: But, O my precious savior, O my lord, forgive me! I am a rotten blind man, wretchedly sick in my eyes. I didn't see you! If I had known, if I had seen you, I wouldn't have done such a thing. Now then, O my precious savior, forgive me! I am a rotten sinner, wretchedly sick in my eyes.

(Then all come down. They lower our lord Jesus Christ from the cross.)

53. According to medieval legend, this is the name of the soldier who pierced Christ's side with a lance. In some accounts, like here in the play, this man was going blind but is miraculously healed (Farmer 1992, 302).

54. A motet, or short polyphonic choral composition, by the Spanish composer Francisco Guerrero (1528–1599). The text in English is: O lord Jesus Christ, / I worship you, wounded on the cross, / with gall and vinegar to drink. / I beseech you / that your wounds and your death / may be my life.

Dialogue on the Apparition of the Virgin Saint Mary of Guadalupe

The earliest Nahuatl text telling the full story of how a Nahua man named Juan Diego encountered the Virgin Mary in 1531—the story of Our Lady of Guadalupe—is called *Nican mopohua*, or "Here is told," after its first two words. A priest named Luis Laso de la Vega published this text in 1649, in a book known as *Huey tlamahuizoltica* ("By means of a great miracle"), which also included other Nahuatl texts about the Guadalupan devotion.[1] Laso de la Vega was a *criollo*, or "creole," a person of Spanish descent born in the colony. One or more native speakers of Nahuatl probably collaborated with him, but whether the text draws on any earlier written or oral tradition in Nahuatl is uncertain.

The story assigns a miraculous origin to the image of the Virgin Mary that is housed at the shrine of Guadalupe in Tepeyacac (or Tepeyac), a pilgrimage center now visited by millions of people each year. In colonial times this settlement lay on the lakeshore north of Mexico City; today it falls within the city's urban expanse. This image of Mary as the Immaculate Conception,[2] painted on a large piece of cloth, may have hung at the popular shrine since it was founded in the mid-1550s. A 1556 account speaks of an image recently painted by an indigenous artist. The style of the painting resembles the works of early colonial native artists. The Spaniards who founded the shrine named it after Our Lady of Guadalupe in Estremadura, Spain, a popular Marian shrine dating to the fourteenth century. The Mexican Guadalupe soon gained a reputation for curing devotees or rescuing them from danger.[3]

The *Nican mopohua* story loosely follows a European model for apparition legends. The Virgin or another saint appears to a person of humble origin, often a herder of livestock. The saint requests that a shrine be built on a certain site. Authorities do not believe the lowly messenger's report until a miracle provides proof. For example, a statue of the saint may be found on the remote site, which is then impossible to move or, if taken elsewhere, returns to its chosen spot. Finally the authorities believe the messenger and agree to the request.[4]

In the Mexican case, Guadalupan devotees apparently adapted this story line to fit a Native American protagonist and a cloth image that already existed. In this story, and the play, three miracles support the protagonist's claims. First, flowers blossom on the dry hilltop at Tepeyacac, which Mary orders Juan Diego to gather into his *tilmatli*, the rectangular cloth that Nahuas wore as a cloak. Second, Mary's image appears on the cloak when Juan shakes it open in front of Bishop Zumárraga, Mexico's first bishop and the story's doubting authority figure. Third, Juan's uncle, called Juan Bernardino, miraculously recovers from a severe illness.

The story of Guadalupe gave criollos a symbolic focus as they began to identify more with Mexico, the land of their birth, than with Spain, their ancestral homeland. They found in this story a sign that God had shown special favor to Mexico. Priests taught the story to indigenous people as well, spreading it far beyond the Mexico City area. To speak of how the Virgin appeared to a humble Nahua man who had recently turned Christian, entrusted him with an important mission, saved his uncle's life, and left her image imprinted on his cloak would have seemed like a good way to persuade indigenous people to be proper Christians and revere the Virgin. The dramatization presented here comes from this project of spreading and popularizing the *Nican mopohua* story among Nahuatl speakers. The play probably dates to the late seventeenth or early eighteenth century. All the stage directions are in Spanish, which suggests priestly involvement in the text's preparation.[5]

The author or authors of this play drew heavily on the *Nican mopohua*, quoting chunks of its dialogue. But they made it into a longer and more complex story. They embellished the established narrative in two principal ways.

First, they provide a solid and seemingly comfortable home life for Juan Diego. He has a wife, a father, and fellow altepetl residents in addition to his uncle (the only relative mentioned in the *Nican mopohua*). Another part of Laso de la Vega's book stated that Juan Diego's wife,

Subio Juan Diego, y siendo Invierno hallo las Flores tomo en
su tilma las que pudo, bajo, y las mostró ála S.ª q.ⁿ las tomo en
sus divinas manos, se las compuso, y mandó le dije se alobpo, q ai esta
ban las señas q pedia. En el sitio donde esperó N.ª S.ª al felicisimo Indio
brotáron milagrosamente unas saludables aguas. q asta oi exosisten

Juan Diego gathers flowers on the hilltop, and the Virgin places them in his
cloak. Engraving from Francisco de Florencia's *La estrella del norte de Mexico*,
1785. (Courtesy of The John Carter Brown Library at Brown University.)

given the name María Lucía, died two years before the apparitions. However, in 1666 another criollo priest, Luis Becerra Tanco, claimed that she died two years after those events, providing a model for her presence in the play.[6] Both Becerra Tanco and Laso de la Vega maintained that Juan and María, influenced by a Franciscan friar's preaching about sex, practiced abstinence.

Although their celibacy is unusual, a wife who cooks tortillas for her husband and worries about him when he is delayed on the road makes Juan more realistic, more connected to everyday life, and thus easier for spectators to identify with. Juan's father also shows love and concern for him. It is he who dispatches Juan to Tlatelolco, site of a Franciscan establishment, to find a priest for the sick uncle. The *Nican mopohua* never places Juan at his own home, although it says he was from the Nahua altepetl of Cuauhtitlan.

Second, following seventeenth-century Spanish theatrical conventions, the story is stretched into three acts and embellished with comedy and with music and dancing between the acts. In the Mexico City scenes, two pages who wait upon Bishop Zumárraga provide some laughs with their squabbling and idle chitchat. Livening up the altepetl scenes, a phony doctor peddles his useless cures and offends the local folks. In the play's raucous finale, the people play a trick on the doctor and beat him up. Juan Diego himself does not participate in the collective thrashing, but his father and (now healthy) uncle orchestrate it. The doctor's outrageousness highlights the Virgin's role as a true provider of health. Nevertheless, to end the play in this way suggests a less-than-reverential attitude toward the material. The story had not yet attained sacred, Gospel-like status.

The playwright(s) use another motif introduced by Becerra Tanco: the bishop's retainers suspect Juan Diego of being a sorcerer. Since the Spanish classified native religion as devil worship, indigenous people carried an aura of black magic, an association they could sometimes manipulate as a source of power.[7] Just as the Virgin Mary differs from the phony doctor, Juan Diego contradicts Spanish stereotypes of indigenous people: he is not a sorcerer, he surprises the bishop by stating that he has never drunk alcohol, and he avoids sexual intercourse. Under Spanish Christian values, he is a "good Indian"; how native people viewed him would depend on the extent to which they accepted or rejected those values.

Juan's celibacy receives special emphasis in the play, because the text starts with Juan and María's mutual decision to abstain from sex. In doing this, they imitate the Virgin Mary and Joseph, who, according to Roman Catholic tradition, had a celibate marriage. Just after Juan and María declare this vow, the Virgin selects Juan as her messenger. So she seems to be rewarding him for his abstinence. Nahuas, generally less prudish than Catholic churchmen, might understand this motif in terms of ritual purity: the kind of abstinence required, in preconquest as well as many other religious traditions, of people who are about to come into contact with sacred powers. According to Laso de la Vega, Juan would devote the rest of his life to the Virgin, living in a little house at the shrine and keeping the site well swept. Before and after the conquest, Nahuas served their sacred powers by sweeping their temples, churches, and household shrines, keeping them free of polluting debris. Juan's celibacy suits his new vocation as a servant of the divine lady.

Just before the Virgin appears, at dawn, Juan hears the singing of birds that were associated with the Nahua sacred realm, and he sees a rainbow-like radiance at the hilltop site. Later he tells the bishop how the radiance made the stones and plants shine like gemstones and gold. Later, he gathers flowers that have suddenly blossomed there. The play, like the *Nican mopohua*, calls these "Castilian flowers"—that is, roses, flowers imported from Spain and associated with the Virgin Mary. Nevertheless, these motifs of light, color, flowers, birds, and precious stones link the apparition scenes to Nahua concepts of the sacred, invoking associations that carried over from preconquest religion to the Nahua practice of Christianity.

When Juan carries the roses to the bishop, their miraculous transformation occurs in two stages, heightening the dramatic tension. The chaplain sees actual flowers, but when he tries to touch one, they suddenly seem to be painted or embroidered on Juan's cloak. The bishop comes in. Then, presumably, Juan shakes open the cloth to reveal the image of the Virgin. This climactic moment is missing, however. Someone defaced the script by yanking this page right out of it, perhaps from disapproval of how the miracle was presented, or from a wish to carry off the most important bit. Two later copies have the same gap, so the earlier script was mutilated before the copies were made. On the next page, the bishop finishes a gushy speech directed at Mary's image, and then kisses it: his skepticism has turned to wonder and devotion.

This play provides a fascinating glimpse of how Nahuas of the later colonial period participated in the developing Guadalupan tradition. As a model of Christian values, this play encourages sexual purity and a reliance on God and the Virgin—rather than indigenous (or other earthly) healers—to cure disease, two topics that the *Nican mopohua* did not stress. With its loving relatives, its bored pages, and its rowdy humor, the play plants the miraculous events in a more earthy, human, and realistic setting.

Notes

1. Laso de la Vega 1649; Sousa et al. 1998.
2. This phrase refers to the doctrine that Mary was conceived free of original sin. Paintings show her as a young woman standing on a crescent moon.
3. Documentation on this early history of the shrine is in Torre Villar and Navarro de Anda 1982.
4. On these legends, see Christian 1981.
5. The earliest surviving script of this play is in Mexico's Biblioteca Nacional de Antropología e Historia, Archivo Histórico, Colección Antigua, vol. 872. Later copies are in the Bibliothèque Nationale in Paris and the New York Public Library.
6. Becerra Tanco 1982.
7. Laura Lewis (2003) explores the unsanctioned power that indigenous people gained from their association with witchcraft.

DIALOGUE ON THE APPARITION OF THE VIRGIN SAINT MARY OF GUADALUPE

Cast of characters in order of appearance

Juan Diego
María (*Juan Diego's wife*)
Virgin Mary
Chaplain
Bishop (*Juan de Zumárraga*)
First Page
Second Page
Father (*of Juan Diego*)
Doctor
Juan Bernardino (*Juan Diego's uncle*)
Sick Person
(Second) Sick Person
Crazy Person

Act One
Scene One

(Juan Diego and his wife enter from the left of the set.)

JUAN DIEGO: O my precious wife, since God, giver of life, bound us together in holy matrimony, just as our loving elders lovingly wanted, I can't hide from you something that I've been keeping in my heart. You must know what's happened to me. Our lord made me think, and inspired me, when I heard from our teachers, the precious priests, God's spokesmen, about the wondrous life of the heavenly eternal virgin,[1] the precious mother of our lord God, Saint Mary. Right after she was born, she vowed that she would always keep herself chaste, that she would live in purity. And with her pure life she greatly pleased and delighted the lord of heaven, God. Even though later on, by command of the lord God and her guardians, she married her precious husband, Saint Joseph, she didn't break her vow. They loved each other much more. They remained chaste. And then our lord set my heart on fire in just the same way. I longed for a pure life, as if it were precious food and drink. I prayed to our lord to give me the ability to live like his precious mother and her precious guardian, Saint Joseph, with a pure life. And I promised, I resolved that I would serve our lord in this way. And so I tell the truth before you, I reveal my heart to you. O my precious wife, don't let your heart be troubled. Let's just love each other, just as the mother of God and her guardian loved each other in a religious way. Let's just go on serving each other in mutual love, since our lord truly did not create us for earthly pleasures, but only for the life of heaven.

MARÍA: O my dear son, O boy, how fortunate am I, a poor little such-and-such, that our lord, who is my precious husband in heaven, has done me the favor by which you now show me the life of heaven! And who am I that I should serve the heavenly virgin with a pure life? May her admired and good heart grant it, may she give us her help, by which I will carry out your wishes. All I too want is to serve you in this way, with religious love, because I belong to you.

JUAN DIEGO: O my wife, O my precious dear, when I heard your words, your wish, by which you agree with your whole heart to serve the heavenly virgin with your life, you set my heart on fire. Come here, let me hug you. And may the lord of heaven, who has united us in holy

---

1. Or maiden, young woman.

matrimony here on earth, give us his blessing so that we may live out the pure life to which we will promise ourselves. And afterward may he bring us together in his fine land, where, it is said, people love one another forever in a life of perfect sweetness. But today let me leave you with my elders, for I am going to Mexico City. Tomorrow, Sunday, I will obtain God's holiness in our home in Tlatelolco. That's where our lord's representatives gather us together for holy things.²

MARÍA: May our lord go with you.

(He leaves by one door and she by the one where they entered and then chirimías³ are played, also cornets, and the Virgin and little angels appear on a small mountain and they go down to the foot of the stage.)

VIRGIN: Even though the Mexica do not want truly to believe in him,⁴ he does not despise them for it. For those who are still keeping and honoring their false deities will be coming to their senses little by little, from their aimlessness and their blindness, with which those who confuse people⁵ keep their heads spinning. But I, the mother of God's precious child, will turn around those who are my children and supporters. They will see and deserve my love. I want to build myself a house here, where they will come to know me. And one of them, whose heart I have looked into, is about to come by here. He wants very much to love me, to serve me, to follow my way of life. To him I will show myself and reveal what I want. He will go now to present my case to those who will give the orders to build my house for helping people.

(Juan Diego enters with his small pilgrim's staff and looks toward the hill and says:)

JUAN DIEGO: Am I so fortunate, am I so favored that I'm hearing this, like precious birds singing? Their voices are chattering, and it's as if the hill keeps on answering them. Their song is very agreeable and pleasing, entirely surpassing how the bell bird, the trogon, and the other precious birds sing. Am I so fortunate, am I so favored that I am seeing this? Am I now in the land of heaven, where perfect happiness and delight arise? The ground is shining like gold and shimmering like a rainbow!

VIRGIN: O dear Juan, O dear Juan Diego, please come here, please come up.

2. The Franciscan friars, who teach Christian doctrine at their church in Tlatelolco.
3. Shawms, or double-reed instruments, introduced from Spain.
4. God or Jesus Christ.
5. The devils or false gods, or their remaining worshippers.

JUAN DIEGO: Who's calling me? Who knows my name, here in her dwelling place? The light of dawn is just now brightening the land. It's still very early in the morning. Someone's already moving about on top of the hill. Let me pay very close attention. Let me see who summons me, and what will be said to me. *(He goes toward the hill and catches sight of the Most Holy Virgin before reaching it.)* Now I do truly perceive a royal noblewoman, a wondrous virgin, sitting over there. How fortunate I am that I am worthy of beholding her splendor and brilliance, with which she's striking everything here on top of the hill! She's changing it into riches of gold and jade!

VIRGIN: Do listen, O my youngest child, O dear Juan. *(Juan Diego falls to his knees.)* Where are you going?

JUAN DIEGO: O my lady, O noblewoman, O my daughter, I'm going to your home, Mexico-Tlatelolco. I'm going after the holy things that our great lord's representatives give and teach us.

VIRGIN: Know, be assured, O my youngest child, that I am the ever-perfect virgin, Saint Mary, mother of the very true deity, God, giver of life, the creator of people, the lord of the near, the lord of the close, the lord of heaven, the lord of earth. I greatly wish and desire that they build my temple for me here, so that there I will manifest, make known, and give to people all my love, my compassion, and my tender mercy. For I am the compassionate mother of you and of all you people here in this land and of the various other peoples who love me, who cry out to me, who seek me, and who trust in me. At that place I will listen to their weeping and their sorrows in order to remedy and heal all the various afflictions, their miseries and torments. And in order that the merciful thing I'm contemplating may come to pass, go to the holy home of the ruler-priest, the archbishop, in Mexico, and tell him how I am sending you to put before him how I want very much for him to build me a house, to erect a temple for me on the level ground here. You're to relate every single thing that you've seen and beheld, and what you've heard. And you can be sure that I will be very grateful for it. And I will reward and repay your efforts, for I'll make you rich and happy. And then you'll deserve and gain many things, as you are going to carry out everything I send you for. And so, O my youngest child, you have heard my breath, my words.[6] Get on your way, make every effort.

6. My important message.

JUAN DIEGO: O my lady, O noblewoman, now I am going to carry out your breath, your words. Let me, your poor little vassal, take leave of you.

VIRGIN: It gives me very much joy, it makes me rejoice, that poor people are like that. In their humble wisdom they live a pure life, they follow my own life. And I reward them for it by guarding them, and helping them before my precious child.[7]

(The curtain closes at the sound of cornets or chirimías.)

Scene Two

(A servant of the bishop, dressed as a clergyman, enters.)

CHAPLAIN: This is the time when poor people seek out the priest-ruler.[8] Let me go look, let me go ask. Someone might be waiting. I will have him enter, I will bring him in.

(Juan Diego enters.)

JUAN DIEGO: O my lord, O dear priest, may God, the lord of the world, be seated at your side. Don't let your good heart be troubled in any way because I humbly ask for something in your presence. Is it possible for me to see him? Is it possible for me to stretch myself humbly on the ground right in front of our great priest-ruler?

CHAPLAIN: He's coming out now. He's going to the church. Stand there in front of him.

(The bishop enters with two other servants, one of whom carries his train, one his hat. And Juan Diego places himself in front and kneels and kisses his hand.)

BISHOP: May God keep you. Do you have some grievance for which you've come? Or are you a messenger? Did someone send you here? What did you come to say? Stand up. Even though you are just a poor little fellow, judging by the appearance of your face I believe that you are good and honorable.

JUAN DIEGO: Who am I? Am I so fortunate, so favored as to go and appear before you, poor little Indian[9] that I am? Don't let me give you

---

7. Mary prays to Jesus Christ on behalf of people who serve her.

8. The text sometimes calls the bishop "ruler-priest," sometimes the more common "priest-ruler," and sometimes the Spanish *obispo* or *arzobispo* (Zumárraga was appointed Mexico's first archibishop but died before actually assuming the post). The stage directions, which are in Spanish, use *obispo*.

9. During the colonial period the word *macehualli* (commoner) took on the meaning of "Indian," which is probably intended here as Juan addresses a high-ranking Spaniard.

a headache or a stomachache with the message I've come to deliver. Know what happened to me. Today while it was still very early in the morning, while it was still dawn, on the road in the place called Tepeyacac, I was coming to pursue holy things here in our home in Tlatelolco. And by chance I looked on top of the hill. A very great radiance spread out, arranged like the rays of a rainbow. And the singing was more pleasing than the voices of all the various birds. It seemed to me that it wasn't real, what I was seeing and marveling at, nor the precious singing that I heard. I kept asking myself, am I asleep? Am I merely dreaming? And then again I heard someone call me from over there. With my very own name she said to me, "O dear Juan, O dear Juan Diego, please come here, come up." As for me, your poor little vassal, I was not at all afraid, my heart was undisturbed as I went up to the top of the hill where I heard myself summoned. And when I arrived there, I saw a splendid, royal noblewoman. She was standing. A light, a radiance was coming right from inside of her, which made the top of the hill shimmer in golden rainbow colors. Yet again she called to me. She said, "Please listen. O my youngest child, O dear Juan, be assured that I am the mother of God, the only true deity. My name is Ever-Virgin Saint Mary. And I greatly wish and desire that they build my temple for me here so that there I will reveal, make known, and give to people all my love, compassion, aid, and protection. For I am the compassionate mother of you and of all of you peoples here in this land, and of the various other peoples who love me, who cry out me, who seek me, who trust in me. There I'll listen to their tears, their sorrows, and their troubles. Go to the palace of the priest-ruler, the bishop. You're to tell him how I sent you in order to make known how I very much desire that he build a house for me here. You're to relate to him absolutely everything you've seen, heard, beheld. And when you've told him my message, how I came to appear before you, report to me."

BISHOP: What are you saying, O little fellow? Maybe it's true that, as you say, in your sleep and in your dreams the night made fun of you. That is what showed and said to you what you came to recount to me. It's true that you Indians are just like you used to be. You really consider what you dream to be true. And if this is the case, are you making fun of us as well? Will you confuse us?

JUAN DIEGO: O my ruler-priest, the master, the ruler, God himself, is watching me. It wasn't in my sleep. It was on the road. I was coming along walking, very much alive I was coming along breathing when God's precious mother called to me and showed herself to me.

BISHOP: O my child, you are to come again. I'll listen to you at leisure. First I will thoroughly look into and ponder what you've come about, your wish and desire.

(The bishop exits by another door.)

JUAN DIEGO: How wretched I am! I've just come in vain. It seems the ruler-priest can't comply with my message. Isn't it really because it's to someone like me that she appears, a poor little Indian? And now I'm supposed to go appear before my royal noblewoman! Since her breath, her words weren't believed, let me turn around and go home. She herself knows how to make it happen that her wishes are carried out. *(He starts to walk toward the hill and sees that again the Virgin is revealing herself, to the sound of the cornets, and he falls to his knees.)* O my lady, O mistress, O noblewoman, O my youngest child, O my daughter, I went where you sent me to carry out your breath, your words. Although it was very difficult for me to enter the quarters of the priest-ruler, I did see him and I put before him your breath, your words, as you ordered me. He received me kindly and heard it out, but when he answered me, he didn't seem to be satisfied or to take it seriously. He told me, "You're to come again and I'll listen to you at leisure. First I will thoroughly look into what you have come about, your wish and desire." I could easily see from how he answered me that he thought I might just be making up how you want them to build your temple for you there and that maybe it isn't by your order. I beg of you, O my lady, O noblewoman, O my daughter, entrust someone else, one of the high nobles, who are recognized, respected, and honored, to carry and convey your message, so that he will be believed. For I'm a poor person. I'm a carrying strap, a carrying frame, a carrier, a bearer.[10] Where you're sending me is not a place for me to be standing around, O my daughter, O my youngest child, O mistress, O noblewoman. Pardon me if I cause you concern, if I incur or bring upon myself your frown or your anger.

VIRGIN: Do listen, O my youngest child. Be assured that my servants and messengers whom I entrust to carry my breath, my words, and to fulfill my wishes are not high-ranking people. Rather it is highly necessary that you yourself be involved and speak strongly in favor

10. A commoner, a humble working man.

of it. It is very much by your hand that my will and wish are to be carried out and accomplished. I give you strict orders, O my youngest child, to go and see the bishop once again. Instruct him on my behalf, make him fully understand what I want and wish for, so that he will build my temple that I'm asking him for. And be sure to tell him again how it's really me, ever-virgin Saint Mary, the mother of God, who is sending you.

JUAN DIEGO: O my lady, O noblewoman, O my daughter, don't let me cause you concern, for with all my heart I will go there and carry out your wishes. I won't abandon it under any circumstances. Although I find the road painful, I will go. The only thing is that I might not be heard out, or when I have been heard, I might not be believed. However, tomorrow, late in the afternoon, when the sun is going down, I'll come, bringing back whatever answer the priest-ruler should give me to your words. Now, O my youngest child, O my daughter, I am taking leave of you. May you get some sleep. *(He leaves.)*

VIRGIN: Although I already know that my messenger, whom I send for the second time today, will not be believed, nevertheless through a great miracle my wish, my will is going to be carried out. For my precious child's vassals need me to build my house here, so that they may go about crying out to me and obtaining my help.

(Let the curtain fall to the sound of the cornets, and if there is dancing, it can come here.)

Act Two

(The bishop's two little pages, First and Second, enter.)

FIRST PAGE: Now when everything's ready, now when it's time for rest, for sleep, the lord bishop has gone to sleep. Isn't there something we can have fun with, to cheer each other up?

SECOND PAGE: And how, O Palaton,[11] are we going to have fun, since we've already eaten? As for me, I'm very happy when my little drum, my little pouch, my little gut is full.

FIRST PAGE: And what will there be that we can have fun with? Please tell me, what were you doing at home when you were with your mother?

---

11. A Nahuatl name derived from Francisco, equivalent to "Little Frankie."

SECOND PAGE: You want to know what I was doing. I was going around hunting hares.

FIRST PAGE: I think you're lying to me. How were you able to catch them? It's like they really fly, they run so fast.

SECOND PAGE: What do you know? It's not hard. When I saw a hare go scurrying off, I would go right out and chase after it a little. I'd drop down on its tail from above, like a bird of prey. I take it home. I'm going to keep them there.

FIRST PAGE: God help me![12] What a great . . .

SECOND PAGE: A great what? And now you're saying it's a lie?

FIRST PAGE: Not at all. But though it may be true, does it equal what I myself was up to in my home?

SECOND PAGE: And what is it? Let me hear it.

FIRST PAGE: I used to go around catching very many birds: some pigeons, some that they call crested guans, the yellow-headed parrot, the eagle, the black vulture. None escaped from my hands! There was just one barn owl that I had captured, which spurted crap right in my face, so I quickly let it go from my hands.

SECOND PAGE: Jesus, Jesus! That's really great! But how did you catch them?

FIRST PAGE: If I went in some place and startled them, after I've put them to flight, and they're fleeing, I simply go looking for them again, I jump up and down, I string them up by their tails. I take them home and take care of them, and I keep feeding them.

SECOND PAGE: And what will you do with them?

FIRST PAGE: O my friend, they'll fight with your hares, that you were catching. You're just going to hang them by their tails. I entrust you with it. I can count on you to forget it.

SECOND PAGE: Still, O my little brother, you're just making fun of me.

FIRST PAGE: Or not. But who told you? You just want to tell lies about everything. But as for me, aren't I a person too? For my mother gave birth to me.

SECOND PAGE: I won't tell you anything else. You're a real knucklehead.

FIRST PAGE: And as for you, you're a real toad, you're a little mud creature. *[Spying Juan Diego]* Damn him! He's watching. Now he's come back here, the person who came yesterday, who came to say he'd been shown a so-called miracle. Maybe he's come again to tell his dreams.

---

12. This oath is in Spanish. The pages have picked up some Spanish slang.

JUAN DIEGO: O pages, O my lords, is it possible for me to see the priest-ruler?

SECOND PAGE: Wait some more, O little father. He's still resting.

(The bishop rings a bell offstage, summoning the pages.)

FIRST PAGE: He's summoning us now. Maybe he's going to the church.

(They leave.)

JUAN DIEGO: O heavenly ever-virgin mother of God, may it be your will that I can be believed. It frightens me very much when I consider that I'm a poor little Indian, a digging stick, a carrying strap.

(The bishop enters with his servants, and Juan Diego kneels before him.)

BISHOP: You've come back very soon, O my son. Is there some other reason why?

JUAN DIEGO: O master, O ruler, O my lord, don't regard my coming here, my returning here, as a bother to you, since I was sent by the order of the ever-pure virgin, Saint Mary, God's precious mother. And you can be sure that yesterday when I departed from your presence, I was returning to my humble home. Right in the very place where I first saw her and she called to me, I saw the heavenly noblewoman again! She was waiting for me. She called to me, and she asked me what your answer was. And I, your poor little vassal, threw myself down on the ground before her. I beseeched her, I said to her, "O my lady, O noblewoman, I think that your breath, your words were not heard as something true. And when I received an answer, it was just that I should go again to deliver and speak the words by which it will be looked into thoroughly, whether it was truly you who gave the order." And although I humbled myself before her, as I begged her to appoint someone else, one of the honored people, the worthy ones, her precious ones, who would deliver it to you so that it would be heard as true, that's not what she wants at all. She said to me, "No matter what, it will be by your very own hand that you now go ask on my behalf that I want my house. You must go back. You're to go tell the bishop that it is I myself, the ever-perfect virgin, Saint Mary, the mother of God, who is sending you." And that's why I am appearing before you so soon.

BISHOP: Please come here. O my dear child, answer my questions. Where is your home? What kind of work do you do? Are you married? Are you of age? Do you know if you were instructed when you were baptized? Do you now believe in good things? Or, is there still a suspicion that you remember and serve the false gods that your fathers and grandfathers worshipped? Answer me very honestly so that I'll be able to see if it might be believable, if perhaps it is true, that the heavenly noblewoman herself summoned you.

JUAN DIEGO: O master, O ruler, I was born in your home, Cuauhtitlan. And I travel this way in my work, where we come to set up our little fields, every year since the deity, God, our lord Jesus Christ, came to reveal himself to us, came to illuminate people. I came to be so fortunate as to obtain the faith. Also when I was baptized I was well instructed, because I was already of age, already grown up. The only deity I worship is the one God, but there are many images of the demon. I live with my honored father and my dear wife.

BISHOP: Please say, please admit that perhaps you give yourself very much to drinking, perhaps it has turned your head.

JUAN DIEGO: O ruler, you may be certain that with my very own ears I have heard from our teachers, the precious priests, that where there is drunkenness, there is sin. It frightened me very much, although ever since I came to appear on our lord God's earth, at no time did I take into my hands nor did I taste pulque or any other intoxicating drink that confuses people's heads.

BISHOP: What you tell me I consider a very great marvel. And with what prayers do you give joy to our lord every day? Do you do very much for his sake?

JUAN DIEGO: But who am I, to think that I would see this? If I am able, if I do what is good and right, it is a service to our lord. In everything I dedicate myself entirely to her. I call on his precious mother, I pray to her to make her precious child known to me, and the life of heaven, so that I will deserve to go to that place of light and see all the things that are told of, that I hear about from others, God's wondrous riches.

BISHOP: Everything you say is good and correct, if that's truly how it is. Nevertheless, please tell me what God's mother was like, for whom you were full of admiration. Were you frightened? Did something disorient you, or make you feel anxious?

JUAN DIEGO: O master, O my lord, it's not possible for me to explain what she's like, whom I saw. I'm a poor little fellow, but I have eyes, I have ears. She was more splendid than anything. Her clothes gleamed and shone very much like the sun. Her radiance struck the stones and boulders that she stood next to, so that they seemed like precious emeralds and jeweled bracelets. The ground sparkled like a rainbow. And the mesquite, the prickly pear cactus, and the various other little plants that grow there seemed like emeralds, and their foliage seemed like fine turquoise, and their stalks, their thorns, and their spines gleamed like gold. And with the noblewoman's words, her breath, moreover, my heart was content. Nothing frightened me at all. Rather, I thought that maybe I died and was in heaven, forever delighted and enriched.

BISHOP: This is quite a breathful of words that you have spoken! Our faces, our hearts take much delight in her precious face, and especially yours, if it's so, if it's true that you marveled at it with your own eyes. Nevertheless, O my precious child, so we won't be confused by anything that's just useless or false, go back again, go to your home. And if she who says that she is the ever-perfect virgin Saint Mary sends you again, say to her, by my orders, that if she really is commanding me to build her temple where she says, in Tepeyacac, let her give people some sign, some indication by which it will be verified, by which our doubts will be satisfied, that it's truly she who gives the command. You're to tell her what my answer is. Get going.

JUAN DIEGO: O my lord, O master, be at rest, for now I am going. I go to deliver your message, your wish. *(He leaves.)*

BISHOP: O my precious children, you must go. Follow after this little fellow. Don't lose him. I wonder if you might be able to see who talks to him.

CHAPLAIN: Let us carry out your command.

(The bishop leaves.)

FIRST PAGE: As for me, let me tell you, I know this for sure: he's playing a trick.

SECOND PAGE: And as for me, shall I go? Shall I go along with you two?

CHAPLAIN: Stay here near your lord. He might summon you about something. Please get the little [horses] ready. They'll carry us.

(They exit and Juan Diego enters, as if on a journey.)

JUAN DIEGO: Oh, I am four hundred times wholly unfortunate! Maybe it's because of some great sin of mine that I'm not believed. My face, my heart are disturbed, so they weep and feel sad. How am I to go and appear before my royal noblewoman? I might fall into her anger and vexation because her desire, her wish, was not carried out. However, I won't follow the road over there, on which she stands. Let me just go on the other side as I return home. I don't want to cause her concern.

(He leaves and enters among the branches of the underbrush, and the servants enter before Juan Diego disappears from view.)

CHAPLAIN: Damn the animals! Let's just travel on foot. Let's hurry, so the fellow won't get away from us. Please see: is that him, approaching near the hill over there?

FIRST PAGE: It's him! I recognize him because of the worn-out little cloak he's wearing.

CHAPLAIN: Go, watch him closely. We mustn't lose sight of him.

FIRST PAGE: Jesus! I think he's hiding from us now. I no longer see him like I was seeing him just now. Maybe he's a *nahualli*![13]

CHAPLAIN: True, he's out of sight now. Let's search. Please go see that no one is here.

FIRST PAGE: There's no one here either, no one's in that direction. Nobody can be seen anywhere around here now. Maybe the earth swallowed him!

CHAPLAIN: And what are we going to return with? What are we going to say? Will the priest-ruler believe that he just disappeared, that he just tricked us and hid from us?

FIRST PAGE: What else are we to do? Does he know that he might be a nahualli? Their deeds have always confounded people. They mock people in order to confuse them.

CHAPLAIN: It's impossible to say that he's like that. But I'm sure we're going to see some great marvel involving him. Let's go tell [the bishop] the truth about what happened to us.

FIRST PAGE: If he should come again, I myself will know what to do to him. Let's go back. (*They leave, and Juan Diego enters with his pilgrim's staff.*)

JUAN DIEGO: May our lord be thanked that he has returned me to my humble home, at my humble corner. Are they home? Let me summon someone.

(*He knocks at the door, and his father enters.*)

FATHER: Oh, O my youngest child, now you've come back! But what happened to you? Did you get into some kind of trouble?

JUAN DIEGO: O my lord, O master, you deserve thanks. I was not so fortunate and favored as to obtain God's holy things, with which my face, my heart, would find great contentment. And you, who are my precious wife, how has our lord kept you during the day?

13. A shaman or sorcerer with the ability to change shape.

MARÍA: O my lord, O my dear child, it's just like dawn has risen upon me when I see you. Were you detained somewhere? Just a moment ago I was calling to you.

FATHER: O my youngest child, O my precious child, we are four hundred times unfortunate! In what way did we anger, in what way did we cause pain to our lord, that he's now sent his scorpion, his nettle upon us?[14] He is repaying, he is punishing my older brother, your uncle, dear Juan Bernardino. He's getting very weak. He hasn't slept all night because he's overcome by fever. How will we come out of this? Now we're waiting for the doctor who's coming to see him. Come inside to eat a tortilla and some atole[15] that my daughter has prepared for you, while she was waiting for you.

JUAN DIEGO: I hope it's not because of my four hundred sins that our lord is punishing my precious uncle! Let's go inside. We are completely in our lord's own hands. What's the use? Maybe for the sake of his precious mother he'll take pity on us and give health to the poor sick one.

(All exit. A doctor enters by another door.)

DOCTOR: As I recall, they summoned me here to heal a sick person. Nevertheless, so they'll pay well for my cure, and so I'll show that I'm a really great doctor, I must stretch my neck, so that I'll speak my words with a deep voice, which the sick person will find hard to understand. But if I admit the real truth, it's that I don't know anything. I'm a big idiot. I deceive people only in order to eat. Whatever medicine I prescribe, it's useless for them to order it. Let me have my food and drink. And whether the sick person gets better or doesn't get better, what's the difference? There will always be people dying. O my mothers, you who are here, know me well.[16] If anyone summons me, if they fall into my hands, I'll kill them. Nevertheless, I am summoned here; they don't know me yet. Let me summon someone. *(He knocks on the door.)* Is this the place where I'm summoned?

(Juan Diego's father enters.)

FATHER: O master, welcome! Here in your home[17] a poor sick person needs you.

---

14. His punishment.
15. *Atolli*, a beverage made from maize dough.
16. Women in the audience should watch out for phony healers like him.
17. An expression of courtesy.

DOCTOR: And where is he? Can he still see a bit? Is he able to come outside? Let me see him here in daylight so I can see what his illness is.

FATHER: It just started yesterday. But he was still walking yesterday. Let him come outside.

DOCTOR: Let him come outside quickly, for sick people are waiting for me in lots of other places.

(Juan Bernardino enters along with Juan Diego and his wife, and the sick person should wear a cloth on his head, and they should come in holding him.)

BERNARDINO: Ay, Jesus, really, I'm about to pass away!

DOCTOR: Sit down, O little sick person. It's a strong illness that's come upon you. What you have is green fever.[18] All of you, hear what is to be done. He is to be given the medicine twice in his rear end.[19] Today he will have a high fever. During the night he should drink a little ice from time to time. And if he isn't much better, he must be given a strong dose in his rear end. Nevertheless, first have someone sent to summon a priest to hear his confession; let him be prepared. In this way I lay a snare for his disease. You are to keep it up until the day after tomorrow. However, I'll do everything I know so that I'll be able to cure him. Don't worry, for we are entirely in God's hands. And I'll come to see him tomorrow. All of you stay here.

FATHER: O master, please listen: forgive us for what we give you. Here are one small turkey, and one small egg-laying hen, a few plums, and some tortillas and, to keep you warm, a small squared log.

DOCTOR: A turkey, an egg-laying hen, fruit, and some bread. You're very kind to me. I am very grateful for it. Let someone go deliver them to my home for me. Now I declare that the sick person will not die. In this way he pays for what helps him. *(He leaves.)*

FATHER: O my precious older brother, go in and lie down. *(The sick person exits and Juan Diego and his father remain on stage.)* O my son, O dear Juan, go to Mexico City to our home, Tlatelolco. You shall summon one of God's representatives. Let him prepare your uncle. And until our lord brings you back, let us who are here think about how we'll cure him. Go right now, hurry!

(Juan Diego's father leaves and Juan Diego remains alone and says:)

---

18. Possibly typhus (Prem 1992, 37–40), one of the infectious diseases brought from the Old World.

19. Rectal administration of medicines was an indigenous practice.

JUAN DIEGO: I shall go. I shall obey you. I'm going to fall right into the hands of the heavenly ever-virgin again. But thus I'll be able to reassure her about why I didn't return to her. She wouldn't get perturbed with me. Even so, let me take another road. I'm going to double around behind the back of the hill so she won't see me. I hope she'll forgive me. *(He leaves.)*

Act Three

(At this point there is singing or dancing and afterward the Virgin will enter through the door that is free, near the hill.)

VIRGIN: My vassal is taking another road so that the poor man won't see me again, for his faith is not yet altogether complete. It's still young. Now his eyes are opening. The light of heaven is dawning everywhere before him. I see absolutely everything on the earth, lying in order. I know absolutely everything that takes place on the earth because I am God's precious mother. And how will he be able to hide from me? Now he's coming in this direction. Now I will intercept him here along the road so he can go to deliver my message for the last time. *(Juan Diego enters by another door, like someone who is traveling, and the Virgin goes to meet him.)* Well, O my youngest child, where are you going? Where are you heading?

JUAN DIEGO: O my daughter, O my youngest child, O noblewoman, greetings! How did you feel on awakening? Is your precious body in good health, O my lady, O my noble one? I'm going to trouble your face, your heart. Know that a vassal of yours, my uncle, lies very gravely ill. A great illness has come upon him. Before he dies of it, I am, meanwhile, as a great doctor, his healer, has commanded, hurrying to your home in Mexico City to summon one of our lord's precious ones, our priests, to go hear his confession and prepare him, for we were born to fulfill our duty of death. And when I've gone and carried this out, then I'll return here again in order to go and carry your message. O mistress, O my daughter, forgive me. Have patience with me in the meantime. I'm not deceiving you, O my youngest child, O my noble one. I'll come out quickly tomorrow.

VIRGIN: Be very well assured, O my youngest child. Don't let anything at all frighten you or worry you. Don't be afraid of the illness, or any other affliction or torment. Aren't I, your mother, here? Aren't you under my protective shade, my shadow? Aren't I your happiness? Aren't you in my lapfold, in my backpack?[20] Do you need anything else? Don't let anything worry you or upset you further. Don't let your uncle's illness worry you any longer, for he won't die of it. Be sure of it, for he has already recovered.

JUAN DIEGO: O noblewoman, O my lady, with all my heart I am grateful for your compassion and your love! And if you've favored my uncle in this way, you've been merciful to him, so that he's already cured, do send me after all. Let me deliver your breath, your words to the master, the ruler, the bishop. Let me take something to him, his sign, his verification, by which he will believe it.

VIRGIN: Go up, O my youngest child, to the top of the hill. And where you saw me and I spoke to you, you'll see various flowers lying about. Cut them, gather them, group them together, and then come down. You're to bring them here to me.

JUAN DIEGO: O my lady, O noblewoman, let me carry out your wish in this way. *(He goes up the mountain, where there will be artificial roses,[21] and while he collects the flowers chirimías are played.)* O mistress, O noblewoman, here are the little flowers I went to gather. *(He opens the mantle and the Virgin blesses them and says:)*

VIRGIN: O my youngest child, these various flowers will be the light, the proof, and the sign that you will take to the bishop. You're to tell him, on my behalf, that by this he should see that it is what I want and that he should carry out my will. And you, my trustworthy messenger, I give you very strict orders to unfold your cloak only before the bishop himself and show him what you are carrying. You are to report everything to him, and tell him how I instructed you to climb to the top of the hill to pick the flowers, and everything that you saw and beheld, so that you may be able to inspire the priest-ruler to speak immediately in favor of my temple that I'm asking him to have built. O my youngest child, go, hurry! *(The Virgin exits where she had entered from.)*

JUAN DIEGO: O noblewoman, my heart goes absolutely rejoicing because you have given me the sign by which your words will be believed. Let me go and let people know! *(He exits by another door. The cornets are played a little and the bishop's two little pages should enter.)*

---

20. In the security of my protection.
21. "Castilian flowers" in Nahuatl.

FIRST PAGE: O Palaton,[22] O my little friend, it's very true. I definitely can't put up with the lord bishop's household any longer.

SECOND PAGE: But what's bothering you, O little brother? As for me, I am very content.

FIRST PAGE: Every single day we have to pray, we have to make devotions, we have to read books, we have to go to confession, we have to receive communion. And our insides are as thin as thread. They're full of nothing but air. Are we chameleons, which they say drink and eat only air, which go around swallowing it?[23] This is what bothers me. Let's run away, O Palaton.

SECOND PAGE: And where do you want to go? Do tell, O little idiot. What kind of job are you going to get?

FIRST PAGE: And is there any limit to where and what I'll go and enjoy? I'll go herd sheep, or I'll join up with the singers. I've always longed for their life, for they have total happiness. If there's a feast day in church, they sing, they play drums, they eat. If they're summoned to a banquet, they sing, they play drums and wind instruments, they eat. If somebody died somewhere, then they sing sad songs; nevertheless, they eat with great joy, for everyone sings, plays drums, and eats. Isn't what I'm saying a bit better?

SECOND PAGE: You're a joke. But go, if you want to.

FIRST PAGE: You yourself also really want to get away.

SECOND PAGE: O my friend, if at any time such a thought comes to me, there's the holy water, with which I'll get rid of it. And what do you think I am, crazy?

FIRST PAGE: And as for me, am I crazy?

SECOND PAGE: You seem to be, even if you're not.

FIRST PAGE: Well,[24] if I'm crazy, put up with it. I'll scratch your face, I'll scrape your face! *(He acts as if he is becoming angry and tries to scratch him.)*

SECOND PAGE: Get hold of yourself, restrain yourself, crazy dog![25]

(Juan Diego enters with the flowers in his cloak, and they are partly visible.)

JUAN DIEGO: May you be most happy, O my lords, O dear pages.

FIRST PAGE: Now you've come, O my little father. And why did you come here again?

---

22. In the first act, First Page had this name.
23. This refers to a legend that chameleons lived on air.
24. The Spanish word *pues* is used, here and below.
25. This phrase is in Spanish: *tente, perro loco.*

SECOND PAGE: Didn't he go and have another dream? He must be coming to offer us some bait.

JUAN DIEGO: It's actually the master, the ruler, the bishop, that I've come to see. Arrange it for me, if you please, so that I may be able to counsel him with my message.

FIRST PAGE: And is it for some bit of nonsense that the bishop is to interrupt his priestly work for your sake? Wait some more. Or better, go back to your dreamland.

JUAN DIEGO: Nevertheless, I must wait for him as long as you want.

(He takes his place at the door with much humility, and the chaplain enters.)

CHAPLAIN: O little pages, are you here? What are you doing? Is fooling around the only reason for your existence?

SECOND PAGE: O ruler, we're just conversing with this little fellow here. He's just now returned. He's telling us he wants to see the master, our lord.

CHAPLAIN: You've come back already, O little fellow?

JUAN DIEGO: As for me, I am your poor little vassal, O master, O ruler.

CHAPLAIN: But why have you come? Is it the same thing again that you keep coming to say? It's useless for you to wear yourself out over this unless you bring some sign.

JUAN DIEGO: O master, O ruler, it's precisely for that reason that I'm sent here as a messenger. Forgive me, all of you, that I bother you so much.

CHAPLAIN: And what do you come carrying in your lapfold? It seems to me they're roses. Please give me one. Still, what is it that I see, that I marvel at, that I observe only from a distance? They definitely seem to be real roses. But if I now want to take hold of them, they aren't like that anymore. It seems to me they're painted on the mantle, the cloak, or just worked in rabbit fur. Earlier they truly were roses. There's some great wonder associated with them. O my little father, let me summon the great bishop, let him come forth, let him come to see you. *(He exits.)*

JUAN DIEGO: Thank you very much.

FIRST PAGE: O my little father, give me one of your flowers with your own hands. And if not, I'll grab it.

JUAN DIEGO: O dear page, O my youngest child, they don't belong to me. I'm only a messenger for the person who's sending the message to the great bishop. It's no use. Let's not make her angry.

FIRST PAGE: Let us admire one. Truly, their color is more pleasing to the eye than all the flowers that usually grow on earth. Nevertheless,

please consider them carefully, O Palaton. It seems to me that they aren't real flowers, that the cloak is just embroidered. Please look at it.
SECOND PAGE: It doesn't look like embroidery to me. The flowers were just inscribed on the cloak with paint.
(*The bishop and the chaplain enter.*)
CHAPLAIN: O master, O ruler, this little person has returned again, who keeps coming to see you, he says, by order of the heavenly noblewoman. And what he brings here, what he comes carrying here in his lapfold, very much surprised me, such that it caused me to marvel, because precious, fresh roses are appearing in different places. At that very moment they blossomed, they bloomed. And when I tried to take one to enjoy it, I couldn't get hold of it, because . . .
[A PAGE WAS REMOVED FROM THE MANUSCRIPT AT THIS POINT.]
[BISHOP?]: . . . image with which you will instruct us and you will give joy to our hearts as much as you will grant favors to others, there where you are sitting. (*He kisses [the cloak].*)
FIRST PAGE: Jesus, is this something that instructs people? Is it something by which we seem to see, to marvel at a great miracle of this kind? Now, truly, an earthly painter did not make it. The one who painted it came from heaven. The one who painted it came here. Ah, O mother of God, may the lord of heaven praise you forever because you now give us your image, through an amazing miracle! (*He kisses it.*)
BISHOP: And as for you, O my precious child, who are precious to the heavenly noblewoman, by means of you we obtain her image. Stay with us another short day. Then tomorrow you will go to your home. The priests will go along with you. You must go right out and show them her level ground where the heavenly noblewoman indicated they are to begin her temple. And when they have learned the way to it, you are to go to your home. But you mustn't go for good. You must keep coming back here. You must come greet your precious mother. And when we've built her a house in that place of hers, I will also build you a house there so that, together with your precious wife, you may take care of it, and sweep it, for the royal virgin.
JUAN DIEGO: O master, O ruler, the heavenly noblewoman has been most generous, as she has verified her message by a miracle. And, O master, O ruler, don't be troubled, only give me your permission, for my uncle's illness worries me very much. Let me go and see him. Is it true that he's already recovered, just as the heavenly noblewoman

said to me when she sent me before you, that I should let nothing distress me, since he had already been cured by her help?

BISHOP: Go, O my precious child. And if he is well, he has already been cured, both of you are to come. You will come and tell me how it happened that he was cured, so that we may praise God's precious mother all the more.

JUAN DIEGO: Let me do just as you command me. And you, who are my precious mother, my joy, do stay here. I am truly going to leave my face, my heart, by your side. I'll come back so that I can sweep for you, until I die.

BISHOP: O my children, order the bells to be rung everywhere, and let them know everywhere the great miracle by which the precious and admired image of the heavenly noblewoman has come to appear. Come into my humble home, O queen!

(*Chirimías are played and everyone leaves. The doctor enters.*)

DOCTOR: I'm remembering another turkey here. They won't hear me. Let me knock on the walls of the house. Are you there?

(*Juan Bernardino and Juan Diego's father enter.*)

BERNARDINO: You'll come here, O master, O ruler? Welcome.

DOCTOR: But aren't you the one I came to cure yesterday? But how is it that you're already cured?

BERNARDINO: It's me, O ruler. And how it happened that I've been cured, it wasn't you. I'll show you.

DOCTOR: And do you now mean to say that what cured you wasn't the medicine I gave you?

BERNARDINO: No. A greater doctor cured me.

DOCTOR: Do not believe this, that there's anyone better than me. Admit it, it's rather that you don't want to pay me for my cure.

FATHER: O ruler, leave. Go away. You aren't needed. We've already shown that our great healer has cured us.

DOCTOR: Now you're sending me away! Well, that's not how it's going to be. I will heal people, no matter what. Your turkeys that you raise here are very tasty. Call and bring here all the sick people in your altepetl, for I'm going to cure them. I'm not going home like this.

BERNARDINO: Then let them come. Let me go and call them. (*He goes to summon and bring sick people.*)

DOCTOR: Now everyone will say, will recognize that I am a great and wise doctor.

(Juan Diego's father enters, bringing a sick person by the hand.)
FATHER: O ruler, here now is a sick person.
SICK PERSON: Oh, Jesus, my belly is about to explode. Oh, my guts!
DOCTOR: Ay, ay, ay! But what's wrong with you? What ails you?
SICK PERSON: Ay, O my lord, I've gotten inflated in my stomach, I've
   gotten bloated.
DOCTOR: Perhaps it was something you ate?
SICK PERSON: Just one little squash cake, and I also drank a little
   something.
DOCTOR: Ho, ho, get away from here. You have a bad case of indiges-
   tion, so there is gas in your belly. But the good medicine I'll prescribe
   for you will set you right. O my children, grab hold of this sick person
   and take him up to the top of the bell tower. Let him get on all fours
   there. Let him take off his trousers. Let him spurt his diarrhea toward
   our grandmothers and our mothers. Let him send on them the gas
   with which his intestines are bloated. Quickly, take him away. He
   mustn't let anything loose here in front of us that would disgust us.
   Go, O gluttonous pig!
SICK PERSON: May our lord cure you the same way you cure people,
   you demonic doctor! *(He leaves.)*
FATHER: Another sick person has arrived.
(A person with a very twisted neck enters.)
SICK PERSON: Oh, the back of my neck! I can't straighten myself out
   at all.
DOCTOR: And what did you do, you bow neck?
SICK PERSON: I met up with a really powerful wind.
DOCTOR: If you'd just stayed in the house, it wouldn't have bent you.
   Speak honestly, because my thinking is that you've undertaken some-
   thing evil.
SICK PERSON: O ruler, I tried to conjure the hail.
DOCTOR: Isn't that what I said? So it turns out that you're a conjurer of
   hail. Well, it serves you right. Put up with your pain, you demon. I
   won't cure you. Go. Let him cure you by whose order you conjure hail.[26]
SICK PERSON: By God, as I was born, I curse the conjuring of hail!

---

26. This refers to the devil. Practitioners of magic in both Spain and Mexico claimed
to be able to send or prevent hailstorms, which could destroy crops in the fields. See
Christian 1981, 29; Sahagún 1950–1982, 7:20. Catholic priests considered such conjuring
to be diabolical.

DOCTOR: If it's true that you curse it, listen to how you'll be able to get better. O my children, when the hail is coming, a great sky-darkening hailstorm, make him eat it. Then he'll get better. Or else the one who orders him to conjure the hail will take him. Go, O deer,[27] O troublemaker. Conjure hail somewhere else.

SICK PERSON: May they cure you the same way you cure people!

BERNARDINO: Someone else has come.

(A person pretending to be crazy enters, whom they all bring in tied up, and everyone carries bulls' bladders filled with air for striking the doctor, and first they say, aside:)

CRAZY PERSON: O my friend, they say he's just a buffoon, the way the little doctor cures people. They say he just mocks the poor sick people. Let's mock him back. Is this the only way he'll stop making fun of people?

BERNARDINO: But how will it be? How will we do it?

CRAZY PERSON: I'll come as if I'm tied up. Stand me up in front of him. When you see me beating him, you hurry up and beat him in just the same way.

FATHER: It's good that you've thought of it! Let's do it.

DOCTOR: Who comes tied up? What makes him ill?

BERNARDINO: O ruler, he's a crazy person.

DOCTOR: And what's the matter with him, that he is crazy?

FATHER: O master, what happened to him was that he used to be a good friend of his.[28] But now he says that all the people he sees are demons, whereupon he follows them around, especially if they're doctors. He really thinks they're devils, and he hates them most of all.

DOCTOR: I've never, ever, heard of a disease like that. What does he want now?

BERNARDINO: O ruler, maybe there's something you can cure him with.

DOCTOR: Untie the poor man. I will cure him.

FATHER: O ruler, just leave him the way he is. He's really fierce. Don't let him beat you!

DOCTOR: Is he a wild beast? He's a human being. What are you afraid of? Just untie him now. *(They untie him.)* Do you know me, O young man?

CRAZY PERSON: I know you. You're considered a doctor. You're a devil! You keep going around killing people. But now you've fallen

27. Metaphor for an immoral or uncivilized person.
28. Of Juan Bernardino's, presumably.

into my hands. You'll pay, you devil! *(Hitting him with the bladders.)* Here's the turkey, here are the tamales, here's the hen! Eat them! Chug them down! May your belly just explode with them! Here's a tamale!

DOCTOR: Restrain him, hold him back! Ay, ay, ay!

(Everyone on him.)

[CRAZY PERSON:] Here's the turkey, O dog!

(They exit.)

FATHER: And now, O precious and noble people, ends the great miracle by which the image of the ever-virgin Saint Mary appeared. If in any way your children have done wrong, may forgiveness be in your hearts.[29]

---

29. The "father" speaking here may be Juan Diego's father, or it may be a real priest who addresses the audience here at the end. The children referred to are probably young actors who have put on the play, perhaps with some mistakes.

The Animal Prophet and the
Fortunate Patricide

At the core of this play lies a medieval legend, the story of Saint Julian the Hospitaler. In the legend, Julian is a young nobleman who goes hunting and kills a deer. The deer predicts that Julian will murder his parents. To avoid committing such an act, Julian flees his homeland for another kingdom, where he marries and establishes a household. His parents go looking for him and arrive at his new home while Julian is away. His wife invites her in-laws to sleep on the bed she shares with Julian. Coming home after dark and finding two people in his bed, Julian assumes his wife is sleeping with another man. He kills them both, only to discover the deer's prophecy has come true. For many years Julian tries to atone for the murders by doing good deeds, such as ferrying travelers across a river or running a hospital. Eventually Jesus Christ visits him to let him know that his sin has been forgiven.

A Spanish playwright named Antonio Mira de Amescua adapted this story to fit the theatrical fashions of seventeenth-century Spain. Mira de Amescua favored plots that revolved around "a Baroque mixture of sex, violence, and repentance."[1] The Julian story offered all three, and the playwright spiced it up further by adding two sexually charged subplots. In the first, Julian has a sweetheart in his original home whom he seduces and then abandons when fleeing to protect his parents' lives. The jilted woman adds her own curse to the deer's prophecy. In the second subplot a powerful nobleman in Julian's new home, the younger brother of the duke who has become Julian's patron, is intent on seducing or raping Julian's wife. Julian unfairly suspects that his wife plans to sleep with this man and pretends to leave town in order to catch them together. Of course, he finds his newly arrived parents in his bed and kills them in the darkness.

Mira de Amescua added two other important characters to the story. The first is Julian's servant and sidekick, named Bulcano, or Vulcan. The name comes from the Roman god of fire, who is not only lame but also constantly cheated on by his wife, Venus, the goddess of love. Vulcan is the play's *gracioso*, a comic character whose lower-class status, earthy humor, cowardice, and realistic outlook on life contrast with the nobility, idealism, and bravery of the dashing young hero. In Spanish plays of the time, the gracioso acted as a mediator between the audience and the play, commenting on the action and making jokes but also helping the spectators to sympathize with the hero.[2]

The second character is a devil who infiltrates Julian's hospital disguised as a patient. He wants to make Julian think that God will never forgive him, so that he will stop doing penance. Then the devil will be able to claim his soul. The gracioso, immune to illusions, sees this character's diabolical nature right from the start. His rude treatment of the devil adds much humor to the play's third act.

In 1640, this Spanish play was adapted into Nahuatl by don Bartolomé de Alva. Three of Alva's four grandparents were Spaniards, but through his mother he was descended from the royal lineage of Tetzcoco, the second most powerful altepetl in the Aztec Empire. His direct ancestors included the famous rulers Nezahualcoyotl and Nezahualpilli. His mother, and later his oldest brother, held the *cacicazgo*, or native rulership, of the Nahua altepetl San Juan Teotihuacan. Don Bartolomé became a Catholic priest, partly on the strength of his fluency in Nahuatl, and with financial support from his Spanish relatives. He ministered to Nahua communities and also helped Jesuit priests improve their knowledge of Nahuatl. This play and his other writings (other plays and a confession manual) show that he wanted Nahuas to comprehend Christianity at a sophisticated level, not just to learn the basics.[3]

Alva's family background was not unusual. Some Nahua noblewomen married Spaniards. Their children sought to retain traditional noble privileges while also taking advantage of their connections to Spanish society and adopting many Spanish cultural traits. Meanwhile, the basic status divide between indigenous nobles and commoners lasted through the colonial period.

Alva gave some characters Nahuatl names, moving the Spanish play into New Spain's multi-ethnic society. He removed European place names, so the action occurs in anonymous altepetl. Characters have different degrees of indigenous identity, according to differences of rank and generation.

To Julian's hometown sweetheart, Irene in the Spanish play, Alva gave the name Malintzin. This is the Spanish (and Christian) name Marina, adapted to Nahua pronunciation and embellished with the suffix –tzin, indicating affection or respect. This name is famous in Mexican history because it belonged to the Nahua woman who was Hernando Cortés's interpreter and lover during the time of the Spanish conquest.[4] By having her mention flowers and birds that are typically evoked in Nahua religious poetry, Alva made his Malintzin sound very indigenous: she is a Nahua noblewoman. Alva, as a priest, would certainly not condone her willingness to meet Julian for a lovers' tryst.

Malintzin's father's name is Colhua Lord, or lord of the Colhuas of Colhuacan. This Nahua group was enjoying a civilized lifestyle long before the ragtag Mexica migrated into Central Mexico. The Mexica established their own ruling dynasty by intermarrying with the Colhuas. The name says, in effect, "old-timey big shot." In the Spanish play, this man is Alexander, a name that recalls the ancient empire of Alexander the Great.

For the comic character Vulcan, Alva cleverly replaced the name of a pathetic Roman god with the name of a pathetic Aztec emperor: Tizoc. After ruling the Aztec Empire only from 1481 to 1486, with no notable successes, Tizoc died; by some accounts, he was murdered to make way for a more talented brother. So the name suggests a man who is not only unbaptized (or he would have a Christian name) but a bumbler as well.

The play's Tizoc gets drunk on pulque, the native brew. Although he knows a lot about Christianity, he also knows the names and functions of Aztec gods. From Alva's priestly perspective, Tizoc's familiarity with Aztec gods might enhance his ability to know a devil when he sees one. As a virtual pagan, Tizoc is also well cast in the scene where he poses as a seller of magic stones.

While Julian's parents use some old-fashioned Nahuatl speech formulas, such that they can be seen as Christianized Nahua nobles, Julian himself does not. Alva may have imagined him as a young colonial nobleman more Hispanicized than his parents' generation. The woman Julian marries, Laurencia, is more Hispanicized than Malintzin in her name and speech patterns, but she too may be seen as an indigenous noble. Her deceased father is called a *huey tlatoani*, the Nahuatl title for a powerful ruler like the Aztec emperor. The word *tlatoani* is also used for the duke whom Julian serves in Act Two, his nasty brother, and the duke who briefly lusts after Laurencia at the beginning of Act Three; however, in these contexts the Spanish title *duque* is used as well, indicating that these three men are not indigenous.

If Julian has been recast as an indigenous man (or a man of mixed descent, like Alva), his social position relative to those Spanish lords is insecure not only because he is a stranger in their midst. He also belongs to a conquered people. When Federico, the duke's brother, insults him, he uses a word that in Alva's time meant "Indian" as well as commoner or peasant. When Federico claims sexual rights to Julian's wife, an indigenous audience might well think of how Spanish men sexually exploited native women.

The animal prophet—the deer who tells Julian that he will murder his parents—carried particular meanings for Nahuas. A day sign in the old ritual calendar, Deer was associated with extreme cowardice and fearfulness—and with the west, where the life-giving sun lost power and passed into the underworld. The day One Deer was one of five days when the Cihuateteo, dangerous goddesses associated with death in childbirth, descended to earth and caused diseases in children. Nahuas also linked the deer with the uncivilized Chichimeca of northern Mexico, nomadic hunters and gatherers who dressed in skins or, at best, raggedy cloth garments. In Nahuatl, "to turn oneself into a deer" or "to follow the road of the deer" meant to go morally astray.[5]

When Julian kills the deer, he is in a dangerous state of disorder. Lusting after Malintzin, he has lost control over his desires. He has further de-civilized himself by putting on ragged clothes (so he can pass unrecognized into Malintzin's garden) and by passing into the forest. Pursuing a deer, like a Chichimec hunter, he is literally following "the road of the deer," an act that might also lead him into moral danger. Through these acts he makes himself vulnerable to an otherworldly experience that will challenge his moral integrity.

Catholic priests dismissed Nahua beliefs about animals as superstition or deviltry. In the play, though, the deer is an authentic prophet: Julian cannot escape its prediction. In this way the play, whether in Spanish or in Nahuatl, challenges the fundamental Christian doctrine of free will and actually presents something closer to a Native American worldview: humans do not control the world or their own fate but are tied to larger cosmic forces. However, this fatalistic story is absorbed into a larger, Christian narrative of salvation: God can forgive any sin, if the person who committed it does enough penance.

For don Bartolomé de Alva, a Catholic priest descended from Nahua kings, this play offered a way to balance the two sides of his heritage. He could present the gallant hero as a Nahua nobleman and give him a loyal and likeable Nahua sidekick and a strong-minded and faithful wife, characters sure to appeal to Nahua audiences. The play acknowledges the dangerous passions that beset human nature, with which Alva, a parish priest and hearer of confessions, was thoroughly familiar. But it shows how, with faith, anyone can rise above these weaknesses. It encourages the Christian values of penance and charity and the Nahua tradition of respect for parents and elders. Of the plays Alva adapted into Nahuatl, this is by far his longest work, and thus the one in which he invested the most effort. He must have thought it well suited to his own place and time.

Notes

1. Wright 2008, 12. See *Nahuatl Theater*, vol. 3, and Mira de Amescua 2005 for recent publications of the Spanish original.
2. Leoni 2000; Asensio 1965, 38–39.
3. See Schwaller's biography of Alva in Sell and Schwaller 1999.
4. On Malintzin, see Townsend 2006, Karttunen 1994, 1997.
5. On the Deer day sign and the goddesses, see Sahagún 1950–1982, 4:10, 37. On the Chichimecs, see ibid., 10:171–74. The moral associations of deer are discussed in Burkhart 1986.

THE ANIMAL PROPHET AND THE FORTUNATE PATRICIDE

Cast of characters in order of appearance

Malintzin (*Julian's sweetheart*)
Tizoc (*Julian's servant*)
Colhua Lord (*Malintzin's father*)
Julian (*a young nobleman*)
Luis (*Julian's father*)
Susana (*Julian's mother*)
Voice (*singing in woods*)
Deer
Lorenza (*Malintzin's servant*)
Juan (*Federico's servant*)
Pedro (*Federico's servant*)
Laurencia (*Julian's wife*)
Federico
Laurencia's Servant
Duke
Enrique (*Duke's servant*)
Demon
Blind Man
Lame Man
Sick Man
Soldier
Voice (*of woman, singing*)
Boy Jesus

[Act One]

MALINTZIN: Everything sprouts anew in the summertime. The birds go around twittering and chirping then. Flowers burst into bloom and the rain falls lightly in the place of delight. My heart takes pleasure in smelling the flowers here. And now, red popcorn flowers and golden flowers, guard my heart and my words. Don't say anything to anyone. Let me open the golden letter. *[She reads a letter from Julian]* O precious and admired Malintzin, you don't truly love me, as you say that your father won't give you up and keeps close watch on you. Let me know your decision, even if I'm only to be frustrated in my hopes. I've given you my heart. If I can't win yours, just return mine to me.

TIZOC: Our heart is poor and miserable.

MALINTZIN: Who are you?

TIZOC: I am your humble slave.

MALINTZIN: It's you?

TIZOC: Now you see that it's me.

MALINTZIN: But how did you dare come in here?

TIZOC: Don't be upset that I just came right in. Have pity on me. It might be a bad omen for me. Something bad might happen to me. Someone might give me a thorough beating with a stick. I think something bad's about to happen to me.

MALINTZIN: Get out of here! Leave!

TIZOC: Absolutely impossible. No matter how they put an end to me, I can't possibly leave. You simply must speak to me first as to why I came.

MALINTZIN: And what do you have to say to me?

TIZOC: What I've come about is my lord Julian's weeping and sadness. *(He gets scared.)* But I've just come and upset you. You're yelling at me here. And he said to me, "Oh, how wretched I am!"

MALINTZIN: What are you afraid of?

TIZOC: I think someone's about to beat me on the back of the neck.

MALINTZIN: What else did he tell you?

TIZOC: *(aside)* Now I'm getting her excited and aroused. *[to Malintzin]* He said to me, in case you can't give him an answer right here, he went with his father to his garden. And you are to go there too. He says, "Let us see each other there so that you can put an end to my uncertainty."

MALINTZIN: What else did he tell you? Is there more?

TIZOC: That's all there is.

MALINTZIN: Don't tell anyone. Don't let anyone know.

TIZOC: Don't be afraid. Reveal your heart to me for his sake.

MALINTZIN: Now, you should be grateful to my heart.

TIZOC: But anyone who is not grateful to it would be behaving crudely.

MALINTZIN: You are a fine person. Nevertheless, my heart is uneasy about whether I should say anything to you.

TIZOC: What are you saying? Am I a blabbermouth? Will someone rip it out of me?

MALINTZIN: What's your name?

TIZOC: I'm Tizoc. My father is Mexicatl.[1] They gave us royal Mexica names that are feared everywhere in the world.

MALINTZIN: Now I've decided. Your lord may have hope that what he's longing for will indeed happen. And I'll tell my father to take me to our garden so that we'll see each other there.

TIZOC: Wonderful! Let me dance!

MALINTZIN: Don't tell anyone.

TIZOC: I'm locking your words up tight inside me.

MALINTZIN: Get going.

TIZOC: Ho! I'm not afraid of anything anymore. Let me take off out of here like something on fire.

MALINTZIN: Oh, poor me! My father's come upon us!

TIZOC: It's like someone beat me on the back of the neck. What am I in for now?

MALINTZIN: I've been caught!

TIZOC: Which tree trunk will he smash my ribs with?

(The father enters.)

COLHUA LORD: Where would I see you, you who are my flowery quetzal feather, except in the garden, since it is your place, where the precious bell bird is always singing to you? But who is here?

TIZOC: *(aside)* Yikes! Oh, poor me! Help me, my wits! [to Colhua Lord] I've been waiting for you for a good while. Are you the father of the noblewoman here?

COLHUA LORD: I am. What do you want?

TIZOC: They told me that this young woman and her mother, who just now left . . .

COLHUA LORD: You're lying! She doesn't have a mother. It was three years ago yesterday that she died, leaving us behind.

TIZOC: But maybe it was some other mother.

---

1. A completely generic name, analogous to "Joe Aztec."

COLHUA LORD: You're lying!

MALINTZIN: I'm in big trouble now.

TIZOC: But maybe it was someone who looks like a woman, for I saw no beard on him.

COLHUA LORD: What do you want? Why did you come?

TIZOC: That's right. I told you that they told me your daughter here is a greedy person. And maybe she'd like one of the precious stones I've brought from the coast.

COLHUA LORD: And what are they? Where do you have them?

TIZOC: Over where I'm staying, for I've just arrived.

COLHUA LORD: And are they wonderful? What are their qualities?

TIZOC: Very many and countless are their qualities, for they are very great precious stones.

COLHUA LORD: List them. State their qualities.

TIZOC: The first is called . . . oh yes . . . what? Did I forget its name? Oh yes, "cricket stone" is its name. And as for this stone, if someone who has started going bald puts it on his head, soon it will make him completely bald. All of a sudden his head will be left just as shiny as the moon.

COLHUA LORD: And that's good?

TIZOC: Why isn't it good? Isn't he better looking with his head completely bald?

COLHUA LORD: Very good.

TIZOC: I have another precious stone called "rattle stone." Now then, with that one, women (we will marry) fall right into our hands.

COLHUA LORD: But do you really have it?

TIZOC: Even if a woman's heart is like a hard stone, it won't be long before she falls into our hands (and we marry her).[2]

COLHUA LORD: Can it be possible? If she doesn't want him, who can move her to it?

TIZOC: These stones, O my nobleman, truly overcome them all. When women see them they all get soft-hearted right away.

COLHUA LORD: Shush. I don't need them.

TIZOC: (aside) Yikes! When can I leave?

MALINTZIN: You will leave now. Don't be afraid.

COLHUA LORD: Get going.

---

2. Here and above, Tizoc's references to marriage were added after the script was written, to make the talk of seduction sound like references to marriage.

TIZOC: I'm very relieved to be going.

COLHUA LORD: Wait a moment.

TIZOC: Maybe he'll beat me now. Enough already!

COLHUA LORD: O my daughter, O Malintzin.

MALINTZIN: What is it? What do you want?

COLHUA LORD: I want to take you to our garden today. We'll amuse ourselves a bit for the few days we will be there.

MALINTZIN: You're going to please me very much by that.

TIZOC: *(aside)* That was it?

MALINTZIN: Tell this to your lord.

TIZOC: I'll explain it to him right away.

COLHUA LORD: Pardon me, O nobleman.

TIZOC: It's you who should pardon me and give me orders, for I'm going now, taking my leave of you.

COLHUA LORD: And the rattle stone you speak of, which works well on women: I really need it.

TIZOC: I'll give it to you, I'll bring it to you.

COLHUA LORD: I love a woman. Maybe it will soften her heart, since she doesn't love me.

TIZOC: *(aside)* We're in big trouble now.

COLHUA LORD: I'll pay you very well for it.

TIZOC: *(aside)* The little old man is in love too. We'll take his money from him.

COLHUA LORD: Get going. Don't make me wait.

TIZOC: I'm going to fool him with a bit of adobe brick.

(At this point they exit and some others enter, Julian's mother and father, named Luis and Susana, and Julian.)

LUIS: And how is it you left behind your good clothes, O my child? Julian, is it because no one else is here that you come so dirty?

JULIAN: Is it the good clothing of honorable people that makes them illustrious? When a precious emerald is placed among rags, does that make it lose its splendor?

SUSANA: Why did you say you came like this, dressed in your rags?

LUIS: Leave him alone. Maybe it's because he's going to go hunting in the forest that he came dressed just in his rags, as though he were a field hand.

JULIAN: You spoke precisely to my liking. That's right, you who are my father.

LUIS: That's right. Don't you sometimes dress yourself up to look as good as the sun itself?

JULIAN: I came here into the woods in this fashion so as not to frighten a deer that has come here searching for hearts. And to make it feel sorry for me I dressed just in my rags to hunt for it.

LUIS: Don't let some misfortune happen to you, for there are real man-eaters here in the forest. If you fell into their clutches, the bad dreams I have dreamt, which I'm always telling you about, will come true. It seems that you will die young.

JULIAN: We all are completely in God's hands. What's frightening you? If I am to die, even if you hid me in a very safe place, wouldn't the word of God reach there, such that you would lose me?

LUIS: True, but you must realize that God places our good judgment in our hands so that we will be careful about death. Even though some people say we are born right into the misfortunes that will befall us, it is also possible for us to escape from the very thing that was to entrap us. Should we just give ourselves to the currents and the cliffs?[3]

JULIAN: Thank you, for I do pay great attention to your teachings.

LUIS: But are you going to go all by yourself?

JULIAN: O my father, I have two companions.

LUIS: And when will you get back?

JULIAN: This very night.

SUSANA: May that be God's will.

LUIS: Don't cry. Isn't he going just right here in the forest? Go into the garden.

JULIAN: Ho! So much the better for you! Now she[4] will fall into my clutches. Will a precious bird come now to fall into my clutches? Where is he? Tizoc's taking a very long time. Maybe he's waiting for the precious one. Isn't that where he's coming from? Let me relax here a bit on the flowery riverbank, where the waters come tumbling down, like threads of silver spilling down. But what do I hear now?

VOICE: (singing) Where are you going, discontented wretch? You will destroy your mother and your father.

JULIAN: Is it me they're talking to? Not me! Aren't I in God's hands? He wouldn't despise me, would he? What I hear is just lies, four hundred times over! But again, it starts up. Let me keep listening carefully. Is it really saying what I think it said?

VOICE: (singing) In a fit of rage you will kill your mother and your father. You will bathe the sword with their blood.

3. Act dangerously and recklessly.
4. Malintzin, the "precious bird" and "precious one," for whom Julian is "hunting."

JULIAN: Me? I will destroy my parents, who raised me? But what did they do? That's what I'll give them in return for all the grief I caused them as they brought me up? How could I begin to roll them in their own blood? Even beasts feel pity for those who engendered them. Maybe it's just someone here in the forest who's mocking me. Just because he hates me and is jealous of my reputation, he came into the woods and sang. Let me look for him. I'll find him, for I'll go around everywhere. Sooner or later he'll fall into my clutches. But there goes a deer! That's what I came for. Quickly now! Let it die! *(At this point he throws a weapon at it.)* It's going into the foliage, but the metal [knife] plunged right into its flank. You will fall here no matter what. Now you've fallen into my clutches!

(At this point Deer calls to him.)

DEER: What are you looking at?

JULIAN: Oh! Poor me! I feel scared to death! It might be a bad omen for me that a deer spoke to me. My head feels like it's gone numb all of a sudden.

DEER: You poor wretch, what have you done? Does it matter that you killed me? Much more important is what you are going to do, that your mother and your father will die at your hands.

JULIAN: Oh no! It seems I must suffer a misfortune that's never happened to anyone else. Let me just disappear once and for all! Let the earth swallow me up, for my heart is much afflicted with the misfortune that's happening to me now. What my precious father said to me, which I didn't believe, is true. But in any case I will believe the deer since it's not in its nature to speak. Why did God make me? I wish you, my parents, had not raised me! Why did you give birth to me? It seems you just engendered your death. Will I destroy you who gave life to me? May the master of the world not want that. How have you offended me? What have you done? No, my parents, however you might vex me, I am your child. Is it my place to speak? In any case this means something. I hope nothing bad happens to me! Let me abandon my altepetl once and for all, let me go and abandon my mother and father, let it be somewhere far away. Let me know nothing of them after I've left them. And you, my precious Malintzin, let me also abandon you. Better that I destroy you than my mother and my father.

(At this point Tizoc enters.)

TIZOC: I wore myself out looking for you and was about to turn back. Give me something.

JULIAN: I'm in trouble just now, and I'm supposed to give something to you?

TIZOC: What danger did you get into? When I'd worn myself out and had barely seen fine and precious Malintzin, her father came upon me. If I hadn't told him I was a seller of precious stones, what would he have done to me? A rattle stone saved me. Malintzin has already come and she's waiting for you in her garden. You can find her over where that big rock lies, for she's already sneaked away from her mother and her father.

JULIAN: What can be done? It has already happened. Thanks for your efforts. Go, tell the precious young woman, Malintzin, to go away, and to forgive me, since I don't deserve to enjoy the precious rose that is her splendid face. But wait a minute, don't bother her. If she sighs over me, she might get hold of me again that way, and soften my heart. Once and for all bring two horses that run like the wind.

TIZOC: What do you want to do?

JULIAN: I want to leave this land.

TIZOC: Are you in danger?

JULIAN: No, but I don't want my mother and my father to die here at my hands. It's better that I forsake them.

TIZOC: What are you telling me? Is it true?

JULIAN: You see this deer whose blood seems to have bathed and sprinkled all the foliage with red?

TIZOC: I see it.

JULIAN: It spoke to me after I killed it.

TIZOC: Really? Is it true? What are you saying?

JULIAN: It told me that I will kill my mother and my father before their time.

TIZOC: I don't think it's a bad omen that it spoke to you, but I think it's a very bad omen that it said you yourself would destroy your mother and your father.

JULIAN: In any case something bad is going to happen to me here in the forest. And I also heard a very piteous song that says the same.

TIZOC: But what are you saying? What should we do?

JULIAN: I don't care. Go quickly, and get a horse that moves like it's flying, and a set of fine clothes. Let's get going so that nothing bad will happen to us.

TIZOC: But you'll leave just like that? Won't you still bid her farewell?

JULIAN: Yes, but the weeping of women is very strong. It mustn't detain us.

TIZOC: But where are you going to end up?

JULIAN: I'll go anywhere.

TIZOC: Let's get going.

JULIAN: I now forsake you, O my mother, O my father. Now I am going on my way, O my precious Malintzin. There's nothing more to be done, for now I am going to forsake you. Forgive me. Now I forsake you, my altepetl. It's over and done with. I'll never see you again.

(Julian then goes. Malintzin enters.)

MALINTZIN: I'm just frustrated in my hopes. I've been waiting here for Julian for a long time. I sneaked away from my father and my mother. But as for him, maybe he hasn't. What's bothering him? When someone's in love, if he is loved in return, he gets presumptuous right away. Let me keep my hopes up here in the garden, where the golden flowers lie sprouting like emeralds, and the holy popcorn flowers lie hatching like roseate spoonbills. It's delightful how the waters go spilling over. Who's coming?

(At this point Lorenza, Malintzin's servant, enters.)

LORENZA: You've already seen him, made your decision, and come to an agreement?

MALINTZIN: At what time did I speak with him?

LORENZA: What a relief! What purpose does it serve? He'll quickly cast you away. That's how men are. I saw them.

MALINTZIN: What are you saying?

LORENZA: It's because I saw Julian going off accompanied by a servant of his. The horses are carrying them along as if they're flying. And he goes along saying, "It's over and done with, it's over and done with, for I'm going to forsake you, my altepetl, and you, my Malintzin."

MALINTZIN: You, woman, should also have an ungrateful man make fun of you!

LORENZA: What's bothering you? If you had seen him, wouldn't he be carrying off your heart? Curses on him! As yet you haven't seen him anywhere. Is he taking something from you?[5]

MALINTZIN: He's carrying off my heart, which is more precious than anything.

LORENZA: Maybe not. Do let us get a bit out of the trees. Maybe we'll see them somewhere.

---

5. Lorenza is relieved that Malintzin has not yet met in secret with Julian and perhaps lost her virginity. In Nahuatl, "to see" someone can refer to sexual relations.

MALINTZIN: But what should I do, for he's carrying off my heart?

LORENZA: It seems he's still got you all bewildered.

MALINTZIN: But if he weren't carrying off my heart, you would have hurt it just now.

(She goes. At this point Julian again enters, with Tizoc.)

TIZOC: Are you bewitched? Have you gone crazy?

JULIAN: What's happening to me now?

TIZOC: You haven't gotten started yet, and you've suddenly gone and changed your mind?

JULIAN: At this moment I remembered my precious Malintzin. And it seems as if my heart just got this way all of a sudden. Let's turn back.

TIZOC: But your father: don't you remember him?

JULIAN: Don't remind me of them, for it gives me much pain. Let me enjoy my splendid flower, Malintzin. But look, I think two women are coming down over there.

TIZOC: One of them is the one you're dying for.

JULIAN: She gives me great contentment.

(At this point Malintzin and Lorenza enter.)

MALINTZIN: May it be God's will that the horse who bears you on its back throws you off a cliff somewhere!

TIZOC: Isn't she trying to tell you something?

JULIAN: She has shown me favor.

TIZOC: She who has shown you favor hates you.

MALINTZIN: Just kill yourself with poison! Curse you! May you suffer the same way you're making me suffer!

LORENZA: Let that be all, O my older sister. Curses on him!

JULIAN: Who on earth are you scolding, O my precious and admired Malintzin?

MALINTZIN: You, inconsiderate person.

JULIAN: Me? Why?

MALINTZIN: Because you deceived me. Don't you say so, O Lorenza?

LORENZA: Stop. Maybe I just made a mistake.

JULIAN: Have I deceived you?

MALINTZIN: You, didn't you send someone to me at my father's place so I'd come here? And I've been waiting for you right here all day. But Lorenza tells me that you and your servant are abandoning your altepetl. It seems you were just making fun of me.

JULIAN: Maybe not. If it is true, how could I forget you? Maybe you judged wrongly, O Lorenza. How could I abandon her?

LORENZA: It's true. I might have just confused you with some travelers.

TIZOC: What you're saying is true. You just made a mistake. Some people were passing on the road, maybe some travelers.

JULIAN: Will I abandon you, abandon your eyes like stars, those precious flowers that gaze out from under your eyebrows? If it's true, perhaps I've forgotten you.

MALINTZIN: Stop talking to me. You're a great big liar.

TIZOC: That's enough of your anger. Have pity on Julian. He's really dying for you.

LORENZA: All you do is talk. Curses on him still! Enough already!

TIZOC: But are we really going now?

JULIAN: Fool, maybe it won't come true. So shall we stay?

MALINTZIN: Will you be my husband?

JULIAN: I will be your slave as long as I live.

MALINTZIN: And as for me, I will be your vassal forever. Hurry up! Tell your father and my father that we're going to get married.

JULIAN: But what shall I do now in the meantime?

MALINTZIN: While I'm still staying here you shall go on seeing me.

JULIAN: I kiss your hands.

MALINTZIN: My hands and my heart.

TIZOC: Is it time for us to leave?

JULIAN: Shut up! Even if my father and my mother die at my hands, I'm going to stay here regardless.

(At this point Luis enters along with Susana, Julian's mother.)

LUIS: What are you doing? Are you enjoying yourself?

JULIAN: I couldn't be happier. Here I've met up with the daughter of our neighbor, Colhua Lord. The young woman, precious Malintzin, has likewise come here to enjoy herself.

SUSANA: She is a really splendid young woman.

LUIS: Your mother was very relieved to see you.

SUSANA: God knows that although it's just a little while since we've seen you, I was very worried.

JULIAN: But what am I up to? What am I doing? It seems certain that my mother and my father will die. Let me go once and for all! For the sake of a woman will I suffer the misfortune of murdering my mother and my precious father? Let it not be God's will. Come, Tizoc.

TIZOC: What do you want? Did the deer talk to you again? What on earth are you up to?

MALINTZIN: Are you in danger? What on earth are you thinking?

JULIAN: Oh! Wretched me! It seems I will abandon you no matter what.

LUIS: What on earth are you doing? Do sit down first.

JULIAN: Oh! Wretched me! Once and for all let me abandon the woman who incites my passion. My poor suffering father: don't let me do anything to him. Don't let anything happen to me. Listen, Tizoc.

TIZOC: Devil take the deer! I wish it hadn't talked to you. You're fixated on it.

JULIAN: Where are the horses?

TIZOC: They're over there under the willow tree.

JULIAN: Hurry up! Let's go!

LUIS: Where are you going? Settle down.

JULIAN: I'm leaving you now. I don't want to do anything bad to you.

LUIS: What's my child up to? Tell me, Tizoc.

TIZOC: I don't know what he's up to. He killed a deer, and it told him to act like this.

LUIS: You're mistreating us. How can you say you're leaving us? What will become of us when we can't see you anywhere? You're really going to make us suffer. What will become of us? We think about you all the time.

JULIAN: I'm going now. I'm starting off. At last I'm forsaking you, my altepetl!

LUIS: Wait a little! Wait a moment and listen!

MALINTZIN: Is it good you deceived me?

JULIAN: What's to be done? Wherever I end up, may you go on living, my precious father.

LUIS: Without a doubt, O Malintzin, it's because of you that our child is leaving us. It's your fault!

SUSANA: Let it be God's will that you too will experience the suffering you give us.

MALINTZIN: Let it also be God's will that he do something bad to you both, and whatever suffering he gives me, let him give you much worse!

Act Two

(Julian and Tizoc enter.)

TIZOC: The old folks say: let us have good luck, for what good would wisdom do us?

JULIAN: If I were back home, would I be enjoying what I've got right here? The place we have come into: they really like us, and I've married a precious and admired young woman from here.

TIZOC: Don't let anything make you leave her! Don't let another deer ruin things for you again by getting you mixed up about something.

JULIAN: But I've been married for a month and we couldn't be happier, even though some who get married are always scolding each other.

TIZOC: There's no greater bliss than when we are newly married. But afterward some misery comes along and then we have to put up with it. Most especially we get suspicious about something. But how fortunate you are! You're rich, and your wife loves you more than anything. Won't you and she be happy forever?

JULIAN: If it weren't for the deer, would I have come? He did me a favor. What good would it have done me to be over in my altepetl? See, I arrived here on a night when I helped the lord here, whom they were trying to stab to death. And he honors and esteems me very much. He has married me to, and given me, my precious wife, the noblewoman Laurencia.

TIZOC: Haven't you come for good? Will you ever go back to our home?

JULIAN: What else am I to do? Would it be good for some misfortune to happen to me there?

TIZOC: If it was God's will that your mother and your father should die at your hands, given that it could be anywhere, it will happen no matter what.

JULIAN: As long as I don't go there, how is it possible? What harm can I do to my mother and my father, and what are they going to come here and do? Do they know we're here? It can't possibly come true.

TIZOC: Fool that I am, what can I say to you?

JULIAN: It seems that the smart thing for you to do in regard to omens is just to run away from them, so that they won't come true.

TIZOC: And as for Malintzin?

JULIAN: But you still think of her? Curse her! For here I have my precious and admired wife, Laurencia, and so that I won't think about anything else, you go on in, and let me go in and see her. Isn't she waiting for me?

(At this point Julian exits. Tizoc is left by himself. He speaks.)

TIZOC: We who marry, suffer. What on earth do we go around doing? At first, when we see our spouses we couldn't be happier, but afterward if something troublesome comes along, then we weep. Isn't that what they say, sweet at the start, and later it becomes just like a bitter poison?

(Tizoc exits. Julian enters again.)

JULIAN: There's no happiness whatsoever on earth. My heart has become extremely bitter, and I'm very troubled. I came upon Laurencia, my wife, speaking to Federico, the younger brother of the ruler, the duke. What's he saying to her? Maybe he's telling her something bad. Maybe they were this familiar with each other before I married her. It was Federico who tried to ruin me when the ruler, his older brother, married me to her. He said: "Why does he get to marry Laurencia? He's a drifter, and her father, Octavio, was a great ruler." Who's coming? It's his servants. Let me get away from them first.

(At this point Julian hides. Then two servants of Federico enter.)

FIRST SERVANT, JUAN: We've been here a long time already, and her husband hasn't come out. Maybe he won't go anywhere.

SECOND SERVANT, PEDRO: Let's wait a little longer, for our lord goes around pining for the splendid young woman, Laurencia. Will he get tired of it even though she's married?

JUAN: She really respects her husband and really loves him. Won't our lord just be frustrated in his hopes?

PEDRO: Sooner or later she'll fall into his clutches. Is he playing around? If he wants her, what's she going to say against a lord?

JULIAN: Let me die.

JUAN: Let's go in. We'll satisfy ourselves as to whether he's left.

(At this point Federico's two servants go off.)

JULIAN: What did I hear? What they say is very disturbing. Sooner or later the ruler will get to my wife and enjoy her whether she wants it or not. But why should I put up with this? Is my heart a stone, to endure everything? Once and for all I am going in. Maybe my wife is up to something. But hold on . . . his servants are coming out now.

(At this point Laurencia, Julian's wife, enters along with Federico and his servants.)

LAURENCIA: If my husband were here, he would have received you.

FEDERICO: Please wait a moment and listen.

(At this point Julian enters.)

LAURENCIA: My husband is here now. Say to him what you want to say.

FEDERICO: Please wait a moment and listen.

LAURENCIA: But now my husband has come. Talk to each other. *[to Julian]* The ruler has come here to greet us.

JULIAN: We thank him for his generosity.

LAURENCIA: Be sure to thank him very much.

FEDERICO: *[to Laurencia]* Now I'm dying for you. Where are you going?

LAURENCIA: My husband is over there.

FEDERICO: May God go with you; may he guard you. *(At this point Laurencia exits.) (Aside)* Go where you will, for no matter what, you will fall into my clutches. *(He comes toward Julian and speaks to him.)* How are things turning out for you, Julian? Aren't you and your wife very happy? Doesn't she love you a lot? Wait a little. Do go on being content for a little while.

JULIAN: All owe you thanks. Nobles of honored blood are always of one heart, like the sun that always shines and is troubled by nothing.[6]

FEDERICO: What sun? What light?

JULIAN: It's true. But if you've got something to confide, let us speak of it in private. Those who are here must leave us.

FEDERICO: Let them leave. *[to his servants]* Go away.

TIZOC: I'll leave too. *[aside]* But do they see me here? Let me stay here listening to them.

(At this point Federico's servants leave and Tizoc hides.)

FEDERICO: They're gone.

TIZOC: *[aside]* Great! What's happening now?

JULIAN: What bad things will be said about me with you coming in here? Will meddlesome, no-good people think such things? Won't they gossip about me now? I hold myself in respect although, as you see, I'm not from around here. My mother and my father are nobles in my altepetl. Everyone honors us. If I hadn't suffered a misfortune there, what would I be doing here? I arrived right when they were trying to hurt the lord duke, your older brother. If not for me he would have died, for I'm the one who saved him when four people tried to stab him during the night. I stood beside him and defended him. This is my sword by whose grace he lives and with which I saved him. And he held me in great esteem for it. He was most grateful. How much of his esteem have I seen? Afterward he bestowed on me the noblewoman Laurencia, my wife, the precious daughter of a great ruler who is now deceased. Now then, I've been told that some time ago, when my wife there, Laurencia, was still single, you had asked for her and you desired her very much. I beg your pardon, but will they say good things about

---

6. Julian means his marriage is as steady and constant as the sun.

us? I beg your honor, do not enter my home again. I thank you very much for honoring me, for I am undeserving and unworthy. What will they say about me when they see that you come in when I'm not here? Won't my honor be lost in this way?

FEDERICO: Commoner,[7] how dare you answer me like that? What makes you so presumptuous? What is it, that you speak to me so disrespectfully? Don't you know, commoner, that I rule over you, since you're a vassal of my older brother? How dare you! Drifter, we don't know where you came from and where your home is. Now you tell me I won't come in here anymore? Fool! Beast! You know who I am. Don't you know we rulers are like the sun that navigates the heavens? Its radiance goes into everyone's home. Regardless of whose home it is, it illuminates and honors it. I am the sun. I come in here and everywhere. No one will stop me.

JULIAN: If you're the sun, then I'm the clouds and the thunder. And if your shining rays come flooding around me, like you want, then I'll be like a wolf that will thunder and flash at you as I take my revenge on you.

FEDERICO: What are you saying?

JULIAN: You heard it.

FEDERICO: You dare with me, O commoner?

JULIAN: I too am a nobleman and a ruler, even though you don't know me. You're the younger brother of the duke, the ruler. I know you.

FEDERICO: And what of it?

JULIAN: Respect for others.

FEDERICO: Shut up!

JULIAN: If you want something, it won't be here.

FEDERICO: All right, then!

JULIAN: All right, then! Even if it makes my ruler the duke angry, I don't give up my honor for anyone. Come. Here in the fields we'll fight each other. I'll wait for you over there.

FEDERICO: Go. I'll meet you there, even though you're a commoner. What good would it do for us to come to blows here? Wouldn't my relatives and vassals destroy you right away? I'll meet you there at the edge of the water, where we were yesterday.

JULIAN: All right, then! I'll wait for you there.

---

7. This word, *macehualli*, could also be understood to mean "Indian," here and in the following dialogue.

FEDERICO: *[aside]* He can be sure I'm going to enjoy his wife while he's waiting for me over there.

JULIAN: *[aside]* I will annihilate him, whatever happens to me.

FEDERICO: Look at me and remember.

JULIAN: Go, you poor wretch! You'll see what happens to you!

(At this point Julian and Federico leave. Then Tizoc enters.)

TIZOC: They're gone now. They'll kill each other! Oh! Let another deer talk to us here and tell us what's going to happen. Now the noblewoman's coming out. What good would it do for her to hear about this? Let me follow the others. May God calm Federico's heart. How will he destroy us? Aren't my lord and I like little dogs that he'll shake in his teeth, or like little flies that he'll crush between his hands?

(Tizoc exits. At this point Laurencia, Julian's wife, enters.)

LAURENCIA: My heart is very troubled by what's happening now. What's [Federico] sniffing around for? What's he looking for? Aren't my husband and I happy? He's tormenting us. I must tell my husband to be careful, for [Federico] says he'll do something to me tonight. What's happening to me? I'm dying to get some sleep. Let me rest a while. Maybe that way I'll forget my troubles.

(At this point Laurencia sits on a chair. She falls asleep there. Then her husband, Julian, enters.)

JULIAN: What did I hear my enemy say? I went and eavesdropped on him by the partition. And when he left here he went straight to the palace to consult with two people, saying to them: "O my friends, it will be today if you want to help me. While Julian waits for me in the place where we're supposed to fight each other, help me, for I'll go straight to his home to enjoy his wife. What's the use of us killing each other? Who can stop me? But you go on and keep watch for me." Then they said, "We'll go with you." What's going to happen? What will become of me? Shall I just go and wait for my enemy? I should just keep watch over my wife. *(At this point Julian speaks to his wife, but just in a calm and peaceful way. And the woman just keeps on sleeping.)* Splendid star that God created perfect, sleeping there, what do you know of how my heart is suffering now, because of you? Are you guilty of something? Are you worthy of me? Tell me: do you know something? *(aside)* This way she'll speak to me, saying "What am I guilty of? How am I offending you?" Let me keep quiet.

(At this point Laurencia talks in her sleep. Julian keeps quiet.)

LAURENCIA: Let that be all, O my heart, don't torment me any longer! Tonight my love will be put into effect. Oh, Federico!

JULIAN: What's happening to me now? What's my wife saying in her sleep? Let her die once and for all! What will she put into effect tonight? *(She speaks again.)*

LAURENCIA: Let that be all, O my heart, for you will love someone very much, but perhaps they won't love you.

JULIAN: This is how she loves me, this is how she keeps from hurting me—talking to my enemy in her sleep? *(She speaks again.)*

LAURENCIA: Tonight you'll see how you will love someone. Don't let it be God's will that my husband be deceived . . .

(At this point he acts like he will throw himself on her to stab her, then he stops.)

JULIAN: Enough already! Let my wife die at my hands! What am I up to? What am I doing? And is it just her and not the two of them who are offending me? They will die together. It's true, what my enemy told me when he said, "I'll do you harm tonight." Haven't the two of them made a pact with one another? Let me wait some more. They'll both die at my hands.

(At this point Tizoc enters.)

TIZOC: I can't find my lord anywhere.

JULIAN: Where were you? You've come at a very good time.

TIZOC: In my whole life, have I ever come at a good time?

JULIAN: Come quickly.

TIZOC: What are you up to? Wait a little. Settle down. What's bothering you?

JULIAN: I know you by now, and up to now I've always trusted you. And now, there's something you have to do.

TIZOC: I'll always obey you. Will I ever abandon you? Don't be ashamed to tell me. What is it?

JULIAN: Quick, saddle a horse, for I want to leave tonight. And as for you, you have to be on guard and keep an eye on a certain person.

TIZOC: Oh no! I'm such a sleepyhead! What's going to happen?

JULIAN: And when I whistle to you, go open the back door right away.

TIZOC: But at that hour, aren't I just groping around in the dark?

JULIAN: Don't talk back to me. Just do it.

TIZOC: Do get going. *(Tizoc exits.)*

JULIAN: Laurencia, Laurencia!

LAURENCIA: Who are you? What is it? What do you want?

(At this point Julian addresses his wife and speaks loudly to her.)

JULIAN: It's me, O my wife. The ruler is sending me away all of a sudden. Here's a letter I'm taking. Goodbye. You must forgive me, for we who serve others can't pay attention only to our own affairs.

LAURENCIA: Please go, then. Will I hold you up, since it's necessary?

JULIAN: *(aside)* She's quick to take comfort in whatever she's thinking. Wait a little. Soon the whole world will know that they died at my hands. *(At this point Julian leaves.)*

LAURENCIA: If Federico enters my quarters tonight, he might get bold because I'm alone. Let him have no doubt that he shall torment me no longer. But now it's getting dark. Let me lock myself up and strengthen my resolve. Heaven will defend and help me.

(At this point a servant of the noblewoman Laurencia enters.)

LAURENCIA'S SERVANT: I don't know where they come from, but two courteous people are asking about your husband.

LAURENCIA: I don't know what's come over me. My husband isn't here. What do they want? Let them come in.

HER SERVANT: They're coming in now.

(At this point Luis enters again, with Susana, Julian's mother. They come in search of their child, Julian.)

LUIS: What will become of us if we don't find him?

LAURENCIA: What are you looking for, O honored people?

LUIS: *(speaking to his wife)* The noblewoman is very splendid. It seems like we already see, in her face, our child whom we lost. *(Speaking to Laurencia)* O splendid highborn noblewoman, O my daughter, we've been told that this place is the home of a child of ours named Julian, who abandoned us long ago. We've come a long way, following behind him.

LAURENCIA: What shall I say to you? Let me embrace you both! It seems your precious child is my husband. Come on in. Rest your bodies. The young man isn't here, for he's still on an errand for the ruler. But here am I, your daughter. Do have a seat.

SUSANA: O precious child, O my precious daughter, we thank you, O my older sister, O jade.

LUIS: Truly indeed she is our daughter and our child, since she is so loving and generous to us.

(At this point Laurencia takes Luis and Susana inside.)

LAURENCIA: Do come in, for it is your home. Do stay a while.

LUIS: O my daughter, O noblewoman, O little one, don't let us be a bother to you, since that's what old folks are like. I am extremely tired, as is your mother. Don't go to any trouble. Let us rest our earth, our mud, somewhere here at the corner of the mat.[8]

LAURENCIA: Very well. Relax, sleep, rest your bodies. Here is the bed on which the young man your child and I sleep. I will see you later.

LUIS: *(to his wife)* O my wife, O noblewoman, do go in.

SUSANA: Now our daughter is here. What a comfort it is for us to have seen her.

LUIS: *(to his daughter)* Please go in, O my daughter.

LAURENCIA: *[aside]* Now nothing troubles me anymore, for they're looking after me now.

(At this point she leaves. Then Tizoc enters.)

TIZOC: What in the world am I doing? I was so terribly sleepy! This is what happens to me. But it seems it's because of the burden and orders I was given. The pulque I drank really settled in me. I think I'll sip a bit from the drinking gourd. *(At this point someone whistles offstage.)* Who's hanging around whistling? What's he want at this hour? Let him keep waiting until dawn if he wants. *(He whistles again.)* Devil take him, if I'm to be disturbed. No matter what, I'll stay happy and sleep. I feel like I'm plunged in cotton. I've been softened up by a touch of pulque. I'm looking up at the stars, all dancing, led by a moon with a face like a drum.

(At this point Tizoc lies down to sleep. Julian enters with a firepot in his hand.)

JULIAN: Did I have to put my trust in this fool? If I hadn't climbed over the wall, how would I have gotten in? Everyone's asleep. But my enemy's not in the house yet? I've made up my mind about them. All right then, let me take out what they will die with.[9] Let me calm down. Will I take off my shoes first? Let me leave them on. Let me hurry straight to my bedroom. What am I still waiting for? That is all. Let me hide the pine torch first. Let it remain here. Done. May heaven strengthen my resolve.

8. The diphrase "earth, mud," referring to the body, and the offer to sleep out of the way, "at the corner of the mat," are expressions of formal, old-fashioned speech.

9. He draws his dagger.

TIZOC: Who are you, going around there? What do you want at these hours, going around with a light? Truly indeed, if there were a pitcher of water here I'd pour it all on top of your head. Are you trying to make fun of me, going around with a light? Come, I'll blow out your pine torch for you. Just let me sleep.

(Julian enters with a dagger in his hand. It is full of blood, which is dripping.)

JULIAN: It's done! I've bathed the weapon in their blood four hundred times. It seemed like someone tried to catch hold of my hand. Maybe what I undertook was bad, but so be it. What they were doing was bad too. There was a time when I loved Laurencia. Let her die! Let honor be celebrated and let shame be despised! Enough already! Let me go! Let me go out over the wall again where I left my horse. I'm out of here once and for all. Who's here?

TIZOC: Don't run me over! Who the devil are you?

JULIAN: Get up, idiot commoner!

TIZOC: Who are you?

JULIAN: It's me!

TIZOC: Pardon me, but I was sound asleep. Truly indeed, what happened to me?

JULIAN: Do you have the key to the back door?

TIZOC: Here it is.

JULIAN: Bring it right here.

TIZOC: Are you going now?

JULIAN: Don't ask me anything, for it's over. I've taken my revenge. Now let me save myself and go. What am I doing now? What's happening to me now? What am I seeing?

(At this point Laurencia enters and meets up with her husband, Julian. She brings a light.)

LAURENCIA: O my husband!

JULIAN: What are you doing at this hour, that you haven't gone to bed yet?

LAURENCIA: I was still at devotions and am just now coming in to lie down.

JULIAN: Do come. Who are the two people sleeping on our bed?

LAURENCIA: Give me something and I'll tell you.

JULIAN: So be it. Tell me: who are they?

LAURENCIA: It's your precious mother and your precious father, who have followed you all this time.

JULIAN: Jesus! What are you saying?

LAURENCIA: You don't believe it? Please look at them.

JULIAN: Leave them be. Don't uncover them.

LAURENCIA: What are you doing?

JULIAN: I absolutely do not want to see them.

LAURENCIA: What's wrong with you?

JULIAN: Oh, how wretched I am, four hundred times over! Oh no!

(At this point they uncover Julian's father and mother, whom he stabbed. Then Laurencia says:)

LAURENCIA: Please look at them. Here is the cloak with which they are covered. Ah, O my deity, O my ruler, O God, they're soaking in blood! Who killed them?

JULIAN: How wretched I am! It was me! Here is the weapon with which I tormented them. I thought it might be you and Federico.

LAURENCIA: Come. Your heart is extremely bitter and now you have inflicted suffering on your own blood and kin. What did you see wrong with me? Did you see something amiss sometime? Wasn't my life as pure as emerald and turquoise, I offending you in nothing? O wretched me! For it is with much suffering that your doubts are now satisfied.

JULIAN: Leave me be, Laurencia. Let that be all. Don't torment me. Each drop of the blood of my father and my mother is an arrow that pierces my very heart. Once and for all let the earth open and swallow me up. Is there anyone in the world who would do what I have done? I gave myself to the cliffs, the currents, the waters. The judgment of heaven has been carried out. It didn't stop when I abandoned them. Cover them up! I don't want to look at them. Let me die once and for all. Let me be destroyed by this weapon here with which I killed them.

(At this point he acts like he is about to stab himself. Laurencia quickly grabs his hand.)

LAURENCIA: Enough! Stop it!

JULIAN: Indeed what else can I do, for God won't ever forgive me!

LAURENCIA: Why? Aren't you a Christian, that you say such a thing?

JULIAN: May it be true, what you say. I thank you, for God is indeed merciful. Let me go quickly to where the royal priest of the world is, he who is God's representative,[10] for he will help me. Isn't it true? I'm going to leave you here.

LAURENCIA: I'm to be left behind? Absolutely not! I won't abandon you, since I love you. Let's go. Let me go with you so you won't ever

10. The pope.

think such things again.[11] Will those who truly love each other ever leave one another? Let's go!

TIZOC: And as for me, no way will I ever abandon you two.

JULIAN: Many boats have come to the shore. We'll take to the water right away. Let's go, O my wife.

(At this point Federico enters again with his servants. They try in vain to detain the others.)

FEDERICO: Where are you going? Wait!

JULIAN: You poor wretch, that you've come to meet me right now.

FEDERICO: It's me, Federico.

JULIAN: What do you want?

FEDERICO: We will take your wife away from you now.

JULIAN: For some reason I used to feel intimidated by you, but now you've brought on my rage!

LAURENCIA: Here, I took the weapons from them. Let them die!

JULIAN: Now would this be what you were searching so hard for?

TIZOC: If I had my sword . . .

(At this point they exit. They go stabbing them repeatedly. From offstage Federico cries out, saying:)

FEDERICO: That's all, I'm dying, they've stabbed me! *(At this point he dies.)*

TIZOC: You must die!

JULIAN: I destroyed my mother and my father, and you're going to stay alive?

TIZOC: What the deer said was true.

JULIAN: Follow me!

TIZOC: We're following you. God knows, if a deer talks to me again, I'll become a priest.

Act Three

(At this point a ruler, a duke, enters along with a servant of his.)

ENRIQUE, HIS SERVANT: O my ruler, are we going all by ourselves?

DUKE: It's better that we go by ourselves. I want to marvel at this splendid woman. She is really carrying off my heart.

ENRIQUE: But is there anybody really splendid here? For they're all just poor folks. Where's the one who's like a flower? I don't get it.

---

11. So he will not suspect her of cheating on him.

DUKE: As for me, yes, I've seen her and marveled at her. She's carried off my heart. Because you see only their rags, you don't recognize her. If a precious pearl is wrapped in rags, do they destroy its splendor and beauty?

ENRIQUE: What you're saying is true.

DUKE: In the same way, you saw the rags and didn't see the face. But who are they, coming here? It seems to me they're carrying a poor sick person on their shoulders. Don't let them see us.

ENRIQUE: Here they come.

DUKE: Yes. Sometimes they walk around with the woman I'm talking about.

ENRIQUE: One of them might be her husband. Did you find out about him?

DUKE: Even if she's married, it doesn't bother me.

(Duke exits. At this point Julian enters along with Tizoc. They come sharing the task of carrying Demon on their shoulders. Demon is disguised as a poor sick person.)

TIZOC: May four hundred devils take anyone who'd try to move him.

JULIAN: Aren't we sharing this task? Get going; move along.

TIZOC: It's well enough that you're here, since you murdered people and are paying for your sin, but I've never killed even a beetle. Do you want me to suffer the way you suffer?

JULIAN: You will be blessed for that and God will show you favor.

TIZOC: I'd be blessed if this devil's orphan weren't so heavy. Maybe then I'd be able to budge him.

DEMON: *[aside]* I'll do my hunting like this, so that Julian won't escape my clutches, for he is steadfast in seeking favor from God. Did I come out of hell for no purpose? He may carry on. I'm disguising myself as a poor person. He's carrying me off in order to take care of me, but there are lots of things that I will do.

TIZOC: Tell, infernal invalid, what on earth you've filled yourself with, that you're so heavy! Have you gorged yourself on corn stew and chopped squash? What on earth makes you so heavy?

JULIAN: Please put up with it, just for my sake.

TIZOC: Let the devil put up with it.

DEMON: That could happen.

TIZOC: Furthermore, the way he stinks, whether he's a poor person or a devil he's giving me a terrible headache, because while I go at the back, his stench flows right onto me.

JULIAN: Let me go in back. Don't wear yourself out with him.

TIZOC: Go peacefully. Don't go aggravating us. If you make me mad, I'll throw you on the ground and whack you against it.

DEMON: Please wait a moment and listen.

TIZOC: Get over there, devil! How you stink! Maybe your liver has gone rotten. Don't come near me! You stink like something out of hell. Don't infect me! Maybe you have some bad disease. Julian, if you want to transport this sick person, hire him four people to carry him on their shoulders.

JULIAN: Don't talk like that. Truly indeed you are really pathetic.

TIZOC: More pathetic is the one who's carrying this devil on his shoulders! Maybe he came out of hell. Maybe he just came to spy on us.

DEMON: Don't let me trouble you. Let me just go on my own feet, for it's not much farther. Let me get walking. Where on earth do you live?

TIZOC: Get walking. Don't you have feet?

JULIAN: Leave him alone. Let me be in charge of carrying him. Will it embarrass us? What can be done? Let me do penance.

DEMON: Please wait a moment and listen.

JULIAN: Let me be. When I carry a poor person on my shoulders, it's the same as carrying God on my shoulders.

(At this point Julian exits along with the devil he carries on his shoulders.)

TIZOC: Julian's poor nose suffers. What does he want? Must all my bones get broken?

(At this point Duke enters again.)

DUKE: Let me just ask a question of this one here. Do you recognize me, O my friend?

TIZOC: I'm just a little poor guy. Where have we seen each other?

DUKE: We might have spoken to each other somewhere.

TIZOC: *[aside]* Maybe he means to do me some favor.

DUKE: Please come and tell me, who is that very troubled-looking woman who came out of there yesterday?

TIZOC: I'll tell you what I think! You're smitten with desire. But please give me something, for you're a rich man.

(The duke gives him a purse.)

DUKE: *[aside]* He recognized me. *[to Tizoc]* Here's what you require.

TIZOC: Oh my! O God, since you see how poor I am, wouldn't it be ungrateful of me not to accept it? Jesus! But do bring it here. Let me take it. And do please wait a moment and listen. Please pay attention and let me sum up for you what happened. Maybe then you'll understand. The woman you're asking about isn't from around here. And as for her husband, who passed by here a little while ago carrying a sick person on his shoulders, even though he was in rags, he was a great noble back home. His name is Julian. But a bad thing happened to him: by God's orders he killed his mother and his father. But he travels around doing penance. The pope gave him his blessing. And now everywhere we end up, we keep on doing penance. And in this place, it's been God's will that we made a hospital, where poor sick people can be restored to health, and where he can give rest to all the travelers. This, then, O my ruler, is what you were asking about. But if you want to get his wife for yourself, you're wasting your time, for there's no way you'll manage it. Laurencia's not interested in that, for she's a great penitent. She never stops whipping herself and fasting. Here it is; you've heard it. May God keep you, for it's late and I take my leave of you.

(Tizoc exits. Duke and his servant remain there and speak to each other.)

DUKE: I'm really astonished at what he told me.

ENRIQUE: Now you have your answer.

DUKE: You speak the truth. I won't trespass against God, but will be especially helpful to Laurencia. I'm a rich man. I'll be generous toward them, so they won't need to look for another place somewhere else. Let's leave them alone, for I'm not someone who would kick at service to God.

ENRIQUE: Love has left you now.

DUKE: Rather, I love her even more because of God. Now I honor her.

(At this point Duke and his servant leave. Julian enters again, with his wife and Demon, a firepot in Laurencia's hand.)

JULIAN: Hang the firepot over there. And go fetch some rags with which to heal the poor sick person.

(Laurencia goes to fetch rags.)

DEMON: *(aside)* How will I be able to do this? He's really trying to save himself. He may carry on for a time. No matter what, I will make him give up.

(Laurencia enters with rags in her hands.)

LAURENCIA: Here's what I went to get.

JULIAN: You've done well. Right there you show, my precious wife, how you will serve God. And as for you, you poor sick person, sit and rest your body.

DEMON: *(aside)* What might give rest to someone who is constantly on fire?[12]

12. A devil, he is constantly burning in the flames of hell.

JULIAN: Now the poor sick people are coming in.

(At this point Tizoc enters, a syringe in his hand.)

TIZOC: Watch out, Lucifer.

JULIAN: Wait. Where are you going?

TIZOC: I hear tell he's going to take his medicine later, or tomorrow. Who is he to be putting it off? He'd better not irritate me too much.

JULIAN: Who?

TIZOC: Who would it be except this devil? Don't you see that big talker on his bed over there, writing something?

JULIAN: Don't let him bother you so much.

TIZOC: He really gives me a hard time. This is what he keeps doing. This is how he thinks it is. He just gave the medicine back to me and told me a gift from me is no medicine. "And if you put it on me I'll cause a fright."

JULIAN: But what can be done, how can it be otherwise? It's already paid for. Please take it back.

TIZOC: Absolutely impossible, cannot be done. I'll give him medicine now, for the potion's already been prepared. Are we just going to fool around with it after spending the money?

JULIAN: You're bothering him. Leave him alone.

TIZOC: Sick sorcerer,[13] roll over! Hurry up! I'm going to give you medicine up your rear end![14]

DEMON: What do you want?

JULIAN: You're bothering him. Leave him alone.

TIZOC: Enough already! On with the medicine, for the devil really stinks. Maybe it'll get rid of whatever's inside of him.

JULIAN: Don't let him die from it.

TIZOC: He'll be given something else right away. There's a really icy medicine he can take!

JULIAN: Please wait until someone goes with you.

(At this point a blind man and a lame man enter.)

BLIND MAN: May God's precious name be totally praised!

JULIAN: May that be done forever.

TIZOC: Now what's your day's take, O my blind friend?

BLIND MAN: If I can't see, how can I carry out what you're saying?

---

13. Tizoc calls the devil a *tlahuipochin*, a sorcerer thought to go about at night spitting fire and frightening his enemies to death (Bautista 1600, 1:112r–v).

14. The indigenous practice of applying medicines through the rectum is exploited here for comic effect.

TIZOC: The lame man and the blind man really abuse Two Rabbit. How many times has he been applied to your heads?[15]

LAME MAN: Not many times.

TIZOC: You guys come and really waft the smell around, which is a comfort to me.[16]

LAURENCIA: What on earth are you saying? That's enough. Stop it.

DEMON: If he doesn't leave, he's going to make me really sick.

JULIAN: Something bothering you?

DEMON: I'm all right.

TIZOC: Blind man, lame man, help me! Grab him! Now's the time! Let him get his medicine up his rear! Get a good grip on him!

DEMON: Oh, poor me!

TIZOC: If you don't get a good strong hold on him, I'll spread the medicine on you!

JULIAN: Leave him alone! You're bothering him.

TIZOC: What on earth's bothering you? I think he makes you feel sorry for him.

(At this point two other poor sick people enter.)

SICK MAN: May the wondrous name of the heavenly royal virgin, mother of God, be praised!

EVERYONE: Let it be done!

DEMON: Now I'm burning and suffering![17]

TIZOC: I think I'll break your ribs with a tree trunk.

JULIAN: O my wife, sit down. Let's take comfort through God's poor sick people.

LAURENCIA: Let's take comfort. I want that as well.

(At this point a soldier enters.)

SOLDIER: O our friends, what are you doing?

TIZOC: You've run away, O little soldier boy.

SOLDIER: Can you really have just a pine torch for light?

TIZOC: If you want some more torches, go to hell.

SOLDIER: God knows, fool, that I'll break your head!

(At this point they all beat the soldier vigorously.)

TIZOC: What's going on? Beat him, little sick people!

BLIND MAN: Then he'll die at my hands!

---

15. Two Rabbit was a major pulque god. Tizoc is accusing the men of being very drunk and also shows that he is familiar with the old Aztec gods.

16. The smell of pulque.

17. The devil suffers whenever anyone prays or calls on God or the Virgin Mary.

JULIAN: What are you doing? Have you no shame?

BLIND MAN: We're leaving him alone, but we're only doing it for your sake.

SOLDIER: They broke my ribs! Just wait, it'll be dawn in a little while, and they'll pulverize me.

TIZOC: Tomorrow I'll hang around with the sick people. I don't want to get hurt.

(At this point there is singing. From offstage they say:)

VOICE: Julian abandoned his altepetl as well as his mother and his father. But why? I will tell you now.

JULIAN: Who's singing? What they're saying is what happened to me.

TIZOC: Maybe it's not you. Does anyone recognize you? It's a woman who's singing. Isn't she just making herself feel better?

LAME MAN: But who is the Julian they're talking about?

TIZOC: Is it your business, fool? Just go back to sleep.

DEMON: It really exasperates and torments me that he is praying.

TIZOC: And as for you, you don't want to shut your mouth! Talk again and I really will give you some medicine up your rear!

(At this point there is singing again.)

VOICE: Julian tried as hard as he could not to kill his father and his mother. He abandoned them quickly when the deer told him what he would do to them.

BLIND MAN: Ah, she sings very well.

TIZOC: Fool, is it your business whether it's good or bad?

JULIAN: Oh no! O my deity, O my ruler, O God, it seems that the whole world now knows what I did. Have pity on me.

DEMON: He speaks to God with all his heart.

LAURENCIA: What are you doing? You're not asleep.

DEMON: I feel like I'm about to faint.

LAURENCIA: O my husband, arrange for some refreshment for our patient, for he feels faint.

JULIAN: Tizoc, go warm up a few eggs. The poor sick person will down them and feel better for it.

TIZOC: Wouldn't it be better for that devil to choke on a few slippery stones?[18]

(At this point Tizoc exits. Again there is singing offstage.)

---

18. Tizoc's insult relies on the similarity between the Nahuatl word for eggs, *totoltetl* (literally "turkey stones"), and *tealactetl*, "slippery stones."

VOICE: And when he got where he was going, he and a young woman, Laurencia, a splendid noblewoman, got married there.
(Then Tizoc enters again. He brings out two eggs on a plate.)
TIZOC: Here they are. I hope you bust your gut with them.
DEMON: As for me, I never fill myself with food.
TIZOC: You don't want to eat them?
DEMON: No.
TIZOC: Thank you. Please let me swallow them to comfort my soul.
(Tizoc swallows the eggs.) Wonderful! On with it! Let me gulp you guys right down.
JULIAN: How do I know what would have happened to me?
LAURENCIA: Don't think about it anymore. Just have complete confidence in your deity and ruler, God.
TIZOC: What do you say? Was I pleased?
DEMON: Very well.
TIZOC: I just gulped them down like I was a snake.
JULIAN: Maybe he wants more. Give them to him.
TIZOC: Do you want more eggs?
DEMON: That's enough.
TIZOC: Ask for some more. Don't you see that I really know how to swallow them?
SOLDIER: Wait a little. Please be quiet for a while.
LAME MAN: Is someone talking?
(Again there is singing.)
VOICE: What Julian's wife said in her dreams is the reason why he was suspicious and had doubts.
JULIAN: It was because of what you said in your sleep that I started thinking about the bad thing I did.
LAURENCIA: You insulted me very deeply.
JULIAN: Well, that's what it's like for someone who's in love.
SOLDIER: Whoever is singing sure doesn't want to say it all at once. Do be quiet. Devil take you all! All you do is talk.
SICK MAN: But is someone talking?
(Again there is singing.)
VOICE: He pretended that he would deliver a letter. How is it possible that right then his father and his mother came? That's when he stabbed them and killed them.
LAME MAN: Isn't Julian's soul already in hell?
SICK MAN: Why? Is it his fault?

LAME MAN: Why isn't it his fault?

TIZOC: Is it your business?

LAME MAN: Why wouldn't it be his fault? Can't he see? And supposing he were blind like our friend here, then he might not have seen them.

BLIND MAN: His salvation is in danger before God.

DEMON: Thank you. You all are really helping me.

JULIAN: What I'm hearing is very painful, O my wife, and the bad things being said about me cause my heart much torment.

LAURENCIA: Don't let it trouble you, O my precious husband.

TIZOC: What do they know? The beasts don't understand. Isn't God very merciful?

DEMON: No way can he have mercy on him. Is it just some minor thing that he did?

TIZOC: Shut up, stinky. Do you talk like that around other people too? Is it your business? Come, mange from hell. Isn't the deity, God, powerful? Why can't he have mercy on him? Maybe you'd say Tezcatlipoca is giver of life, and very merciful?[19] It's the same with a ruler on earth: if someone who's offended him humbles himself before him, the ruler pardons him. How much more merciful is the ruler of heaven? You're just fools to say that.

JULIAN: Tizoc's words are most comforting. Maybe God will have mercy on me. Maybe I'll inspire pity in him.

DEMON: [aside] He took great comfort in hearing that. Hold on—I know what I'll say to him. Let's have the people here leave him alone, and I shall do my job. Let me scare them, so they'll run away and leave him alone.

(Offstage they make sounds of thunder.)

TIZOC: What's going on? There are really blinding flashes of light, there's lightning everywhere, and the thunder's very strong.

SOLDIER: I think there's about to be a big hailstorm.

LAME MAN: It's like the sky's about to collapse!

BLIND MAN: Come on! Everybody leave! Let's go inside.

(At this point all the poor sick people exit. Julian and his wife and the demon and Tizoc remain by themselves.)

JULIAN: O my wife, what are you doing? It's night now. Go in and sleep, for I want to stay here for a while with this poor sick person.

---

19. Tizoc, again revealing his familiarity with Aztec gods, suggests that the demon character is loyal to Tezcatlipoca, the Aztec god that the friars considered to be most like Lucifer himself. He was not known for being merciful.

LAURENCIA: I shall go. Please rest a while.

TIZOC: [to Demon] Do keep it short. Where will you go to? You'll see, I'll count your ribs with a tree trunk.

(Laurencia exits along with Tizoc.)

JULIAN: The rainstorm is over. Rest, both of you.

DEMON: Enough already! I feel a little better.

JULIAN: Come. How do you know Julian's soul can't be saved? Doesn't God have a lot of mercy?

DEMON: All the great scholars have mulled it over, and what they see in the books is that he can't possibly be saved.

JULIAN: But do the wise men know how it happened? Don't they say that maybe he didn't intend to do what he did?

DEMON: Even though he didn't know what he was doing, in any case he can't be saved.

JULIAN: What's to be done? I am four hundred times unfortunate! Let weeping and tears swell up. Can I still be healed?

DEMON: The sin you committed is without equal because your father and your mother died in sin. They came to an end in anger.[20]

JULIAN: Is it really true? Is it certain?

DEMON: A saint saw them burning in hell.

JULIAN: Oh no! What will become of me? I wish I hadn't been born! What shall I do, I, whose mother and father are in hell? Hasn't God already rejected me? Will he have pity on me now?

DEMON: I take my leave of you now for I want to rest a while.

JULIAN: I thank you. Be going along.

DEMON: (aside) Now I've taken my revenge, not on this person but on God. But so he'll really believe it, all right then, let me do my job. Let me show him his father among the flames. He'll talk to him there to no good and he'll scorn him completely! (At this point the demon leaves.)

JULIAN: O my deity, O my ruler, O God, I am four hundred times unfortunate. Where will I go? You've already rejected me! Can I flee from you? Where can I hide? Poor me! Isn't it all over? But you know that I didn't plan to kill my father and my mother. My heart wasn't in it. If I'd known, would I have done such a thing? I tried as hard as I could to get away from them. Don't you know that? Help me, have pity on me. O my deity, aren't you compassionate? Aren't you gentle?

---

20. The demon says that Julian's parents were in a state of mortal sin when they died and so were sent to hell, rather than purgatory or heaven.

Let your heart be merciful. Poor me! Don't let me fall into any more of your anger, for my heart is extremely tormented. Jesus, what's happening to me now? What am I being forced to see? The earth has opened and what's coming out of there is very frightening. I think that's my father looking at me, and he comes burning in flames!

(At this point Luis, Julian's father, again appears, from under the stage. He looks like he is on fire. He says:)

LUIS: It's me, your father. Is this how you paid me back, that now you've cast me into hell, where I suffer eternal pain and misery? Let the day you were born be completely scorned, as well as when I engendered you. It's as if you tormented me. But soon you too will go there, for the terrifying seat in hell, made all of fire, where you're going to sit, is already there. *(At this point Luis exits quickly.)*

JULIAN: It's over. What more can I do? Aren't I the demon's slave? What more do I want? I wish I'd strangled myself once and for all. Let me hang myself. Yet what can I do? But maybe God's heart will be mollified. Let me still have confidence in him. Yet if he has already spurned me and there is already a seat waiting for me in hell, what more can be done, even though I still had hope? But isn't God the ladder of mercy? Isn't he the fountain of mercy? So I'm the only one who won't enjoy his mercy? Doesn't he show favor to other great sinners? And as for me: why won't he show favor to me? Let me go on putting my trust in God. However I'm to come to an end, I won't abandon God.

(At this point Laurencia enters along with Boy Jesus, who accompanies her. He will look just like a poor needy person; he will be disguised as a poor sick person.)

LAURENCIA: Here is my husband, whom you came looking for. This is the Julian you were asking about.

BOY JESUS: I've come to comfort him today. Something might be worrying him.

LAURENCIA: This splendid child here is looking for you.

JULIAN: What do you want? Your face is very heavenly.

BOY JESUS: I'm exhausted, for the sun is very strong. With your leave I'll cool off from the heat here for a while.

JULIAN: I wouldn't want to demean you by having you sit in such a place, for here where I am is not a good place. Do put up with it and rest. Your face shows that you are a great and highborn noble. What do you want? What are you looking for?

BOY JESUS: Something has been giving me pain. That's why I've come here.

JULIAN: O my heart, speak to me: what's giving you pain? Maybe I can heal you, for I am here to heal the sick.

BOY JESUS: I'm sick with love.

JULIAN: And love troubles you?

BOY JESUS: It torments me very much and tires me out.

JULIAN: Do you have a father?

BOY JESUS: And I have a mother.

JULIAN: Where have you come from?

BOY JESUS: From the place of perfect delight, glory.

JULIAN: It seems I'm not going to enjoy it.

BOY JESUS: Why not?

JULIAN: Because of my sins, God has already consigned me to hell.

BOY JESUS: Maybe not. Aren't you still alive?

JULIAN: Although I'm alive, he's already passed judgment on me in this way.

BOY JESUS: Who has passed judgment?

JULIAN: God himself.

BOY JESUS: You just deceive yourself. It's not true.

JULIAN: And he has already cast my father and my mother into hell.

BOY JESUS: You've just been deceived, that you say those things. Be certain of it. If you saw your father in purgatory now, what would you say?

JULIAN: How can I see them in purgatory? For my father is in hell now. He showed himself to me like that.

BOY JESUS: All heaven and earth are in my hands. Look, see your mother and your father, who are in purgatory and are about to go to heaven.

JULIAN: Heaven and earth are entirely in your hands. I didn't recognize you, wondrous and holy child. You are my deity and ruler.

(At this point Boy Jesus exits, going to sit where heaven is. And then from above appear the mother and father of Julian with very clean garments. And then there is singing.)[21]

SONG: When will you be so generous as to show favor to us who are going to be worthy of your precious face?

---

21. Presumably it is Susana and Luis who are to sing, but there could be other actors playing souls in purgatory who sing with them.

BOY JESUS: In a very short while you will go into heaven. I will show favor to you now, since your child did penance for his sins. And as for you, Julian, do not falter. Serve me. You too will be saved, for I am savior and deity. Although I punish people, even more do I show them favor and pity.

(Demon enters.)

DEMON: Granted, you have tremendous love for the people of earth, but these people must not receive it. As you know, their sins are very great.

BOY JESUS: Come and be happy forever, you who are the totally good and blessed ones of my precious father, God.

(At this point heaven appears above. Boy Jesus is seated there in authority, and a ladder is placed there, by means of which Julian's father and mother will go up.)

DEMON: All you accursed ones, come with me. You will go to hell.

BOY JESUS: Be happy forever with me.

DEMON: Suffer pain forever with me.

BOY JESUS: Now the residents of heaven go to meet you.

DEMON: With weeping the residents of hell will go to meet you.

BOY JESUS: Now they open up heaven for you.

DEMON: Now flames and smoke come forth from hell.

(Heaven closes. Demon exits. Then Julian and his wife and Tizoc enter again.)

LAURENCIA: Didn't I tell you that God is very merciful?

JULIAN: I'm very grateful to him, for his love is immense.

TIZOC: Now right away I'll burn the bed where that infernal pig was lying.

JULIAN: It really needs it.

TIZOC: I still wish I would have given him the medicine.

JULIAN: Let us all praise God, who has shown us favor. Let's go inside.

(It ends with all exiting.)

APPENDIX

Extant Colonial-Era Plays

Title	Type	Place, date, author or copyist, if known	Location	Publication
Souls and Testamentary Executors	Morality play	17th century?	William L. Clements Library, University of Michigan	*Nahuatl Theater* vol. 1, Ravicz 1970, Horcasitas 2004
Final Judgment	Morality play	17th century?	Library of Congress, Washington, D.C.	*Nahuatl Theater* vol.1, Ravicz 1970, Horcasitas 1974
The Merchant	Morality play	San Juan Bautista Tollantzinco, 1687, Don Joseph Gaspar	Library of Congress, Washington, D.C.	*Nahuatl Theater* vol. 1, Ravicz 1970, Horcasitas 2004
*How to Live on Earth** (also called *Tlacahuapahualiztli*)	Morality play	17th century?	Library of Congress, Washington, D.C. (two versions)	*Nahuatl Theater* vol. 1, Horcasitas 2004, Cornyn and McAfee 1944
The Life of Don Sebastián	Morality play	Huaxtepec, 1692	Graduate Theological Union Library, Academy of American Franciscan History Collection, Berkeley, California	*Nahuatl Theater* vol. 1
*The Nobleman and His Barren Wife**	Morality play	c. 1700?	Biblioteca Nacional de Antropología e Historia, Mexico City	*Nahuatl Theater* vol. 4
*Don Rafael**	Morality play	Mexico City, Fray Agustín de Vetancurt, José Maximiano Juárez, Tomás Valdés, 1718/1749	The John Carter Brown Library, Brown University	*Nahuatl Theater* vol. 4

Extant Colonial-Era Plays (*continued*)

Title	Type	Place, date, author or copyist, if known	Location	Publication
*The Grandfather and His Orphan Grandchild**	Morality play	unknown	Archivo General de la Nación, Mexico City	Silva Cruz 2001 (transcription only)
*Julián and His Guardian Angel**	Morality play (incomplete)	1767?	Archivo General de la Nación, Mexico City	none
*Doña Francisca**	Morality play (fragmentary)	Ozumba, 1740?	Archivo General de la Nación, Mexico City	none
The Sacrifice of Isaac	Old Testament play	1678/1760, Bernabé Vázquez	William L. Clements Library, University of Michigan	*Nahuatl Theater* vol. 1, Paso y Troncoso 1899, Ravicz 1970, Horcasitas 1974
*The Three Kings** (also called *The Adoration of the Kings*)	Epiphany play	17th century?	William L. Clements Library, University of Michigan	*Nahuatl Theater* vol. 1, Paso y Troncoso 1900, Ravicz 1970, Horcasitas 1974
*The Star Sign**	Epiphany play	Metepec, 1717, Carlos de San Juan	Biblioteca Nacional de Antropología e Historia, Mexico City	*Nahuatl Theater* vol. 4 (lost earlier version from Tlatelolco, published Paso y Troncoso 1902, Horcasitas 1974, as *La Comedia de los Reyes*)

Extant Colonial-Era Plays (*continued*)

Title	Type	Place, date, author or copyist, if known	Location	Publication
Holy Wednesday	Holy Week play	c. 1590	Princeton Collections of Western Americana, Princeton University Libraries	Burkhart 1996
Untitled Passion play	Passion play	Tepaltzingo, Morelos, 18th century	Latin American Library, Tulane University (photostat only)	*Nahuatl Theater* vol. 4, Horcasitas 1974
Untitled Passion play	Passion play (incomplete)	San Simón Tlatlauhquitepec, Tlaxcala, c. 1700?	Archivo de la Fiscalía, San Simón Tlatlauhquitepec, Tlaxcala	*Nahuatl Theater* vol. 4
Passion of Our Lord Jesus Christ according to Matthew	Passion play	Axochiapan, Morelos, 1732	Latin American Library, Tulane University (photocopy from Horcasitas papers)	none
Untitled Passion play	Passion play	Amacuitlapilco, Morelos, 1757	Archivo General de la Nación, Mexico City	none
The Precious and Admired Passion of Our Lord Jesus Christ	Passion play	18th century?	Princeton University Library, Princeton Mesoamerican Manuscript no. 13	none
La Passion de Nro Señor Jesu christo	Passion play	18th century	Berendt-Brinton Collection, University of Pennsylvania Museum Library	none

Extant Colonial-Era Plays (*continued*)

Title	Type	Place, date, author or copyist, if known	Location	Publication
The Destruction of Jerusalem	Historical play	c. 1700?	Biblioteca Nacional de Antropología e Historia, Mexico City	*Nahuatl Theater* vol. 4, Paso y Troncoso 1907, Ravicz 1970, Horcasitas 1974
The Destruction of Jerusalem	Historical play (one-leaf fragment)	1745	Latin American Library, Tulane University	*Nahuatl Theater* vol. 4
Colloquy of How the Blessed Saint Helen Found the Precious and Admired Wooden Cross	Historical/ saints play	Santa Cruz Cozcaquauh-atlauhticpac, 1714, Don Manuel de los Santos y Salazar	John Carter Brown Library, Brown University	*Nahuatl Theater* vol. 4, Paso y Troncoso 1890, Ravicz 1970, Horcasitas 1974
The Great Theater of the World	Auto sacramental	c. 1640, Don Bartolomé de Alva	Bancroft Library, University of California at Berkeley	*Nahuatl Theater* vol. 3, Hunter 1960
The Animal Prophet and the Fortunate Patricide	Comedia/ saints play	1640, Don Bartolomé de Alva	Bancroft Library, University of California at Berkeley	*Nahuatl Theater* vol. 3
The Mother of the Best	Comedia/ saints play	c. 1640, Don Bartolomé de Alva	Bancroft Library, University of California at Berkeley	*Nahuatl Theater* vol. 3
Entremés	Comic intermezzo	c. 1640, Don Bartolomé de Alva	Bancroft Library, University of California at Berkeley	*Nahuatl Theater* vol. 3

Extant Colonial-Era Plays (*continued*)

Title	Type	Place, date, author or copyist, if known	Location	Publication
Dialogue on the Apparition of the Virgin Saint Mary of Guadalupe	Comedia/ saints play (Guadalupan)	late 17th or early 18th century	Biblioteca Nacional de Antropología e Historia, Mexico City	*Nahuatl Theater* vol. 2
The Wonder of Mexico	Saints play (Guadalupan)	c. 1715, Don Joseph Pérez de la Fuente	no colonial script survives; later copies are in New York Public Library and Bibliothèque Nationale, Paris	*Nahuatl Theater* vol. 2, Horcasitas 2004

Note: * denotes arbitrary title

224

REFERENCES

Alva Ixtlilxochitl, Fernando de. 1975–1977. *Obras históricas*. Edited by Edmundo O'Gorman. 2 vols. Mexico: Universidad Nacional Autónoma de México.

Arróniz, Othón. 1979. *Teatro de evangelización en Nueva España*. Mexico: Universidad Nacional Autónoma de México. Second edition, ed. Félix Báez-Jorge, Jalapa, Universidad Veracruzana y Gobierno del Estado de Veracruz, 1994.

Asensio, Eugenio. 1965. *Itinerario del entremés desde Lope de Rueda a Quiñones de Benavente*. Madrid: Editorial Gredos.

Bautista, fray Juan. 1600. *Advertencias para los confesores de los naturales*. 2 vols. Mexico: Melchor Ocharte.

———. 1606. *Sermonario . . . en lengua mexicana*. Mexico: Diego López Dávalos.

Becerra Tanco, Luis. 1982. "Origen milagroso del santuario de Nuestra Señora de Guadalupe." In Torre Villar and Navarro de Anda 1982, 309–33.

Boone, Elizabeth Hill. 2007. *Cycles of Time and Meaning in the Mexican Books of Fate*. Austin: University of Texas Press.

———. 2008. *Stories in Red and Black: Pictorial Histories of the Aztec and Mixtec*. Austin: University of Texas Press.

Bricker, Victoria Reifler. 1981. *The Indian Christ, the Indian King: The Historical Substrate of Maya Myth and Ritual*. Austin: University of Texas Press.

Burkhart, Louise M. 1986. "Moral Deviance in Sixteenth-Century Nahua and Christian Thought: The Rabbit and the Deer." *Journal of Latin American Lore* 12:107–39.

———. 1988. "The Solar Christ in Nahuatl Doctrinal Texts of Early Colonial Mexico." *Ethnohistory* 35:234–56.

———. 1989. *The Slippery Earth: Nahua-Christian Moral Dialogue in Sixteenth-Century Mexico*. Tucson: University of Arizona Press.

———. 1992. "Flowery Heaven: The Aesthetic of Paradise in Nahuatl Devotional Literature." *Res: Anthropology and Aesthetics* 21:89–109.

———. 1993. "The Cult of the Virgin of Guadalupe in Mexico." In *World Spirituality: An Encyclopedic History of the Religious Quest*, vol. 4, *South and Meso-American Native Spirituality*, ed. Gary H. Gossen and Miguel León-Portilla, 198–227. New York: Crossroad Press.

———. 1996. *Holy Wednesday: A Nahua Drama from Early Colonial Mexico*. Philadelphia: University of Pennsylvania Press.

———. 1998. "Pious Performances: Christian Pageantry and Native Identity in Early Colonial Mexico." In *Native Traditions in the Postconquest World*, ed. Elizabeth Hill Boone and Tom Cummins, 361–81. Washington, D.C.: Dumbarton Oaks.

———. 2001. *Before Guadalupe: The Virgin Mary in Early Colonial Nahuatl Literature*. Albany: Institute for Mesoamerican Studies, University at Albany, State University of New York.

———. 2008. "Meeting the Enemy: Moteuczoma and Cortes, Herod and the Magi." In *Invasion and Transformation: Interdisciplinary Perspectives on the Conquest of Mexico*, ed. Rebecca P. Brienen and Margaret A. Jackson, 11–23. Boulder: University Press of Colorado.

———. 2010. "The Destruction of Jerusalem as Colonial Nahuatl Historical Drama." In *The Conquest All Over Again: Nahuas and Zapotecs Thinking, Writing, and Painting Spanish Colonialism*, ed. Susan Schroeder, 74–100. Brighton, England: Sussex Academic Press.

Carrasco, David. 2001. *Quetzalcoatl and the Irony of Empire: Myth and Prophecies in the Aztec Tradition*. Boulder: University Press of Colorado.

Cartas de Indias. 1970. Edited by Edmundo Aviña Levy. Facsimile of 1877 Madrid edition. 2 vols. Guadalajara.

Chimalpahin Quauhtlehuanitzin, Don Domingo de San Antón Muñón. 1965. *Relaciones originales de Chalco Amaquemecan*. Edited and translated by Silvia Rendón. Mexico: Fondo de Cultura Económica.

———. 2006. *Annals of His Time: Don Domingo de San Antón Muñón Chimalpahin Quauhtlehuanitzin*. Edited and translated by James Lockhart, Susan Schroeder, and Doris Namala. Stanford: Stanford University Press.

Christian, William A., Jr. 1981. *Local Religion in Sixteenth-Century Spain*. Princeton: Princeton University Press.

Ciudad Real, fray Antonio de. 1976. *Tratado curioso y docto de las grandezas de la Nueva España*. Edited by Josefina García Quintana and Victor M. Castillo Farreras. 2 vols. Mexico: Universidad Nacional Autónoma de México.

Clendinnen, Inga. 1990. "Ways to the Sacred: Reconstructing 'Religion' in Sixteenth-Century Mexico." *History and Anthropology* 5:105–41.

———. 1991a. *Aztecs: An Interpretation*. Cambridge: Cambridge University Press.

———. 1991b. "'Fierce and Unnatural Cruelty': Cortés and the Conquest of Mexico." *Representations* 33:65–100.

Cline, S. L. 1986. *Colonial Culhuacan, 1580–1600: A Social History of an Aztec Town*. Albuquerque: University of New Mexico Press.

Cornyn, John H., and Byron McAfee. 1944. "Tlacahuapahualiztli (Bringing Up Children)." *Tlalocan* 1:314–51.

Díaz Balsera, Viviana. 2005. *The Pyramid under the Cross: Franciscan Discourses of Evangelization and the Nahua Christian Subject in Sixteenth-Century Mexico*. Tucson: University of Arizona Press.

Durán, Diego. 1971. *Book of the Gods and Rites and The Ancient Calendar*. Edited and translated by Fernando Horcasitas and Doris Heyden. Norman: University of Oklahoma Press.

———. 1994. *The History of the Indies of New Spain*. Edited and translated by Doris Heyden. Norman: University of Oklahoma Press.

Edgerton, Samuel. 2001. *Theaters of Conversion: Religious Architecture and Indian Artisans in Colonial Mexico*. Albuquerque: University of New Mexico Press.

Eire, Carlos M. N. 1995. *From Madrid to Purgatory: The Art and Craft of Dying in Sixteenth-Century Spain*. Cambridge, England: Cambridge University Press.

Farmer, David Hugh. 1992. *The Oxford Dictionary of Saints*. New York: Oxford University Press.

Garibay K., Ángel María. 1978. *Llave del náhuatl*. Mexico: Editorial Porrúa.

Gillespie, Susan. 1989. *The Aztec Kings: The Construction of Rulership in Mexica History*. Tucson: University of Arizona Press.

———. 2008. "Blaming Moteuczoma: Anthropomorphizing the Aztec Conquest." In *Invasion and Transformation: Interdisciplinary Perspectives on the Conquest of Mexico*, ed. Rebecca P. Brienen and Margaret A. Jackson, 25–55. Boulder: University Press of Colorado.

Greer, Margaret R. 2004. "The Development of National Theatre." In *Cambridge History of Spanish Literature*, ed. David T. Gies, 238–50. London: Cambridge University Press.

Grijalva, fray Juan de. 1624. *Crónica de la orden de N.P.S. Augustin en las provincias de la Nueva España*. Mexico: Juan Ruiz.

Gruzinski, Serge. 1989. "Individualization and Acculturation: Confession among the Nahuas of Mexico from the Sixteenth to the Eighteenth Century." In *Sexuality and Marriage in Colonial Latin America*, ed. Asunción Lavrin, 96–117. Lincoln: University of Nebraska Press.

———. 1993. *The Conquest of Mexico.* Translated by Eileen Corrigan. Cambridge, England: Polity Press.

Guzmán Bravo, José. 2007. *La adoración de los reyes: Reconstrucción musical y escénica de un auto novohispano en lengua náhuatl.* Illustrations by Carlos Teja. Mexico: Escuela Nacional de Música and Universidad Nacional Autónoma de México.

Harris, Max. 2000. *Aztecs, Moors, and Christians: Festivals of Reconquest in Mexico and Spain.* Austin: University of Texas Press.

Haskett, Robert. 1991. *Indigenous Rulers: An Ethnohistory of Town Government in Colonial Cuernavaca.* Albuquerque: University of New Mexico Press.

———. 2005. *Visions of Paradise: Primordial Titles and Mesoamerican History in Cuernavaca.* Norman: University of Oklahoma Press.

Hassig, Ross. 2006. *Mexico and the Spanish Conquest.* Norman: University of Oklahoma Press.

Horcasitas, Fernando. 1974. *El teatro náhuatl: Épocas novohispana y moderna.* Mexico: Universidad Nacional Autónoma de México.

———. 2004. *Teatro náhuatl II: Selección y estudio crítico de los materiales inéditos de Fernando Horcasitas.* Edited by María Sten, Óscar Armando García, Ricardo García-Arteaga, and Alejandro Ortiz Bullé-Goyri; translations revised by Librado Silva Galeana. Mexico: Universidad Nacional Autónoma de México.

Hunter, William H. 1960. *The Calderonian Auto Sacramental* El Gran Teatro del Mundo: *An Edition and Translation of a Nahuatl Version.* In *Middle American Research Institute Publication* 27, 105–202. New Orleans: Tulane University.

Karttunen, Frances. 1982. "Nahuatl Literacy." In *The Inca and Aztec States, 1400–1800: Anthropology and History,* ed. George A. Collier, Renato I. Rosaldo, and John D. Wirth, 395–417. New York: Academic Press.

———. 1994. *Between Worlds: Interpreters, Guides, and Survivors.* New Brunswick, N.J.: Rutgers University Press.

———. 1997. "Rethinking Malinche." In *Indian Women of Early Mexico,* ed. Susan Schroeder, Stephanie Wood, and Robert Haskett, 291–312. Norman: University of Oklahoma Press.

Karttunen, Frances, and James Lockhart. 1976. *Nahuatl in the Middle Years: Language Contact Phenomena in Texts of the Colonial Period.* University of California Publications in Linguistics 85. Berkeley and Los Angeles: University of California Press.

Karttunen, Frances, and James Lockhart, eds. and trans. 1987. *The Art of Nahuatl Speech: The Bancroft Dialogues.* Nahuatl Studies Series No. 2. Los Angeles: UCLA Latin American Center Publications.

Kellogg, Susan, 1995. *Law and the Transformation of Aztec Culture, 1500–1700.* Norman: University of Oklahoma Press.

———. 1997. "From Parallel and Equivalent to Separate but Unequal: Tenochca Mexica Women, 1500–1700." In *Indian Women of Early Mexico,* ed. Susan

Schroeder, Stephanie Wood, and Robert Haskett, 123–43. Norman: University of Oklahoma Press.

———. 1998. "Indigenous Testaments of Early-Colonial Mexico City: Testifying to Gender Differences." In Kellogg and Restall 1998, 37–58.

Kellogg, Susan, and Matthew Restall, eds. 1998. *Dead Giveaways: Indigenous Testaments of Colonial Mesoamerica and the Andes*. Salt Lake City: University of Utah Press.

Klor de Alva, J. Jorge. 1982. "Spiritual Conflict and Accommodation in New Spain: Toward a Typology of Aztec Responses to Christianity." In *The Inca and Aztec States, 1400–1800: Anthropology and History*, ed. George A. Collier, Renato I. Rosaldo, and John D. Wirth, 345–66. New York: Academic Press.

———. 1988. "Contar vidas: La autobiografía confesional y la reconstrucción del ser nahua." *Arbor* 131:49–78.

Lara, Jaime. 2004. *City, Temple, Stage: Eschatological Architecture and Liturgical Theatrics in New Spain*. Notre Dame, Ind.: Notre Dame University Press.

Las Casas, fray Bartolomé de. 1967. *Apologética historia sumaria*. 2 vols. Mexico: Universidad Autónoma de México.

Laso de la Vega, Luis. 1649. *Huey tlamahuiçoltica omonexiti in ilhuicac tlatocacihuapilli Santa Maria totlaçonantzin Guadalupe in nican huey altepenahuac Mexico itocayocan Tepeyacac*. Mexico: Juan Ruiz.

Lehmann, Walter, Gerdt Kutscher, and Günter Vollmer, eds. and trans. 1981. *Geschichte der Azteken: Codex Aubin und verwandte Dokumente*. Berlin: Mann.

León-Portilla, Miguel. 2000. *Tonantzin Guadalupe: Pensamiento náhuatl y mensaje cristiano en el "Nican mopohua."* Mexico: El Colegio Nacional and Fondo de Cultura Económica.

Leoni, Monica. 2000. *Inside, Outside, Aside: Dialoguing with the* Gracioso *in Spanish Golden Age Theatre*. New Orleans: University Press of the South.

Lewis, Laura. 2003. *Hall of Mirrors: Power, Witchcraft, and Caste in Colonial Mexico*. Durham, N.C.: Duke University Press.

Leyva, Juan. 2001. *La Pasión de Ozumba: El teatro religioso en el siglo XVIII novohispano*. Mexico: Universidad Nacional Autónoma de México.

Lockhart, James. 1985. "Some Nahua Concepts in Postconquest Guise." *History of European Ideas* 6:465–82.

———. 1991. *Nahuas and Spaniards: Postconquest Central Mexican History and Philology*. Stanford: Stanford University Press and UCLA Latin American Center Publications.

———. 1992. *The Nahuas after the Conquest: A Social and Cultural History of the Indians of Central Mexico, Sixteenth through Eighteenth Centuries*. Stanford: Stanford University Press.

Lockhart, James, trans. and ed. 1993. *We People Here: Nahuatl Accounts of the Conquest of Mexico*. Berkeley and Los Angeles: University of California Press.

López Austin, Alfredo. 1988. *The Human Body and Ideology: Concepts of the Ancient Nahuas*. Translated by Bernard R. Ortiz de Montellano and Thelma Ortiz de Montellano. 2 vols. Salt Lake City: University of Utah Press.

McKendrick, Melveena. 1989. *Theatre in Spain, 1490–1700*. Cambridge: Cambridge University Press.

Mendieta, fray Gerónimo de. 1980. *Historia eclesiástica indiana*. Edited by Joaquín García Icazbalceta. Mexico: Editorial Porrúa.

Mira de Amescua, Antonio. 2005. *El animal profeta*. Edited by Aurelio Valladares Reguero. In *Teatro completo*, 5:31–152. Agustín de la Granja, coordinator. Granada: Universidad de Granada.

Mosquera, Daniel. 2005. "Consecrated Transactions: Of Marketplaces, Passion Plays, and Other Nahua-Christian Devotions." *Journal of Latin American Cultural Studies* 14:171–93.

Motolinia, fray Toribio de Benavante. 1979. *Historia de los indios de la Nueva España*. Edited by Edmundo O'Gorman. Mexico: Editorial Porrúa.

Nahuatl Theater. 2004–2009. Vol. 1: *Death and Life in Colonial Nahua Mexico*, ed. Barry D. Sell and Louise M. Burkhart. Norman: University of Oklahoma Press, 2004. Vol. 2: *Our Lady of Guadalupe*, ed. Barry D. Sell, Louise M. Burkhart, and Stafford Poole. Norman: University of Oklahoma Press, 2006. Vol. 3: *Spanish Golden Age Drama in Mexican Translation*, ed. Barry D. Sell, Louise M. Burkhart, and Elizabeth R. Wright. Norman: University of Oklahoma Press, 2008. Vol. 4: *Nahua Christianity in Performance*, ed. Barry D. Sell and Louise M. Burkhart. Norman: University of Oklahoma Press, 2009.

Nicholson, H. B. 2001. *Topiltzin Quetzalcoatl: The Once and Future Lord of the Toltecs*. Boulder: University Press of Colorado.

Noguez, Xavier. 1993. *Documentos guadalupanos: Un estudio sobre las fuentes de información tempranas en torno a las mariofanías en el Tepeyac*. Mexico: El Colegio Mexiquense and Fondo de Cultura Económica.

Pardo, Osvaldo F. 2004. *The Origins of Mexican Catholicism: Nahua Rituals and Christian Sacraments in Sixteenth-Century Mexico*. Ann Arbor: University of Michigan Press.

Partida, Armando. 1992. *Teatro de evangelización en náhuatl*. Mexico: Consejo Nacional para la Cultura y las Artes.

Paso y Troncoso, Francisco del. 1890. *Invención de la Santa Cruz por Santa Elena*. Mexico: Museo Nacional.

———. 1899. "El sacrificio de Isaac." In *Biblioteca Náuatl*, vol. 1. Florence: Salvador Landi.

———. 1900. "La adoración de los Reyes." In *Biblioteca Náuatl*, vol. 1. Florence: Salvador Landi.

———. 1902. "La comedia de los Reyes." In *Biblioteca Náuatl*, vol. 1. Florence: Salvador Landi.

———. 1907. "La destrucción de Jerusalén." In *Biblioteca Náuatl*, vol. 1. Florence: Salvador Landi.

Peck, George T. 1980. *The Fool of God: Jacopone da Todi*. University: University of Alabama Press.

Pérez de Ribas, Andrés. 1645. *Historia de los trivmphos de nuestra santa fee.* Madrid: Alonso de Paredes.

Poole, Stafford. 1981. "Church Law on the Ordination of Indians and *Castas* in New Spain." *Hispanic American Historical Review* 61:637–50.

———. 1995. *Our Lady of Guadalupe: Origins and Sources of a Mexican National Symbol, 1571–1797.* Tucson: University of Arizona Press.

———. 2006. *The Guadalupan Controversies in Mexico.* Stanford: Stanford University Press.

Prem, Hanns J. 1992. "Disease Outbreaks in Central Mexico during the Sixteenth Century." In *"Secret Judgments of God": Old World Disease in Colonial Spanish America,* ed. Noble David Cook and W. George Lovell, 20–48. Norman: University of Oklahoma Press.

Ramos Smith, Maya, Tito Vasconcelos, Luis Armando Lamadrid, and Xabier Lizárraga Cruchaga, eds. 1998. *Censura y teatro novohispano (1539–1822): Ensayos y antología de documentos.* Mexico: Consejo Nacional para la Cultura y las Artes, Instituto Nacional de Bellas Artes, Centro Nacional de Investigación e Información Teatral Rodolfo Usigli, and Escenología, A.C.

Ravicz, Marilyn Ekdahl. 1970. *Early Colonial Religious Drama in Mexico: From Tzompantli to Golgotha.* Washington, D.C.: Catholic University of America Press.

Restall, Matthew. 2003. *Seven Myths of the Spanish Conquest.* Oxford: Oxford University Press.

Reyes García, Luis. 1960. *Pasión y muerte del Cristo Sol (Carnaval y cuaresma en Ichcatepec).* Xalapa, Mexico: Universidad Veracruzana.

Reyes Valerio, Constantino. 1960. *Tepalcingo.* Mexico: Instituto Nacional de Antropología e Historia.

Ricard, Robert. 1966. *The Spiritual Conquest of Mexico.* Translated by Lesley Byrd Simpson. Berkeley and Los Angeles: University of California Press.

Rouanet, Léo, ed. 1979. *Colección de autos, farsas, y coloquios del siglo XVI.* 4 vols. Hildesheim and New York: Georg Olms.

Sahagún, fray Bernardino de. 1950–1982. *Florentine Codex, General History of the Things of New Spain.* Edited and translated by Arthur J. O. Anderson and Charles E. Dibble. 12 vols. Santa Fe, N.M.: School of American Research and University of Utah.

———. 1993. *Psalmodia Christiana (Christian Psalmody).* Edited and translated by Arthur J. O. Anderson. Salt Lake City: University of Utah Press.

———. 1999. *Psalmodia Christiana y Sermonario de los sanctos del año, en lengua mexicana.* Edited and translated by José Luis Suárez Roca. León, Spain: Diputación Provincial de León and Instituto Leonés de Cultura.

Schechner, Richard. 1985. *Between Theater and Anthropology.* Foreword by Victor Turner. Philadelphia: University of Pennsylvania Press.

Sell, Barry D. 1993. *Friars, Nahuas, and Books: Language and Expression in Colonial Nahuatl Publications.* Ph.D. dissertation, University of California at Los Angeles.

Sell, Barry D., and John Frederick Schwaller, eds. and trans., with Lu Ann Homza. 1999. *Don Bartolomé de Alva*, Guide to Confession Large and Small in the Mexican Language. *Critical edition of the 1634 edition*. Norman: University of Oklahoma Press.

Shergold, N. D. 1967. *A History of the Spanish Stage from Medieval Times until the End of the Seventeenth Century*. Oxford: Oxford University Press.

Silva Cruz, Ignacio. 2001. "Del cómo el nieto desobedeció a su abuelo y por ello fue arrastrado al infierno." *Boletín del Archivo General de la Nación, Nueva Época* 1:9–40.

Sousa, Lisa, Stafford Poole, C.M., and James Lockhart, eds. and trans. 1998. *The Story of Guadalupe: Luis Laso de la Vega's "Huei tlamahuiçoltica" of 1649*. Stanford: Stanford University Press and UCLA Latin American Center Publications.

Sten, María. 1982. *Vida y muerte del teatro náhuatl*. Jalapa: Biblioteca Universidad Veracruzana.

Sten, María, Oscar Armando García, and Alejandro Ortiz Bullé-Goyri, eds. 2000. *El teatro franciscano en la Nueva España: Fuentes y ensayos para el estudio del teatro de evangelización en el siglo XVI*. Mexico: Universidad Nacional Autónoma de México and Consejo Nacional para la Cultura y las Artes.

Sullivan, Thelma. 1966. "Pregnancy, Childbirth, and the Deification of the Women Who Died in Childbirth." *Estudios de cultura náhuatl* 6:63–95.

Taylor, William. 1979. *Drinking, Homicide, and Rebellion in Colonial Mexican Villages*. Stanford: Stanford University Press.

———. 1987. "The Virgin of Guadalupe: An Inquiry into the Social History of Marian Devotion." *American Ethnologist* 14:9–33.

———. 2003. "Mexico's Virgin of Guadalupe in the Seventeenth Century: Hagiography and Beyond." In *Colonial Saints: Discovering the Holy in the Americas*, ed. Allan Greer and Jodi Blinkoff, 277–98. New York: Routledge.

Torquemada, fray Juan de. 1975–1983. *Monarquía indiana*. 7 vols. Mexico: Universidad Nacional Autónoma de México.

Torre Villar, Ernesto de la, and Ramiro Navarro de Anda, eds. 1982. *Testimonios históricos guadalupanos*. Mexico: Fondo de Cultura Económico.

Townsend, Camilla. 2003. "Burying the White Gods: New Perspectives on the Conquest of Mexico." *American Historical Review* 108:659–87.

———. 2006. *Malintzin's Choices: An Indian Woman in the Conquest of Mexico*. Albuquerque: University of New Mexico Press.

———. 2009. *Here in This Year: Seventeenth-Century Nahuatl Annals of the Tlaxcala-Puebla Valley*. Stanford: Stanford University Press.

Vetancurt, fray Agustín de. 1971. *Teatro mexicano, Crónica de la provincia del Santo Evangelio de México, Menologio franciscano*. Mexico: Editorial Porrúa.

Wake, Eleanor. 2009. *Framing the Sacred: The Indian Churches of Early Colonial Mexico*. Norman: University of Oklahoma Press.

Williams, Jerry. 1992. *El teatro del México colonial: Época misionera.* New York: Peter Lang.

Wright, Elizabeth R. 2008. "A Dramatic Diaspora: Spanish Theater and Its Mexican Interpretation." In *Nahuatl Theater*, 3:3–25.

Zapata y Mendoza, don Juan Buenaventura. 1995. *Historia cronológica de la noble ciudad de Tlaxcala.* Edited and translated by Luis Reyes García and Andrea Martínez Baracs. Tlaxcala, Mexico: Universidad Autónoma de Tlaxcala and Centro de Investigaciones y Estudios Superiores en Antropología Social.